A Casebook on Candida

A *Casebook on* Candida

Edited by

STEPHEN S. STANTON

University of Michigan

THOMAS Y. CROWELL COMPANY

New York, Established 1834

To Jane and Deborah Jane

Preface

Now, nearly twelve years after his death, it is surely unnecessary —even superfluous—to praise George Bernard Shaw as a dramatist and thinker; the world has eloquently paid him tribute. Students find his plays irresistible, despite his claim that art should be didactic (a term sometimes synonymous in our minds with "preachy"). *Candida* is an invigorating and delightful introduction both to Shaw's more difficult plays and to the fervent activity and thought which inspired them.

As literature, *Candida* blends four ingredients essential to a good drama: economical structure, heated conflict, boldly realized characters, and the interplay of ideas. Trenchantly dramatizing the eternal conflict between the artist-intellectual and the average person, and raising incisive questions concerning the freedom of the individual, *Candida* examines the nature of love, the basis of marriage, the relationship of the sexes, and Woman's place in the scheme of things—as an agent of what Shaw later called the "Life Force." It questions some fundamental assumptions about capitalism and Shavian socialism; it deeply and compassionately studies the ratio of human suffering to moral strength. In short, this drama gives the student the purest quintessence of Shaw's credo and dramatic technique, and also acquaints him with Shaw's satirical method of inversion: here, of the traditional roles of hero, heroine, and villain.

A Casebook on Candida aims to provide an abundance of materials for student research and papers. It offers a valuable collection of Shaw's own views on one of his most controversial and rewarding plays, as well as on art and life generally, in writings unknown to most college students and often hard to obtain; it scans sixty-five years of changing critical standards and tastes in the form of chronologically arranged essays, letters, and reviews by eminent European and American writers; it provides an introduction to nineteenth-century literature and thought through selections from authors whose ideas directly or indirectly influenced Shaw, such as Shelley, De

Quincey, Carlyle, Ruskin, Nietzsche, and Schopenhauer; and it concludes with a selected bibliography and suggestions for discussion and
research papers.

Not all readers need use this book in the same way. The student of
composition may write research papers of various lengths (see topics
at the end of the book), perhaps best beginning with short ones and
progressing to longer ones, all based on materials found in this book.
With the aid of the bibliography, he may go even further, undertaking
projects involving extensive library research. He may compare or
contrast, as examples of agrumentation, critical essays written over a
period of more than half a century.

The student of literature and criticism, after reading the play, may
wish to make a chronological study of the criticism, or compare
French, English, and American critics, or compare Shaw's own interpretation of *Candida* with those of several critics. For such purposes, the essays of Professors Nethercot and King will be particularly
helpful in charting and summarizing the critical attitudes—the extreme
along with the generally accepted—of the past half century.

The student of theater might begin with Archibald Henderson's
accounts of the earliest British and American performances of both
Candida and its farcical offspring *How He Lied to Her Husband*
(available in the Penguin paperback edition of Shaw's one-act plays),
and go on to trace the many interpretations by leading actresses and
actors up to the present, drawing for details upon such reviewers as
Oliver Elton, A. B. Walkley, Desmond MacCarthy, Brooks Atkinson,
Stark Young, Joseph Wood Krutch, and John Mason Brown. With
its superb photographs of outstanding Shaw productions, the informa-
tive *Theatrical Companion to Shaw* (see bibliography) might well
serve as a starting point for a study of British performances of *Candida*.

The essays are not of uniform critical excellence, and the student
need not regard all their judgments as infallible. Nor should he infer
that Shaw deliberately or consciously used the source materials included in this book when he wrote *Candida* (although the selection
from *Confessions of an English Opium-Eater* is a representative extract from a work Shaw did claim to have in mind). Rather, these
materials contribute clear and vigorous literary statements of the
important ideas given free play, in one way or another, in this Shavian
comedy—those ideas, that is, helping to compose the intellectual cli-
mate in which Shaw thrived at the time of *Candida*'s creation. And

they faithfully exemplify the writing styles of the leading spokesmen for those viewpoints.

Throughout the book bracketed figures indicate the end of a page on which the selection appeared in the cited source. If the page of the original ended with a hyphenated word, the page number here precedes the word. Most of the footnotes have been renumbered for this reprinting; brackets within or around footnotes denote my editorial insertions. Typographical errors have been corrected throughout.

I wish to thank the authors, editors, and publishers who gave me permission to reprint materials here. I am indebted to The Public Trustee and The Society of Authors, London, for permission to use Shaw's writings. I am especially grateful to Jane Stanton for assistance in preparing the manuscript and to Marian Reiner and John T. Hawes for their invaluable advice.

STEPHEN S. STANTON

Ann Arbor, Michigan
December, 1961

Contents

Preface   v

THE "CANDIDA" THEME

Candida   3
GEORGE BERNARD SHAW

From "Candida Accepted, Rejected"   63
ARCHIBALD HENDERSON

From "Arnold Daly Startles Broadway"   65
ARCHIBALD HENDERSON

From "Playlets and Farces"   67
ARCHIBALD HENDERSON

SHAW ON ART AND LIFE

From Love Among the Artists   71

From The Quintessence of Ibsenism
     "*Ideals and Idealists*"   73
     "*The Womanly Woman*"   79

On Shelley and Wagner   86

From Ellen Terry and Bernard Shaw: A Correspondence   87

From Preface to Pleasant Plays   91

From Captain Brassbound's Conversion   94

From "*Epistle Dedicatory*" to Man and Superman   94

Heaven, Hell, and Woman   96

From Preface to Androcles and the Lion   99

From Preface to Pygmalion   99

Miscellaneous Critiques   99

SOME OF SHAW'S SOURCES

IDEAS: *1. Adolescence, Work, and Happiness*

From "The Pains of Opium"   103
THOMAS DE QUINCEY

From "The Everlasting Yea"   106
THOMAS CARLYLE

From "The Mystery of Life and Its Arts"   110
JOHN RUSKIN

IDEAS: *2. Women, Marriage, and Happiness*

"Even Love Is Sold"   113
PERCY BYSSHE SHELLEY

From "On Women"   116
ARTHUR SCHOPENHAUER

From Thus Spake Zarathustra   119
FRIEDRICH NIETZSCHE

From "What Do Ascetic Ideals Mean?"   124
FRIEDRICH NIETZSCHE

IBSEN'S PLAYS

Three Reviews   130
GEORGE BERNARD SHAW

DRAMATIC METHOD

From The Art of Poetry   137
HORACE

Miscellaneous Critiques   137
GEORGE BERNARD SHAW

From The Twentieth Century Molière: Bernard Shaw   138
AUGUSTIN HAMON

Shaw on Shaw and Molière   143
GEORGE BERNARD SHAW

From "Shaw's Debt to Scribe"   144
STEPHEN S. STANTON

From "The Making of a Dramatist (1892–1903)"   154
ERIC BENTLEY

MODELS FROM LIFE

From "Candida Was Not Ellen Terry"   158
GEORGE BERNARD SHAW

From "Bernard Shaw's Beginnings on the London Stage"   159
IRVING MC KEE

From "The Life Force in Action"   160
WILLIAM IRVINE

From "Pleasant Plays"   161
ARCHIBALD HENDERSON

INTERPRETATION OF "CANDIDA"

SHAW ON THE "CANDIDA" SECRET

Letter to James Huneker   165
GEORGE BERNARD SHAW

"The 'Candida' Secret"   166
GEORGE A. RIDING

Note to the Late Editor of The Kansas City Star   169
GEORGE BERNARD SHAW

From "Biographers' Blunders Corrected"   170
GEORGE BERNARD SHAW

THE CRITICS (1895–1960): *Continental*

From "The Dramatist Bernard Shaw" 171
GEORG BRANDES

A Note on Candida 172
HERMANN BAHR

From "From Nora to Candida" 172
MAURICE MURET

THE CRITICS (1895–1960): *British*

From "Miss Janet Achurch and Mr. Charles Charrington
in 'Candida'" 175
OLIVER ELTON

From "Candida" 177
A. B. WALKLEY

From "Shaw the Dramatist" 180
G. K. CHESTERTON

From The Quintessence of Bernard Shaw 184
H. C. DUFFIN

From The Real Bernard Shaw 189
MAURICE COLBOURNE

From Bernard Shaw: A Chronicle 191
R. F. RATTRAY

THE CRITICS (1895–1960): *American*

Two Letters on Candida 194
RICHARD MANSFIELD

From "The Quintessence of Shaw" 197
JAMES HUNEKER

From George Bernard Shaw: His Plays 201
H. L. MENCKEN

A Review of Candida   209
STARK YOUNG

A Review of Candida   212
JOSEPH WOOD KRUTCH

From "Varieties of Comic Experience"   214
ERIC BENTLEY

From "Adventures in Success"   217
WILLIAM IRVINE

"Candida"   223
EDMUND FULLER

From "The Truth about Candida"   227
A. H. NETHERCOT

From "Pleasant Plays"   239
ARCHIBALD HENDERSON

"The Rhetoric of 'Candida' "   243
WALTER N. KING

"Ibsen, Shaw and 'Candida' "   258
JACOB H. ADLER

From " 'Candida' and 'Pygmalion': Shaw's Subversion of
    Stereotypes"   268
PAUL LAUTER

APPENDICES

Selected Bibliography   277
Suggestions for Study, Discussion, and Writing   285

THE "CANDIDA" THEME

Candida

GEORGE BERNARD SHAW

ACT I

A fine morning in October 1894 in the north east quarter of London, a vast district miles away from the London of Mayfair and St James's, and much less narrow, squalid, fetid and airless in its slums. It is strong in unfashionable middle class life: wide-streeted; myriad-populated; well served with ugly iron urinals, Radical clubs, and tram lines carrying a perpetual stream of yellow cars; enjoying in its main thoroughfares the luxury of grass-grown "front gardens" untrodden by the foot of man save as to the path from the gate to the hall door; blighted by a callously endured monotony of miles and miles of unlovely brick houses, black iron railings, stony pavements, slated roofs, and respectably ill dressed or disreputably worse dressed people, quite accustomed to the place, and mostly plodding uninterestedly about somebody else's work. The little energy and eagerness that crop up shew themselves in cockney cupidity and business "push." Even the policemen and the chapels are not infrequent enough to break the monotony. The sun is shining cheerfully: there is no fog; and though the smoke effectually prevents anything, whether faces and hands or bricks and mortar, from looking fresh and clean, it is not hanging heavily enough to trouble a Londoner.

This desert of unattractiveness has its oasis. Near the outer end of the Hackney Road is a park of 217 acres, fenced in, not by railings, but by a wooden paling, and containing plenty of greensward, trees, a lake for bathers, flower beds which are triumphs of the admired

Candida was written in 1894–95, and first published in 1898 in *Plays: Pleasant and Unpleasant*. The present reprinting is from *Plays Pleasant and Unpleasant*, The Standard Edition of Shaw's Works (London: Constable and Company, Ltd., 1952), II: *Pleasant Plays*, 75–141. Reprinted by permission of the Public Trustee and the Society of Authors (London). Bracketed page numbers are to this edition.

3

*cockney art of carpet gardening, and a sandpit, originally imported
from the seaside for the delight of children, but speedily deserted on
its becoming a natural vermin preserve for all the petty fauna of
Kingsland, Hackney, and Hoxton. A bandstand, an unfurnished forum
for religious, anti-religious, and political orators, cricket pitches, a
gymnasium, and an old fashioned stone kiosk are among its attractions.
Wherever the prospect is bounded by trees or rising green grounds,
it is a pleasant place. Where the ground stretches*[1][75] *flat to the grey
palings, with bricks and mortar, sky signs, crowded chimneys and
smoke beyond, the prospect makes it desolate and sordid.*

*The best view of Victoria Park is commanded by the front win-
dow of St Dominic's Parsonage, from which not a brick is visible.
The parsonage is semi-detached, with a front garden and a porch.
Visitors go up the flight of steps to the porch: tradespeople and members of the family go down by a door under the steps to the basement,
with a breakfast room, used for all meals, in front, and the kitchen at
the back. Upstairs, on the level of the hall door, is the drawingroom,
with its large plate g'ass window looking out on the park. In this, the
only sitting room that can be spared from the children and the family
meals, the parson, the Reverend James Mavor More'l, does his work.
He is sitting in a strong round backed revolving chair at the end of a
long table, which stands across the window, so that he can cheer himself with a view of the park over his left shoulder. At the opposite end
of the table, adjoining it, is a little table only half as wide as the other,
with a typewriter on it. His typist is sitting at this machine, with her
back to the window. The large table is littered with pamphlets, jour-
nals, letters, nests of drawers, an office diary, postage scales and the
like. A spare chair for visitors having business with the parson is in
the middle, turned to his end. Within reach of his hand is a stationery
case, and a photograph in a frame. The wall behind him is fitted with
bookshelves, on which an adept eye can measure the parson's casuistry
and divinity by Maurice's Theological Essays and a complete set of
Browning's poems, and the reformer's politics by a yellow backed
Progress and Poverty, Fabian Essays, A Dream of John Ball, Marx's
Capital, and half a dozen other literary landmarks in Socialism. Facing
him on the other side of the room, near the typewriter, is the door. Fur-*

---

[1] [See editor's comment in the Preface regarding bracketed figures and
footnotes.]

*ther down opposite the fireplace, a bookcase stands on a cellaret, with a
sofa near it. There is a generous fire burning; and the hearth, with a
comfortable armchair and a black japanned flower-painted coal scuttle
at one side, a miniature chair for children on the other, a varnished
wooden mantelpiece, with neatly moulded shelves, tiny bits of mirror
let into the panels, a travelling clock in a leather case (the inevitable
wedding[76] present), and on the wall above a large autotype of the
chief figure in Titian's Assumption of the Virgin, is very inviting.
Altogether the room is the room of a good housekeeper, vanquished,
as far as the table is concerned, by an untidy man, but elsewhere
mistress of the situation. The furniture, in its ornamental aspect,
betrays the style of the advertized "drawingroom suite" of the pushing
suburban furniture dealer; but there is nothing useless or pretentious
in the room, money being too scarce in the house of an east end parson
to be wasted on snobbish trimmings.*

*The Reverend James Mavor Morell is a Christian Socialist clergy-
man of the Church of England, and an active member of the Guild of
St Matthew and the Christian Social Union. A vigorous, genial,
popular man of forty, robust and goodlooking, full of energy, with
pleasant, hearty, considerate manners, and a sound unaffected voice,
which he used with the clean athletic articulation of a practised orator,
and with a wide range and perfect command of expression. He is a
first rate clergyman, able to say what he likes to whom he likes, to
lecture people without setting himself up against them, to impose his
authority on them without humiliating them, and, on occasion, to
interfere in their business without impertinence. His well-spring of
enthusiasm and sympathetic emotion has never run dry for a moment:
he still eats and sleeps heartily enough to win the daily battle between
exhaustion and recuperation triumphantly. Withal, a great baby,
pardonably vain of his powers and unconsciously pleased with himself. He has a healthy complexion: good forehead, with the brows
somewhat blunt, and the eyes bright and eager, mouth resolute but
not particularly well cut, and a substantial nose, with the mobile
spreading nostrils of the dramatic orator, void, like all his features, of
subtlety.*

*The typist, Miss Proserpine Garnett, is a brisk little woman of
about 30, of the lower middle class, neatly but cheaply dressed in a
black merino skirt and a blouse, notably pert and quick of speech,*

*and not very civil in her manner, but sensitive and affectionate. She
is clattering away busily at her machine whilst Morell opens the last
of his morning's letters. He realizes its contents with a comic groan of
despair.*[77]

PROSERPINE. Another lecture?

MORELL. Yes. The Hoxton Freedom Group want me to address them on Sunday morning [*he lays great emphasis on Sunday,
this being the unreasonable part of the business*]. What are they?

PROSERPINE. Communist Anarchists, I think.

MORELL. Just like Anarchists not to know that they cant have a
parson on Sunday! Tell them to come to church if they want to hear
me: it will do them good. Say I can come on Mondays and Thursdays
only. Have you the diary there?

PROSERPINE [*taking up the diary*] Yes.

MORELL. Have I any lecture on for next Monday?

PROSERPINE [*referring to the diary*] Tower Hamlets Radical Club.

MORELL. Well, Thursday then?

PROSERPINE. English Land Restoration League.

MORELL. What next?

PROSERPINE. Guild of St Matthew on Monday. Independent Labor
Party, Greenwich Branch, on Thursday. Monday Social-Democratic
Federation, Mile End Branch. Thursday, first Confirmation class.
[*Impatiently*] Oh, I'd better tell them you cant come. Theyre only
half a dozen ignorant and conceited costermongers without five
shillings between them.

MORELL [*amused*] Ah; but you see theyre near relatives of mine.

PROSERPINE [*staring at him*] Relatives of yours!

MORELL. Yes: we have the same father—in Heaven.

PROSERPINE [*relieved*] Oh, is that all?

MORELL [*with a sadness which is a luxury to a man whose voice
expresses it so finely*] Ah, you dont believe it. Everybody says it: nobody believes it: nobody. [*Briskly, getting back to business*] Well,
well! Come, Miss Proserpine: cant you find a date for the costers?
what about the 25th? That was vacant the day before yesterday.

PROSERPINE [*referring to diary*] Engaged. The Fabian Society.

MORELL. Bother the Fabian Society! Is the 28th gone too?

PROSERPINE. City dinner. Youre invited to dine with the Founders'
Company.[78]

MORELL. Thatll do: I'll go to the Hoxton Group of Freedom instead. [*She enters the engagement in silence, with implacable disparagement of the Hoxton Anarchists in every line of her face. Morell bursts open the cover of a copy of The Church Reformer, which has come by post, and glances through Mr Stewart Headlam's leader and the Guild of St Matthew news. These proceedings are presently enlivened by the appearance of Morell's curate, the Reverend Alexander Mill, a young gentleman gathered by Morell from the nearest University settlement, whither he had come from Oxford to give the east end of London the benefit of his university training. He is a conceitedly well intentioned, enthusiastic, immature novice, with nothing positively unbearable about him except a habit of speaking with his lips carefully closed a full half inch from each corner for the sake of a finicking articulation and a set of university vowels, this being his chief means so far of bringing his Oxford refinement (as he calls his habits) to bear on Hackney vulgarity. Morell, whom he has won over by a doglike devotion, looks up indulgently from The Church Reformer, and remarks*] Well, Lexy? Late again, as usual!

LEXY. I'm afraid so. I wish I could get up in the morning.

MORELL [*exulting in his own energy*] Ha! ha! [*Whimsically*] Watch and pray, Lexy: watch and pray.

LEXY. I know [*Rising wittily to the occasion*] But how can I watch and pray when I am asleep? Isnt that so, Miss Prossy? [*He makes for the warmth of the fire*].

PROSERPINE [*sharply*] Miss Garnett, if you please.

LEXY. I beg your pardon. Miss Garnett.

PROSERPINE. Youve got to do all the work today.

LEXY [*on the hearth*] Why?

PROSERPINE. Never mind why. It will do you good to earn your supper before you eat it, for once in a way, as I do. Come! dont dawdle. You should have been off on your rounds half an hour ago.

LEXY [*perplexed*] Is she in earnest, Morell?

MORELL [*in the highest spirits: his eyes dancing*] Yes. *I* am going to dawdle today.

LEXY. You! You dont know how.[79]

MORELL [*rising*] Ha! ha! Dont I? I'm going to have this morning all to myself. My wife's coming back: she's due here at 11.45.

LEXY [*surprised*] Coming back already! with the children? I thought they were to stay to the end of the month.

MORELL. So they are: she's only coming up for two days, to get some flannel things for Jimmy, and to see how we're getting on without her.

LEXY [*anxiously*] But, my dear Morell, if what Jimmy and Fluffy had was scarlatina, do you think it wise—

MORELL. Scarlatina! Rubbish! it was German measles. I brought it into the house myself from the Pycroft Street school. A parson is like a doctor, my boy: he must face infection as a soldier must face bullets. [*He claps Lexy manfully on the shoulders*]. Catch the measles if you can, Lexy: she'll nurse you; and what a piece of luck that will be for you! Eh?

LEXY [*smiling uneasily*] It's so hard to understand you about Mrs Morell—

MORELL. [*tenderly*] Ah, my boy, get married: get married to a good woman; and then youll understand. Thats a foretaste of what will be best in the Kingdom of Heaven we are trying to establish on earth. That will cure you of dawdling. An honest man feels that he must pay Heaven for every hour of happiness with a good spell of hard unselfish work to make others happy. We have no more right to consume happiness without producing it than to consume wealth without producing it. Get a wife like my Candida; and youll always be in arrear with your repayment. [*He pats Lexy affectionately and moves to leave the room*].

LEXY. Oh, wait a bit: I forgot. [*Morell halts and turns with the door knob in his hand*]. Your father-in-law is coming round to see you.

Morell, surprised and not pleased, shuts the door again, with a complete change of manner.

MORELL. Mr Burgess?

LEXY. Yes. I passed him in the park, arguing with somebody. He asked me to let you know that he was coming.

MORELL [*half incredulous*] But he hasnt called here for three[80] years. Are you sure, Lexy? Youre not joking, are you?

LEXY [*earnestly*] No sir, really.

MORELL [*thoughtfully*] Hm! Time for him to take another look at Candida before she grows out of his knowledge. [*He resigns himself to the inevitable, and goes out*].

Lexy looks after him with beaming worship. Miss Garnett, not being able to shake Lexy, relieves her feelings by worrying the typewriter.

LEXY. What a good man! What a thorough loving soul he is! [*He takes Morell's place at the table, making himself very comfortable as he takes out a cigaret*].

PROSERPINE [*impatiently, pulling the letter she has been working at off the typewriter and folding it*] Oh, a man ought to be able to be fond of his wife without making a fool of himself about her.

LEXY [*shocked*] Oh, Miss Prossy!

PROSERPNE [*snatching at the stationery case for an envelope, in which she encloses the letter as she speaks*] Candida here, and Candida there, and Candida everywhere! [*She licks the envelope*]. It's enough to drive anyone out of their senses [*thumping the envelope to make it stick*] to hear a woman raved about in that absurd manner merely because she's got good hair and a tolerable figure.

LEXY [*with reproachful gravity*] I think her extremely beautiful, Miss Garnett. [*He takes the photograph up; looks at it; and adds, with even greater impressiveness*] extremely beautiful. How fine her eyes are!

PROSERPINE. Her eyes are not a bit better than mine: now! [*He puts down the photograph and stares austerely at her*]. And you know very well you think me dowdy and second rate enough.

LEXY [*rising majestically*] Heaven forbid that I should think of any of God's creatures in such a way! [*He moves stiffly away from her across the room to the neighborhood of the bookcase*].

PROSERPINE [*sarcastically*] Thank you. Thats very nice and comforting.

LEXY [*saddened by her depravity*] I had no idea you had any feeling against Mrs Morell.[81]

PROSERPINE [*indignantly*] I have no feeling against her. She's very nice, very good-hearted: I'm very fond of her, and can appreciate her real qualities far better than any man can. [*He shakes his head sadly. She rises and comes at him with intense pepperiness*]. You dont believe me? You think I'm jealous? Oh, what a knowledge of the human heart you have, Mr Lexy Mill! How well you know the weaknesses of Woman, dont you? It must be so nice to be a man and have a fine penetrating intellect instead of mere emotions like us, and to know that the reason we dont share your amorous delusions is that we're all jealous of one another! [*She abandons him with a toss of her shoulders, and crosses to the fire to warm her hands*].

LEXY. Ah, if you women only had the same clue to Man's strength that you have to his weakness, Miss Prossy, there would be no Woman Question.

PROSERPINE [*over her shoulder, as she stoops, holding her hands to the blaze*] Where did you hear Morell say that? You didnt invent it yourself: youre not clever enough.

LEXY. Thats quite true. I am not ashamed of owing him that, as I owe him so many other spiritual truths. He said it at the annual conference of the Women's Liberal Federation. Allow me to add that though they didnt appreciate it, I, a mere man, did. [*He turns to the bookcase again, hoping that this may leave her crushed*].

PROSERPINE [*putting her hair straight at a panel of mirror in the mantelpiece*] Well, when you talk to me, give me your own ideas, such as they are, and not his. You never cut a poorer figure than when you are trying to imitate him.

LEXY [*stung*] I try to follow his example, not to imitate him.

PROSERPINE [*coming at him again on her way back to her work*] Yes, you do: you imitate him. Why do you tuck your umbrella under your left arm instead of carrying it in your hand like anyone else? Why do you walk with your chin stuck out before you, hurrying along with that eager look in your eyes? you! who never get up before half past nine in the morning. Why do you say "knoaledge" in church, though you always say "knolledge"[82] in private conversation! Bah! do you think I dont know? [*She goes back to the type-writer*]. Here! come and set about your work: weve wasted enough time for one morning. Here's a copy of the diary for today. [*She hands him a memorandum*].

LEXY [*deeply offended*] Thank you. [*He takes it and stands at the table with his back to her, reading it. She begins to transcribe her shorthand notes on the typewriter without troubling herself about his feelings*].

The door opens; and Mr Burgess enters unannounced. He is a man of sixty, made coarse and sordid by the compulsory selfishness of petty commerce, and later on softened into sluggish bumptiousness by overfeeding and commercial success. A vulgar ignorant guzzling man, offensive and contemptuous to people whose labor is cheap, respectful to wealth and rank, and quite sincere and without rancor or envy in both attitudes. The world has offered him no decently paid work except that of a sweater; and he has become, in consequence, somewhat hoggish. But he has no suspicion of this himself, and honestly regards his commercial prosperity as the inevitable and so-cially wholesome triumph of the ability, industry, shrewdness, and experience in business of a man who in private is easygoing, affec-tionate, and humorously convivial to a fault. Corporeally he is podgy, with a snoutish nose in the centre of a flat square face, a dust colored beard with a patch of grey in the centre under his chin, and small watery blue eyes with a plaintively sentimental expression, which he transfers easily to his voice by his habit of pompously intoning his sentences.

BURGESS [*stopping on the threshold, and looking round*] They told me Mr Morell was here.

PROSERPINE [*rising*] I'll fetch him for you.

BURGESS [*staring disappointedly at her*] Youre not the same young lady as hused to typewrite for him?

PROSERPINE. No.

BURGESS [*grumbling on his way to the hearthrug*] No: she was young-er. [*Miss Garnett stares at him; then goes out, slamming the door*]. Startin on your rounds, Mr Mill?

LEXY [*folding his memorandum and pocketing it*] Yes: I must be[83] off presently.

BURGESS [*momentously*] Dont let me detain you, Mr Mill. What I come about is private between me and Mr Morell.

LEXY [*huffily*] I have no intention of intruding, I am sure, Mr Burgess. Good morning.

BURGESS [*patronizingly*] Oh, good morning to you.

Morell returns as Lexy is making for the door.

MORELL [*to Lexy*] Off to work?

LEXY. Yes, sir.

MORELL. Take my silk handkerchief and wrap your throat up. Theres a cold wind. Away with you.

Lexy, more than consoled for Burgess's rudeness, brightens up and goes out.

BURGESS. Spoilin your korates as usu'l, James. Good mornin. When I pay a man, an' 'is livin depens on me, I keep him in 'is place.

MORELL [*rather shortly*] I always keep my curates in their places as my helpers and comrades. If you get as much work out of your clerks and warehousemen as I do out of my curates, you must be getting rich pretty fast. Will you take your old chair.

He points with curt authority to the armchair beside the fireplace;

*then takes the spare chair from the table and sits down at an unfamiliar
distance from his visitor.*

BURGESS [*without moving*] Just the same as hever, James!

MORELL. When you last called—it was about three years ago, I
think—you said the same thing a little more frankly. Your exact words
then were "Just as big a fool as ever, James!"

BURGESS [*soothingly*] Well, praps I did; but [*with conciliatory
cheerfulness*] I meant no hoffence by it. A clorgyman is privileged
to be a bit of a fool, you know: it's ony becomin in 'is profession that
he should. Anyhow, I come here, not to rake up hold differences, but
to let bygones be bygones. [*Suddenly becoming very solemn, and
approaching Morell*] James: three years ago, you done me a hil turn.
You done me hout of a contrac; an when I gev you arsh words in my
natral disappointment, you turned my daughrter again me. Well, I've
come to hact the part of a[84] Kerischin. [*Offering his hand*] I forgive
you, James.

MORELL [*starting up*] Confound your impudence!

BURGESS [*retreating, with almost lachrymose depression of this
treatment*] Is that becomin language for a clorgyman, James? And
you so particlar, too!

MORELL [hotly] No, sir: it is not becoming language for a clergyman. I used the wrong word. I should have said damn your impudence:
thats what St Paul or any honest priest would have said to you. Do
you think I have forgotten that tender of yours for the contract to
supply clothing to the workhouse?

BURGESS [*in a paroxysm of public spirit*] I hacted in the hinterest
of the ratepayers, James. It was the lowest tender: you carnt deny
that.

MORELL. Yes, the lowest, because you paid worse wages than any
other employer—starvation wages—aye, worse than starvation wages—
to the women who made the clothing. Your wages would have driven
them to the streets to keep body and soul together. [*Getting angrier
and angrier*] Those women were my parishioners. I shamed the
Guardians out of accepting your tender: I shamed the ratepayers out
of letting them do it: I shamed everybody but you. [*Boiling over*]
How dare you, sir, come here and offer to forgive me, and talk about
your daughter, and—

BURGESS. Heasy, James! heasy! heasy! Dont git hinto a fluster
about nothink. Ive howned I was wrong.

MORELL. Have you? I didnt hear you.

BURGESS. Of course I did. I hown it now. Come: I harsk your pardon for the letter I wrote you. Is that enough?

MORELL [*snapping his fingers*] Thats nothing. Have you raised the wages?

BURGESS [*triumphantly*] Yes.

MORELL. What!

BURGESS [*unctuously*] Ive turned a moddle hemployer. I dont hemploy no women now: theyre all sacked; and the works is done by machinery. Not a man 'as less than sixpence a *hour*; and the skilled ands gits the Trade Union rate. [*Proudly*] What ave you[85] to say to me now?

MORELL [*overwhelmed*] Is it possible! Well, theres more joy in heaven over one sinner that repenteth!—[*Going to Burgess with an explosion of apologetic cordiality*] My dear Burgess: how splendid of you! I most heartily beg your pardon for my hard thoughts. [*Grasping his hand*] And now, dont you feel the better for the change? Come! confess! youre happier. You look happier.

BURGESS [*ruefully*] Well, praps I do. I spose I must, since you notice it. At all events, I git my contrax assepted by the County Council. [*Savagely*] They dussent ave nothink to do with me unless I paid fair wages: curse em for a parcel o meddlin fools!

MORELL [*dropping his hand, utterly discouraged*] So that was why you raised the wages! [*He sits down moodily*].

BURGESS [*severely, in spreading, mounting tones*] Woy helse should I do it? What does it lead to but drink and huppishness in workin men? [*He seats himself magisterially in the easy chair*]. It's hall very well for you, James: it gits you hinto the papers and makes a great man of you; but you never think of the arm you do, puttin money into the pockets of workin men that they dunno ow to spend, and takin it from people that might be makin a good huse on it.

MORELL [*with a heavy sigh, speaking with cold politeness*] What is your business with me this morning? I shall not pretend to believe that you are here merely out of family sentiment.

BURGESS [*obstinately*] Yes I ham: just family sentiment and nothink helse.

MORELL [*with weary calm*] I dont believe you.

BURGESS [*rising threateningly*] Dont say that to me again, James Mavor Morell.

MORELL [*unmoved*] I'll say it just as often as may be necessary to convince you that it's true. I dont believe you.

BURGESS [*collapsing into an abyss of wounded feeling*] Oh, well, if youre detormined to be hunfriendly, I spose I'd better go. [*He moves reluctantly towards the door. Morell makes no sign. He lingers*]. I didnt hexpect to find a hunforgivin spirit in you, James. [*Morell still not responding, he takes a few more reluctant steps[86] doorwards. Then he comes back, whining*]. We huseter git on well enough, spite of our different hopinions. Woy are you so changed to me? I give you my word I come here in peeorr [pure] frenliness, not wishin to be hon bad terms with my hown daughter's usban. Come, James: be a Kerischin, and shake ands. [*He puts his hand sentimentally on Morell's shoulder*].

MORELL [*looking up at him thoughtfully*] Look here, Burgess. Do you want to be as welcome here as you were before you lost that contract?

BURGESS. I do, James. I do—honest.

MORELL. Then why dont you behave as you did then?

BURGESS [*cautiously removing his hand*] Ow d'y'mean?

MORELL. I'll tell you. You thought me a young fool then.

BURGESS [*coaxingly*] No I didn't, James. I—

MORELL [*cutting him short*] Yes, you did. And I thought you an old scroundrel.

BURGESS [*most vehemently deprecating this gross self-accusation on Morell's part*] No you didn't, James. Now you do yourself a hinjustice.

MORELL. Yes I did. Well, that did not prevent our getting on very well together. God made you what I call a scroundrel as He made me what you call a fool. [*The effect of this observation on Burgess is to remove the keystone of his moral arch. He becomes bodily weak, and, with his eyes fixed on Morell in a helpless stare, puts out his hand apprehensively to balance himself, as if the floor had suddenly sloped under him. Morell proceeds, in the same tone of quiet conviction*] It was not for me to quarrel with His handiwork in the one case more than in the other. So long as you come here honestly as a self-respecting, thorough, convinced scoundrel, justifying your scoundrelism and proud of it, you are welcome. But [*and now Morell's tone becomes formidable; and he rises and strikes the back of the chair for greater emphasis*] I wont have you here snivelling about being a model em-

ployer and a converted man when youre only an apostate with your
coat turned for the sake of a County Council contract. [*He nods at
him to enforce the point; then goes to the hearth-rug, where he takes
up a comfortably*[87] *commanding position with his back to the fire,
and continues*] No: I like a man to be true to himself, even in wicked-
ness. Come now: either take your hat and go; or else sit down and
give me a good scoundrelly reason for wanting to be friends with me.
[*Burgess, whose emotions have subsided sufficiently to be expressed
by a dazed grin, is relieved by this concrete proposition. He ponders
it for a moment, and then, slowly and very modestly, sits down in the
chair Morell has just left*]. Thats right. Now out with it.

BURGESS [*chuckling in spite of himself*] Well, you orr a queer
bird, James, and no mistake. But [*almost enthusiastically*] one carnt
elp likin you: besides, as I said afore, of course one dont take hall a
clorgyman says seriously, or the world couldnt go on. Could it now?
[*He composes himself for graver discourse, and, turning his eyes on
Morell, proceeds with dull seriousness*] Well, I dont mind tellin you,
since it's your wish we should be free with one another, that I did
think you a bit of a fool once; but I'm beginnin to think that praps
I was be'ind the times a bit.

MORELL [*exultant*] Aha! Youre finding that out at last, are you?

BURGESS [*portentously*] Yes: times 'as changed mor'n I could a
believed. Five yorr [year] ago, no sensible man would a thought
o takin hup with your hidears. I hused to wonder you was let preach
at all. Why, I know a clorgyman what 'as bin kep hout of his job for
yorrs by the Bishop o London, although the pore feller's not a bit
more religious than you are. But today, if hennyone was to horffer
to bet me a thousan poun that youll hend by bein a bishop yourself, I
dussent take the bet. [*Very impressively*] You and your crew are
gittin hinfluential: I can see that. Theyll ave to give you somethink
someday, if it's honly to stop your mouth. You ad the right instinc
arter all, James: the line you took is the payin line in the long run for
a man o your sort.

MORELL [*offering his hand with thorough decision*] Shake hands,
Burgess. Now youre talking honestly. I dont think theyll make me
a bishop; but if they do, I'll introduce you to the biggest jobbers I can
get to come to my dinner parties.

BURGESS [*who has risen with a sheepish grin and accepted the hand of friendship*] You will ave your joke, James. Our quarrel's[88] made up now, ain it?

A WOMAN'S VOICE. Say yes, James.

Startled, they turn quickly and find that Candida has just come in, and is looking at them with an amused maternal indulgence which is her characteristic expression. She is a woman of 33, well built, well nourished, likely, one guesses, to become matronly later on, but now quite at her best, with the double charm of youth and motherhood. Her ways are those of a woman who has found that she can always manage people by engaging their affection, and who does so frankly and instinctively without the smallest scruple. So far, she is like any other pretty woman who is just clever enough to make the most of her sexual attractions for trivially selfish ends; but Candida's serene brow, courageous eyes, and well set mouth and chin signify largeness of mind and dignity of character to ennoble her cunning in the affections. A wise-hearted observer, looking at her, would at once guess that whoever had placed the Virgin of the Assumption over her hearth did so because he fancied some spiritual resemblance between them, and yet would not suspect either her husband or herself of any such idea, or indeed of any concern with the art of Titian.

Just now she is in bonnet and mantle, carrying a strapped rug with her umbrella stuck through it, a handbag, and a supply of illustrated papers.

MORELL [*shocked at his remissness*] Candida! Why— [*he looks at his watch, and is horrified to find it so late*]. My darling! [*Hurrying to her and seizing the rug strap, pouring forth his remorseful regrets all the time*] I intended to meet you at the train. I let the time slip. [*Flinging the rug on the sofa*] I was so engrossed by— [*returning to her*] —I forgot—oh! [*He embraces her with penitent emotion*].

BURGESS [*a little shamefaced and doubtful of his reception*] How orr you, Candy? [*She, still in Morell's arms, offers him her cheek, which he kisses*]. James and me is come to a nunnerstannin. A honorable unnerstannin. Ain we, James?

MORELL [*impetuously*] Oh bother your understanding! youve kept me late for Candida. [*With compassionate fervour*] My poor love: how did you manage about the luggage? How—[89]

CANDIDA [*stopping him and disengaging herself*] There! there! there! I wasnt alone. Eugene has been down with us; and we travelled together.

MORELL [*pleased*] Eugene!

CANDIDA. Yes: he's struggling with my luggage, poor boy. Go out, dear, at once; or he'll pay for the cab; and I dont want that. [*Morell hurries out. Candida puts down her handbag; then takes off her mantle and bonnet and puts them on the sofa with the rug, chatting meanwhile*]. Well, papa: how are you getting on at home?

BURGESS. The ouse aint worth livin in since you left it, Candy. I wish youd come round and give the gurl a talkin to. Who's this Eugene thats come with you?

CANDIDA. Oh, Eugene's one of James's discoveries. He found him sleeping on the Embankment last June. Havnt you noticed our new picture [*pointing to the Virgin*]? He gave us that.

BURGESS [*incredulously*] Garn! D'you mean to tell me—your hown father!—that cab touts or such like, orf the Embankment, buys pictures like that? [*Severely*] Dont deceive me, Candy: it's a 'Igh Church picture; and James chose it hisself.

CANDIDA. Guess again. Eugene isnt a cab tout.

BURGESS. Then what is he? [*Sarcastically*] A nobleman, I spose.

CANDIDA [*nodding delightedly*] Yes. His uncle's a peer! A real live earl.

BURGESS [*not daring to believe such good news*] No!

CANDIDA. Yes. He had a seven day bill for £55 in his pocket when James found him on the Embankment. He thought he couldnt get any money for it until the seven days were up; and he was too shy to ask for credit. Oh, he's a dear boy! We are very fond of him.

BURGESS [*pretending to belittle the aristocracy, but with his eyes gleaming*] Hm! I thort you wouldnt git a hearl's nevvy visitin in Victawriar Pawrk unless he were a bit of a flat. [*Looking again at the picture*] Of course I dont old with that picture, Candy; but still it's a 'igh class fust rate work of ort: I can see that. Be sure you hintrodooce me to im, Candy. [*He looks at his watch[90] anxiously*]. I can only stay about two minutes.

Morell comes back with Eugene, whom Burgess contemplates moist-eyed with enthusiasm. He is a strange, shy youth of eighteen, slight, effeminate, with a delicate childish voice, and a hunted tormented expression and shrinking manner that shew the painful sensitiveness of very swift and acute apprehensiveness in youth, before the character has grown to its full strength. Miserably irresolute, he does not know where to stand or what to do. He is afraid of Burgess, and would run away into solitude if he dared; but the very intensity with which he feels a perfectly commonplace position comes from excessive nervous force; and his nostrils, mouth, and eyes betray a fiercely petulant wilfulness, as to the bent of which his brow, already lined with pity, is reassuring. He is so uncommon as to be almost unearthly; and to prosaic people there is something noxious in this unearthliness, just as to poetic people there is something angelic in it. His dress is anarchic. He wears an old blue serge jacket, unbuttoned, over a woollen lawn tennis shirt, with a silk handkerchief for a cravat, trousers matching the jacket, and brown canvas shoes. In these garments he has apparently lain in the heather and waded through the waters; and there is no evidence of his having ever brushed them.

As he catches sight of a stranger on entering, he stops, and edges along the wall on the opposite side of the room.

MORELL [*as he enters*] Come along: you can spare us quarter of an hour at all events. This is my father-in-law. Mr Burgess—Mr Marchbanks.

MARCHBANKS [*nervously backing against the bookcase*] Glad to meet you, sir.

BURGESS [*crossing to him with great heartiness, whilst Morell joins Candida at the fire*] Glad to meet you, I'm shore. Mr Morchbanks [*Forcing him to shake hands*] Ow do you find yorself this weather? Ope you aint lettin James put no foolish ideas into your ed?

MARCHBANKS. Foolish ideas? Oh, you mean Socialism? No.

BURGESS. Thats right. [*Again looking at his watch*] Well, I must go now: theres no elp for it. Yore not comin my way, orr you,[91] Mr Morchbanks?

MARCHBANKS. Which way is that?

BURGESS. Victawriar Pawrk Station. Theres a city train at 12.25.

MORELL. Nonsense. Eugene will stay to lunch with us, I expect.

MARCHBANKS [*anxiously excusing himself*] No—I—I—

BURGESS. Well, well I shornt press you: I bet youd rather lunch with Candy. Some night, I ope, youll come and dine with me at my club, the Freeman Founders in Nortn Folgit. Come: say you will!

MARCHBANKS. Thank you, Mr Burgess. Where is Norton Folgate? Down in Surrey, isnt it?

Burgess, inexpressibly tickled, begins to splutter with laughter.

CANDIDA [*coming to the rescue*] Youll lose your train, papa, if you dont go at once. Come back in the afternoon and tell Mr Marchbanks where to find the club.

BURGESS [*roaring with glee*] Down in Surrey! Har, har! thats not a bad one. Well, I never met a man as didnt know Nortn Folgit afore. [*Abashed at his own noisiness*] Goodbye, Mr Morchbanks: I know yore too ighbred to take my pleasantry in bad part. [*He again offers his hand*].

MARCHBANKS [*taking it with a nervous jerk*] Not at all.

BURGESS. Bye, bye, Candy. I'll look in again later on. So long, James.

MORELL. Must you go?

BURGESS. Dont stir. [*He goes out with unabated heartiness*].

MORELL. Oh, I'll see you off. [*He follows him*].

Eugene stares after them apprehensively, holding his breath until Burgess disappears.

CANDIDA [*laughing*] Well, Eugene? [*He turns with a start, and comes eagerly towards her, but stops irresolutely as he meets her amused look*]. What do you think of my father?

MARCHBANKS. I—I hardly know him yet. He seems to be a very nice old gentleman.

CANDIDA [*with gentle irony*] And youll go to the Freeman Founders to dine with him, wont you? [92]

MARCHBANKS [*miserably, taking it quite seriously*] Yes, if it will please you.

CANDIDA [*touched*] Do you know, you are a very nice boy, Eugene, with all your queerness. If you had laughed at my father I shouldnt have minded; but I like you ever so much better for being nice to him.

MARCHBANKS. Ought I to have laughed? I noticed that he said something funny; but I am so ill at ease with strangers; and I never can see a joke. I'm very sorry. [*He sits down on the sofa, his elbows on his knees and his temples between his fists, with an expression of hopeless suffering*].

CANDIDA [*bustling him goodnaturedly*] Oh come! You great baby, you! You are worse than usual this morning. Why were you so melancholy as we came along in the cab?

MARCHBANKS. Oh, that was nothing. I was wondering how much I ought to give the cabman. I know it's utterly silly; but you dont know how dreadful such things are to me—how I shrink from having to deal with strange people. [*Quickly and reassuringly*] But it's all right. He beamed all over and touched his hat when Morell gave him two shillings. I was on the point of offering him ten.

Morell comes back with a few letters and newspapers which have come by the midday post.

CANDIDA. Oh, James dear, he was going to give the cabman ten shillings! ten shillings for a three minutes drive! Oh dear!

MORELL [*at the table, glancing through the letters*] Never mind her, Marchbanks. The overpaying instinct is a generous one: better than the underpaying instinct, and not so common.

MARCHBANKS [*relapsing into dejection*] No: cowardice, incompetence. Mrs Morell's quite right.

CANDIDA. Of course she is. [*She takes up her hand-bag*]. And now I must leave you to James for the present. I suppose you are too much of a poet to know the state a woman finds her house in when she's been away for three weeks. Give me my rug. [*Eugene takes the strapped rug from the couch, and gives it to her. She takes it in her left hand, having the bag in her right*]. Now[93] hang my cloak across my arm. [*He obeys*]. Now my hat. [*He puts it into the hand which has the bag*]. Now open the door for me. [*He hurries before her and opens the door*]. Thanks. [*She goes out; and Marchbanks shuts the door*].

MORELL [*still busy at the table*] Youll stay to lunch, Marchbanks, of course.

MARCHBANKS [*scared*] I mustnt. [*He glances quickly at Morell, but at once avoids his frank look, and adds, with obvious disingenuousness*] I mean I cant.

MORELL. You mean you wont.

MARCHBANKS [*earnestly*] No: I should like to, indeed. Thank you very much. But—but—

MORELL. But—but—but—but—Bosh! If youd like to stay, stay. If youre shy, go and take a turn in the park and write poetry until half past one; and then come in and have a good feed.

MARCHBANKS. Thank you, I should like that very much. But I really mustnt. The truth is, Mrs Morell told me not to. She said she didnt think youd ask me to stay to lunch, but that I was to remember, if you did, that you didnt really want me to. [*Plaintively*] She said I'd understand; but I dont. Please dont tell her I told you.

MORELL [*drolly*] Oh, is that all? Wont my suggestion that you should take a turn in the park meet the difficulty?

MARCHBANKS. How?

MORELL [*exploding good-humoredly*] Why, you duffer—[*But this boisterousness jars himself as well as Eugene. He checks himself*]. No: I wont put it in that way. [*He comes to Eugene with affectionate seriousness*]. My dear lad: in a happy marriage like ours, there is something very sacred in the return of the wife to her home. [*Marchbanks looks quickly at him, half anticipating his meaning*]. An old friend or a truly noble and sympathetic soul is not in the way on such occasions; but a chance visitor is. [*The hunted horror-stricken expression comes out with sudden vividness in Eugene's face as he understands. Morell, occupied with his own thoughts, goes on without noticing this*]. Candida thought I would rather not have you here; but she was wrong. I'm very fond of you, my boy; and[94] I should like you to see for yourself what a happy thing it is to be married as I am.

MARCHBANKS. Happy! Your marriage! You think that! You believe that!

MORELL [*buoyantly*] I know it, my lad. Larochefoucauld said that there are convenient marriages but no delightful ones. You dont know the comfort of seeing through and through a thundering liar and rotten cynic like that fellow. Ha! ha! Now, off with you to the park, and write your poem. Half past one, sharp, mind: we never wait for anybody.

MARCHBANKS [*wildly*] No: stop: you shant. I'll force it into the light.

MORELL [*puzzled*] Eh? Force what?

MARCHBANKS. I must speak to you. There is something that must be settled between us.

MORELL [*with a whimsical glance at his watch*] Now?

MARCHBANKS [*passionately*] Now. Before you leave this room. [*He retreats a few steps, and stands as if to bar Morell's way to the door*].

MORELL [*without moving, and gravely, perceiving now that there is something serious the matter*] I'm not going to leave it, my dear boy: I thought you were. [*Eugene, baffled by his firm tone, turns his back on him, writhing with anger. Morell goes to him and puts his hand on his shoulder strongly and kindly, disregarding his attempt to shake it off*]. Come: sit down quietly; and tell me what it is. And remember: we are friends, and need not fear that either of us will be anything but patient and kind to the other, whatever we may have to say.

MARCHBANKS [*twisting himself round on him*] Oh, I am not forgetting myself: I am only [*covering his face desperately with his hands*] full of horror. [*Then, dropping his hands, and thrusting his face forward fiercely at Morell, he goes on threateningly*] You shall see whether this is a time for patience and kindness. [*Morell, firm as a rock, looks indulgently at him*]. Dont look at me in that self-complacent way. You think yourself stronger than I am; but I shall stagger you if you have a heart in your breast.[95]

MORELL [*powerfully confident*] Stagger me, my boy. Out with it.

MARCHBANKS. First—

MORELL. First?

MARCHBANKS. I love your wife.

Morell recoils, and, after staring at him for a moment in utter amazement, bursts into uncontrollable laughter. Eugene is taken aback, but not disconcerted; and he soon becomes indignant and contemptuous.

MORELL [*sitting down to have his laugh out*] Why, my dear child, of course you do. Everybody loves her: they cant help it. I like it. But [*looking up jocosely at him*] I say, Eugene: do you think yours is a case to be talked about? Youre under twenty: she's over thirty. Doesnt it look rather too like a case of calf love?

MARCHBANKS [*vehemently*] You dare say that of her! You think that way of the love she inspires! It is an insult to her!

MORELL [*rising quickly, in an altered tone*] To her! Eugene: take care. I have been patient. I hope to remain patient. But there are some things I wont allow. Dont force me to shew you the indulgence I should shew to a child. Be a man.

MARCHBANKS [*with a gesture as if sweeping something behind him*] Oh, let us put aside all that cant. It horrifies me when I think of the doses of it she has had to endure in all the weary years during which you have selfishly and blindly sacrificed her to minister to your self-sufficiency: you! [*turning on him*] who have not one thought—one sense—in common with her.

MORELL [*philosophically*] She seems to bear it pretty well. [*Looking him straight in the face*] Eugene, my boy: you are making a fool of yourself: a very great fool of yourself. Theres a piece of wholesome plain speaking for you. [*He knocks in the lesson with a nod in his old way, and posts himself on the hearthrug, holding his hands behind him to warm them*].

MARCHBANKS. Oh, do you think I dont know all that? Do you think that the things people make fools of themselves about are any less real and true than the things they behave sensibly about? [*Morell's gaze wavers for the first time. He forgets to warm his[96] hands, and stands listening, startled and thoughtful*]. They are more true: they are the only things that are true. You are very calm and sensible and moderate with me because you can see that I am a fool about your wife; just as no doubt that old man who was here just now is very wise over your Socialism, because he sees that you are a fool about it. [*Morell's perplexity deepens markedly. Eugene follows up his advantage, plying him fiercely with questions*]. Does that prove you wrong? Does your complacent superiority to me prove that *I* am wrong?

MORELL. Marchbanks: some devil is putting these words into your mouth. It is easy—terribly easy—to shake a man's faith in himself. To take advantage of that to break a man's spirit is devil's work. Take care of what you are doing. Take care.

MARCHBANKS [*ruthlessly*] I know. I'm doing it on purpose. I told you I should stagger you.

They confront one another threateningly for a moment. Then Morell recovers his dignity.

MORELL [*with noble tenderness*] Eugene: listen to me. Some day, I hope and trust, you will be a happy man like me. [*Eugene chafes intolerantly, repudiating the worth of his happiness. Morell, deeply insulted, controls himself with fine forbearance, and continues steadily with great artistic beauty of delivery*] You will be married; and you will be working with all your might and valor to make every spot on earth as happy as your own home. You will be one of the makers of the Kingdom of Heaven on earth; and—who knows?—you may be a master builder where I am only a humble journeyman; for dont think, my boy, that I cannot see in you, young as you are, promise of higher powers than I can ever pretend to. I well know that it is in the poet that the holy spirit of man—the god within him—is most godlike. It should make you tremble to think of that—to think that the heavy burthen and great gift of a poet may be laid upon you.

MARCHBANKS [*unimpressed and remorseless, his boyish crudity of assertion telling sharply against Morell's oratory*] It does not make me tremble. It is the want of it in others that makes me tremble.[97]

MORELL [*redoubling his force of style under the stimulus of his genuine feeling and Eugene's obduracy*] Then help to kindle it in them—in me—not to extinguish it. In the future, when you are as happy as I am, I will be your true brother in the faith. I will help you to believe that God has given us a world that nothing but our own folly keeps from being a paradise. I will help you to believe that every stroke of your work is sowing happiness for the great harvest that all—even the humblest—shall one day reap. And last, but trust me, not least, I will help you to believe that your wife loves you and is happy in her home. We need such help, Marchbanks: we need it greatly and always. There are so many things to make us doubt, if once we let our understanding be troubled. Even at home, we sit as if in camp, encompassed by a hostile army of doubts. Will you play the traitor and let them in on me?

MARCHBANKS [*looking round wildly*] Is it like this for her here always? A woman, with a great soul, craving for reality, truth, freedom; and being fed on metaphors, sermons, stale perorations, mere rhetoric. Do you think a woman's soul can live on your talent for preaching?

MORELL [*stung*] Marchbanks: you make it hard for me to control myself. My talent is like yours insofar as it has any real worth at all. It is the gift of finding words for divine truth.

MARCHBANKS [*impetuously*] It's the gift of the gab, nothing more and nothing less. What has your knack of fine talking to do with the truth, any more than playing the organ has? Ive never been in your church; but Ive been to your political meetings; and Ive seen you do whats called rousing the meeting to enthusiasm: that is, you excited them until they behaved exactly as if they were drunk. And their wives looked on and saw what fools they were. Oh, it's an old story: youll find it in the Bible. I imagine King David, in his fits of enthusiasm, was very like you. [*Stabbing him with the words*] "But his wife despised him in her heart."

MORELL [*wrathfully*] Leave my house. Do you hear? [*He advances on him threateningly*].

MARCHBANKS [*shrinking back against the couch*] Let me alone.[98]

Dont touch me. [*Morell grasps him powerfully by the lapel of his coat: he cowers down on the sofa and screams passionately*] Stop, Morell: if you strike me, I'll kill myself: I wont bear it. [*Almost in hysterics*] Let me go. Take your hand away.

MORELL [*with slow emphatic scorn*] You little snivelling cowardly whelp. [*He releases him*]. Go, before you frighten yourself into a fit.

MARCHBANKS [*on the sofa, gasping, but relieved by the withdrawal of Morell's hand*] I'm not afraid of you: it's you who are afraid of me.

MORELL [*quietly, as he stands over him*] It looks like it, doesnt it?

MARCHBANKS [*with petulant vehemence*] Yes, it does. [*Morell turns away contemptuously. Eugene scrambles to his feet and follows him*]. You think because I shrink from being brutally handled—because [*with tears in his voice*] I can do nothing but cry with rage when I am met with violence—because I cant lift a heavy trunk down from the top of a cab like you—because I cant fight you for your wife as a drunken navvy would: all that makes you think I'm afraid of you. But youre wrong. If I havnt got what you call British pluck, I havnt British cowardice either: I'm not afraid of a clergyman's ideas. I'll fight your ideas. I'll rescue her from her slavery to them. I'll pit my own ideas against them. You are driving me out of the house because you darent let her choose between your ideas and mine. You are afraid to let me see her again. [*Morell, angered, turns suddenly on him. He flies to the door in involuntary dread*]. Let me alone, I say. I'm going.

MORELL [*with cold scorn*] Wait a moment: I am not going to touch you: dont be afraid. When my wife comes back she will want to know why you have gone. And when she finds that you are never going to cross our threshold again, she will want to have that explained too. Now I dont wish to distress her by telling her that you have behaved like a blackguard.

MARCHBANKS [*coming back with renewed vehemence*] You shall. You must. If you give any explanation but the true one, you are a liar and a coward. Tell her what I said; and how you were strong[99] and manly, and shook me as a terrier shakes a rat; and how I shrank and was terrified; and how you called me a snivelling little whelp and put me out of the house. If you dont tell her, I will: I'll write it to her.

MORELL [*puzzled*] Why do you want her to know this?

MARCHBANKS [*with lyric rapture*] Because she will understand me, and know that I understand her. If you keep back one word of it from her—if you are not ready to lay the truth at her feet as I am—then you will know to the end of your days that she really belongs to me and not to you. Goodbye. [*Going*].

MORELL [*terribly disquieted*] Stop: I will not tell her.

MARCHBANKS [*turning near the door*] Either the truth or a lie you must tell her, if I go.

MORELL [*temporizing*] Marchbanks: it is sometimes justifiable—

MARCHBANKS [*cutting him short*] I know: to lie. It will be useless. Goodbye, Mr Clergyman.

As he turns to the door, it opens and Candida enters in her house-keeping dress.

CANDIDA. Are you going, Eugene? [*Looking more observantly at him*] Well, dear me, just look at you, going out into the street in that state! You are a poet, certainly. Look at him, James! [*She takes him by the coat, and brings him forward, shewing him to Morell*]. Look at his collar! look at his tie! look at his hair! One would think some-body had been throttling you. [*Eugene instinctively tries to look round at Morell; but she pulls him back*]. Here! Stand still. [*She buttons his collar; ties his neckerchief in a bow; and arranges his hair*]. There! Now you look so nice that I think youd better stay to lunch after all, though I told you you mustnt. It will be ready in half an hour. [*She puts a final touch to the bow. He kisses her hand*]. Dont be silly.

MARCHBANKS. I want to stay, of course; unless the reverend gentleman your husband has anything to advance to the contrary.

CANDIDA. Shall he stay, James, if he promises to be a good boy and help me to lay the table?

MORELL [*shortly*] Oh yes, certainly: he had better. [*He goes to*[100] *the table and pretends to busy himself with his papers there*].

MARCHBANKS [*offering his arm to Candida*] Come and lay the table. [*She takes it. They go to the door together. As they pass out he adds*] I am the happiest of mortals.

MORELL. So was I—an hour ago.[101]

ACT II

The same day later in the afternoon. The same room. The chair for visitors has been replaced at the table. Marchbanks, alone and idle, is trying to find out how the typewriter works. Hearing someone at the door, he steals guiltily away to the window and pretends to be absorbed in the view. Miss Garnett, carrying the notebook in which she takes down Morell's letters in shorthand from his dictation, sits down at the typewriter and sets to work transcribing them, much too busy to notice Eugene. When she begins the second line she stops and stares at the machine. Something wrong evidently.

PROSERPINE. Bother! Youve been meddling with my typewriter, Mr Marchbanks; and theres not the least use in your trying to look as if you hadnt.

MARCHBANKS [*timidly*] I'm very sorry, Miss Garnett. I only tried to make it write. [*Plaintively*] But it wouldnt.

PROSERPINE. Well, youve altered the spacing.

MARCHBANKS [*earnestly*] I assure you I didn't. I didn't indeed. I only turned a little wheel. It gave a sort of click.

PROSERPINE. Oh, now I understand. [*She restores the spacing, talking volubly all the time*]. I suppose you thought it was a sort of barrel-organ. Nothing to do but turn the handle, and it would write a beautiful love letter for you straight off, eh?

MARCHBANKS [*seriously*] I suppose a machine could be made to write love letters. Theyre all the same, arnt they?

PROSERPINE [*somewhat indignantly: any such discussion, except by way of pleasantry, being outside her code of manners*] How do I know? Why do you ask me?

MARCHBANKS. I beg your pardon. I thought clever people—people who can do business and write letters and that sort of thing—always had to have love affairs to keep them from going mad.

PROSERPINE [*rising, outraged*] Mr Marchbanks! [*She looks severely at him, and marches majestically to the bookcase*].

MARCHBANKS [*approaching her humbly*] I hope I havnt offended you. Perhaps I shouldnt have alluded to your love affairs.[102]

PROSERPINE [*plucking a blue book from the shelf and turning sharply on him*] I havnt any love affairs. How dare you say such a thing? The idea! [*She tucks the book under her arm, and is flouncing back to her machine when he addresses her with awkward interest and sympathy*].

MARCHBANKS. Really! Oh, then you are shy, like me.

PROSERPINE. Certainly I am not shy. What do you mean?

MARCHBANKS [*secretly*] You must be: that is the reason there are so few love affairs in the world. We all go about longing for love: it is the first need of our natures, the first prayer of our hearts; but we dare not utter our longing: we are too shy. [*Very earnestly*] Oh, Miss Garnett, what would you not give to be without fear, without shame—

PROSERPINE [*scandalized*] Well, upon my word!

MARCHBANKS [*with petulant impatience*] Ah, dont say those stupid things to me: they dont deceive me: what use are they? Why are you afraid to be your real self with me? I am just like you.

PROSERPINE. Like me! Pray are you flattering me or flattering yourself? I dont feel quite sure which. [*She again tries to get back to her work*].

MARCHBANKS [*stopping her mysteriously*] Hush! I go about in search of love; and I find it in unmeasured stores in the bosoms of others. But when I try to ask for it, this horrible shyness strangles me; and I stand dumb, or worse than dumb, saying meaningless things: foolish lies. And I see the affection I am longing for given to dogs and cats and pet birds, because they come and ask for it. [*Almost whispering*] It must be asked for: it is like a ghost: it cannot speak unless it is first spoken to. [*At his usual pitch, but with deep melancholy*] All the love in the world is longing to speak; only it dare not, because it is shy! shy! shy! That is the world's tragedy. [*With a deep sigh he sits in the visitor's chair and buries his face in his hands*].

PROSERPINE [*amazed, but keeping her wits about her: her point of honor in encounters with strange young men*] Wicked people get over that shyness occasionally, dont they? [103]

MARCHBANKS [*scrambling up almost fiercely*] Wicked people means people who have no love: therefore they have no shame. They have the power to ask love because they dont need it: they have the power to offer it because they have none to give. [*He collapses into his seat, and adds, mournfully*] But we, who have love, and long to mingle it with the love of others: we cannot utter a word. [*Timidly*] You find that, dont you?

PROSERPINE. Look here: if you dont stop talking like this, I'll leave the room, Mr Marchbanks: I really will. It's not proper.

She resumes her seat at the typewriter, opening the blue book and preparing to copy a passage from it.

MARCHBANKS [*hopelessly*] Nothing thats worth saying is proper. [*He rises, and wanders about the room in his lost way*]. I cant understand you, Miss Garnett. What am I to talk about?

PROSERPINE [*snubbing him*] Talk about indifferent things. Talk about the weather.

MARCHBANKS. Would you talk about indifferent things if a child were by, crying bitterly with hunger?

PROSERPINE. I suppose not.

MARCHBANKS. Well: *I* cant talk about indifferent things with my heart crying out bitterly in its hunger.

PROSERPINE. Then hold your tongue.

MARCHBANKS. Yes: that is what it always comes to. We hold our tongues. Does that stop the cry of your heart? for it does cry: doesnt it? It must, if you have a heart.

PROSERPINE [*suddenly rising with her hand pressed on her heart*] Oh, it's no use trying to work while you talk like that [*She leaves her little table and sits on the sofa. Her feelings are keenly stirred*]. It's no business of yours whether my heart cries or not; but I have a mind to tell you, for all that.

MARCHBANKS. You neednt. I know already that it must.

PROSERPINE. But mind! if you ever say I said so, I'll deny it.

MARCHBANKS [*compassionately*] Yes, I know. And so you havnt the courage to tell him?

PROSERPINE [*bouncing up*] Him! Who?

MARCHBANKS. Whoever he is. The man you love. It might be[104] anybody. The curate, Mr Mill, perhaps.

PROSERPINE [*with disdain*] Mr Mill!!! A fine man to break my heart about, indeed! I'd rather have you than Mr Mill.

MARCHBANKS [*recoiling*] No, really: I'm very sorry; but you mustnt think of that. I—

PROSERPINE [*testily, going to the fire-place and standing at it with her back to him*] Oh, dont be frightened: it's not you. It's not any one particular person.

MARCHBANKS. I know. You feel that you could love anybody that offered—

PROSERPINE [*turning, exasperated*] Anybody that offered! No, I do not. What do you take me for?

MARCHBANKS [*discouraged*] No use. You wont make me real answers: only those things that everybody says [*He strays to the sofa and sits down disconsolately*].

PROSERPINE [*nettled at what she takes to be a disparagement of her manners by an aristocrat*] Oh well, if you want original conversation, youd better go and talk to yourself.

MARCHBANKS. That is what all poets do: they talk to themselves out loud; and the world overhears them. But it's horribly lonely not to hear someone else talk sometimes.

PROSERPINE. Wait until Mr Morell comes. He'll talk to you. [*Marchbanks shudders*]. Oh, you neednt make wry faces over him: he can talk better than you. [*With temper*] He'd talk your little head off. [*She is going back angrily to her place, when he, suddenly, enlightened, springs up and stops her*].

MARCHBANKS. Ah! I understand now.

PROSERPINE [*reddening*] What do you understand?

MARCHBANKS. Your secret. Tell me: is it really and truly possible for a woman to love him?

PROSERPINE [*as if this were beyond all bounds*] Well!!

MARCHBANKS [*passionately*] No: answer me. I want to know: I must know. *I* cant understand it. I can see nothing in him but words, pious resolutions, what people call goodness. You cant love that.

PROSERPINE [*attempting to snub him by an air of cool propriety*] I[105] simply dont know what youre talking about. I dont understand you.

MARCHBANKS [*vehemently*] You do. You lie.

PROSERPINE. Oh!

MARCHBANKS. You do understand; and you know. [*Determined to have an answer*] Is it possible for a woman to love him?

PROSERPINE [*looking him straight in the face*] Yes. [*He covers his face with his hands*]. Whatever is the matter with you! [*He takes down his hands. Frightened at the tragic mask presented to her, she hurries past him at the utmost possible distance, keeping her eyes on his face until he turns from her and goes to the child's chair beside the hearth, where he sits in the deepest dejection. As she approaches the door, it opens and Burgess enters. Seeing him, she ejaculates*] Praise heaven! here's somebody [*and feels safe enough to resume her place

*at her table. She puts a fresh sheet of paper into the typewriter as
Burgess crosses to Eugene].*

BURGESS [*bent on taking care of the distinguished visitor*] Well: so
this is the way they leave you to yourself, Mr Morchbanks. Ive come
to keep you company. [*Marchbanks looks up at him in consternation,
which is quite lost on him*]. James is receivin a deppitation in the
dinin room; and Candy is hupstairs heducating of a young stitcher
gurl she's hinterested in. [*Condolingly*] You must find it lonesome
here with no one but the typist to talk to. [*He pulls round the easy
chair, and sits down*].

PROSERPINE [*highly incensed*] He'll be all right now that he has
the advantage of your polished conversation: thats one comfort, anyhow. [*She begins to typewrite with clattering asperity*].

BURGESS [*amazed at her audacity*] Hi was not addressin myself
to you, young woman, that I'm awerr of.

PROSERPINE. Did you ever see worse manners, Mr Marchbanks?

BURGESS [*with pompous severity*] Mr Morchbanks is a gentleman,
and knows his place, which is more than some people do.

PROSERPINE [*fretfully*] It's well you and I are not ladies and
gentlemen: I'd talk to you pretty straight if Mr Marchbanks wasnt
here. [*She pulls the letter out of the machine so crossly that it*[106]
tears]. There! Now I've spoiled this letter! have to be done all over
again! Oh, I cant contain myself: silly old fathead!

BURGESS [*rising, breathless with indignation*] Ho! I'm a silly ole
fat'ead, am I? Ho, indeed [*gasping*]! Hall right, my gurl! Hall right.
You just wait till I tell that to yore hemployer. Youll see. I'll teach you:
see if I dont.

PROSERPINE [*conscious of having gone too far*] I—

BURGESS [*cutting her short*] No: youve done it now. No huse
a-talkin to me. I'll let you know who I am. [*Proserpine shifts her
paper carriage with a defiant bang, and disdainfully goes on with
her work*]. Dont you take no notice of her, Mr Morchbanks. She's
beneath it. [*He loftily sits down again*].

MARCHBANKS [*miserably nervous and disconcerted*] Hadnt we
better change the subject? I—I dont think Miss Garnett meant anything.

PROSERPINE [*with intense conviction*] Oh, didn't I though, just!

BURGESS. I wouldnt demean myself to take notice on her.

An electric bell rings twice.

PROSERPINE [*gathering up her note-book and papers*] Thats for me. [*She hurries out*].

BURGESS [*calling after her*] Oh, we can spare you. [*Somewhat relieved by the triumph of having the last word, and yet half inclined to try to improve on it, he looks after her for a moment; then subsides into his seat by Eugene, and addresses him very confidentially*]. Now we're alone, Mr Morchbanks, let me give you a friendly int that I wouldnt give to heverybody. Ow long ave you known my son-in-law James ere?

MARCHBANKS. I dont know. I never can remember dates. A few months, perhaps.

BURGESS. Ever notice hennythink queer about him?

MARCHBANKS. I dont think so.

BURGESS [*impressively*] No more you wouldnt. Thats the danger on it. Well, he's mad.

MARCHBANKS. Mad!

BURGESS. Mad as a Morch 'are. You take notice on him and youll see.[107]

MARCHBANKS [*uneasily*] But surely that is only because his opinions—

BURGESS [*touching him on the knee with his forefinger, and pressing it to hold his attention*] Thats the same what I hused to think, Mr Morchbanks. Hi thought long enough that it was ony his opinions; though, mind you, hopinions becomes vurry serious things when people takes to hactin on em as e does. But thats not what I go on. [*He looks round to make sure that they are alone, and bends over to Eugene's ear*]. What do you think he sez to me this mornin in this very room?

MARCHBANKS. What?

BURGESS. He sez to me—this is as sure as we're settin here now—he sez "I'm a fool," he sez; "and yore a scounderl." Me a scounderl, mind you! And then shook ands with me on it, as if it was to my credit! Do you mean to tell me as that man's sane?

MORELL [*outside, calling to Proserpine as he opens the door*] Get all their names and addresses, Miss Garnett.

PROSERPINE [*in the distance*] Yes, Mr Morell.

Morell comes in, with the deputation's documents in his hands.

BURGESS [*aside to Marchbanks*] Yorr he is. Just you keep your heye on im and see. [*Rising momentously*] I'm sorry, James, to ave to make a complaint to you. I dont want to do it; but I feel I oughter, as a matter o right and dooty.

MORELL. Whats the matter?

BURGESS. Mr Morchbanks will bear me hout: he was a witness. [*Very solemnly*] Yore young woman so far forgot herself as to call me a silly ole fat'ead.

MORELL [*with tremendous heartiness*] Oh, now, isnt that exactly like Prossy? She's so frank: she cant contain herself! Poor Prossy! Ha! ha!

BURGESS [*trembling with rage*] And do you hexpec me to put up with it from the like of er?

MORELL. Pooh, nonsense! you cant take any notice of it. Never mind. [*He goes to the cellaret and puts the papers into one of the drawers*].

BURGESS. Oh, Hi dont mind. Hi'm above it. But is it right? [108] thats what I want to know. Is it right?

MORELL. Thats a question for the Church, not for the laity. Has it done you any harm? thats the question for you, eh? Of course it hasnt. Think no more of it. [*He dismisses the subject by going to his place at the table and setting to work at his correspondence*].

BURGESS [*aside to Marchbanks*] What did I tell you? Mad as a atter. [*He goes to the table and asks, with the sickly civility of a hungry man*] When's dinner, James?

MORELL. Not for a couple of hours yet.

BURGESS [*with plaintive resignation*] Gimmie a nice book to read over the fire, will you, James: thur's a good chap.

MORELL. What sort of book? A good one?

BURGESS [*with almost a yell of remonstrance*] Nah-oo! Summat pleasant, just to pass the time. [*Morell takes an illustrated paper from the table and offers it. He accepts it humbly*]. Thank yer, James. [*He goes back to the big chair at the fire, and sits there at his ease, reading*].

MORELL [*as he writes*] Candida will come to entertain you presently. She has got rid of her pupil. She is filling the lamps.

MARCHBANKS [*starting up in the wildest consternation*] But that will soil her hands. I cant bear that, Morell: it's a shame. I'll go and fill them [*He makes for the door*].

MORELL. Youd better not [*Marchbanks stops irresolutely*]. She'd only set you to clean my boots, to save me the trouble of doing it myself in the morning.

BURGESS [*with grave disapproval*] Dont you keep a servant now, James?

MORELL. Yes; but she isnt a slave; and the house looks as if I kept three. That means that everyone has to lend a hand. It's not a bad plan: Prossy and I can talk business after breakfast while we're washing up. Washing up's no trouble when there are two people to do it.

MARCHBANKS [*tormentedly*] Do you think every woman is as coarsegrained as Miss Garnett?

BURGESS [*emphatically*] Thats quite right, Mr Morchbanks: [109] thats quite right. She is corsegrained.

MORELL [*quietly and significantly*] Marchbanks!

MARCHBANKS. Yes?

MORELL. How many servants does your father keep?

MARCHBANKS [*pettishly*] Oh, I dont know. [*He moves to the sofa, as if to get as far as possible from Morell's questioning, and sits down in great agony of spirit, thinking of the paraffin*].

MORELL [*very gravely*] So many that you dont know! [*More aggressively*] When theres anything coarse-grained to be done, you just ring the bell and throw it on to somebody else, eh?

MARCHBANKS. Oh, dont torture me. You dont even ring the bell. But your wife's beautiful fingers are dabbling in paraffin oil while you sit here comfortably preaching about it: everlasting preaching! preaching! words! words! words!

BURGESS [*intensely appreciating this retort*] Har, har! Devil a better! [*Radiantly*] Ad you there, James, straight.

Candida comes in well aproned, with a reading lamp trimmed, filled, and ready for lighting. She places it on the table near Morell, ready for use.

CANDIDA [*brushing her finger tips together with a slight twitch of her nose*] If you stay with us, Eugene, I think I will hand over the lamps to you.

MARCHBANKS. I will stay on condition that you hand over all the rough work to me.

CANDIDA. Thats very gallant; but I think I should like to see how you do it first. [*Turning to Morell*] James: youve not been looking after the house properly.

MORELL. What have I done—or not done—my love?

CANDIDA [*with serious vexation*] My own particular pet scrubbing brush has been used for blackleading. [*A heart-breaking wail bursts*

*from Marchbanks. Burgess look around, amazed. Candida hurries to
the sofa.*] Whats the matter? Are you ill, Eugene?

MARCHBANKS. No: not ill. Only horror! horror! horror! [*He bows
his head on his hands*].

BURGESS [*shocked*] What! Got the orrors, Mr Morchbanks! Oh,
thats bad, at your age. You must leave it off grajally.[110]

CANDIDA [*reassured*] Nonsense, papa! It's only poetic horror, isnt
it, Eugene [*petting him*]?

BURGESS [*abashed*] Oh, poetic orror, is it? I beg your pordon, I'm
shore. [*He turns to the fire again, deprecating his hasty conclusion*].

CANDIDA. What is it, Eugene? the scrubbing brush? [*He
shudders*] Well, there! never mind. [*She sits down beside him*].
Wouldnt you like to present me with a nice one, with an ivory back
with mother-of-pearl?

MARCHBANKS [*softly and musically, but sadly and longingly*] No,
not a scrubbing brush, but a boat: a tiny shallop to sail away in, far
from the world, where the marble floors are washed by the rain and
dried by the sun; where the south wind dusts the beautiful green and
purple carpets. Or a chariot! to carry us up into the sky, where the
lamps are stars, and dont need to be filled with paraffin oil every
day.

MORELL [*harshly*] And where there is nothing to do but to be
idle, selfish and useless.

CANDIDA [*jarred*] Oh, James! how could you spoil it all?

MARCHBANKS [*firing up*] Yes, to be idle, selfish and useless: that
is, to be beautiful and free and happy: hasnt every man desired that
with all his soul for the woman he loves? Thats my ideal: whats
yours, and that of all the dreadful people who live in these hideous
rows of houses? Sermons and scrubbing brushes! With you to preach
the sermon and your wife to scrub.

CANDIDA [*quaintly*] He cleans the boots, Eugene. You will have
to clean them to-morrow for saying that about him.

MARCHBANKS. Oh, dont talk about boots! Your feet should be
beautiful on the mountains.

CANDIDA. My feet would not be beautiful on the Hackney Road
without boots.

BURGESS [*scandalized*] Come, Candy! dont be vulgar. Mr Morchbanks aint accustomed to it. Youre givin him the orrors again. I mean
the poetic ones.

Morell is silent. Apparently he is busy with his letters: really he is puzzling with misgiving over his new and alarming experience that the[111] *surer he is of his moral thrusts, the more swiftly and effectively Eugene parries them. To find himself beginning to fear a man whom he does not respect afflicts him bitterly.*

Miss Garnett comes in with a telegram.

PROSERPINE [*handing the telegram to Morell*] Reply paid. The boy's waiting. [*To Candida, coming back to her machine and sitting down*] Maria is ready for you now in the kitchen, Mrs Morell [*Candida rises*] The onions have come.

MARCHBANKS [*convulsively*] Onions!

CANDIDA. Yes, onions. Not even Spanish ones: nasty little red onions. You shall help me to slice them. Come along.

She catches him by the wrist and runs out, pulling him after her. Burgess rises in consternation, and stands aghast on the hearth-rug, staring after them.

BURGESS. Candy didnt oughter andle a hearl's nevvy like that. It's goin too fur with it. Lookee ere, James: do e often git taken queer like that?

MORELL [*shortly, writing a telegram*] I dont know.

BURGESS [*sentimentally*] He talks very pretty. I awlus had a turn for a bit of poetry. Candy takes arter me that-a-way. Huseter make me tell er fairy stories when she was ony a little kiddy not that igh [*indicating a stature of two feet or thereabouts*].

MORELL [*preoccupied*] Ah, indeed. [*He blots the telegram and goes out*].

PROSERPINE. Used you to make the fairy stories up out of your own head?

Burgess, not deigning to reply, strikes an attitude of the haughtiest disdain on the hearth-rug.

PROSERPINE [*calmly*] I should never have supposed you had it in you. By the way, I'd better warn you, since youve taken such a fancy to Mr Marchbanks. He's mad.

BURGESS. Mad' What! Im too!!

PROSERPINE. Mad as a March hare. He did frighten me, I can tell you, just before you came in that time. Havent you noticed the queer things he says?

BURGESS. So thats what the poetic orrors means. Blame me if[112] it didnt come into my ed once or twyst that he was a bit horff is chump! [*He crosses the room to the door, lifting up his voice as he goes*]. Well, this is a pretty sort of asylum for a man to be in, with no one but you to take care of him!

PROSERPINE [*as he passes her*] Yes, what a dreadful thing it would be if anything happened to you!

BURGESS [*loftily*] Dont you haddress no remorks to me. Tell your hemployer that Ive gone into the gorden for a smoke.

PROSERPINE [*mocking*] Oh!

Before Burgess can retort, Morell comes back.

BURGESS [*sentimentally*] Goin for a turn in the gording to smoke, James.

MORELL [*brusquely*] Oh, all right, all right. [*Burgess goes out pathetically in the character of a weary old man. Morell stands at the table, turning over his papers, and adding, across to Proserpine, half humorously, half absently*] Well, Miss Prossy, why have you been calling my father-in-law names?

PROSERPINE [*blushing fiery red, and looking quickly up at him, half scared, half reproachful*] I—[*She bursts into tears*].

MORELL [*with tender gaiety, leaning across the table towards her, and consoling her*] Oh, come! come! come! Never mind, Pross: he is a silly old fathead, isnt he?

With an explosive sob, she makes a dash at the door, and vanishes, banging it. Morell, shaking his head resignedly, sighs, and goes wearily to his chair, where he sits down and sets to work, looking old and careworn.

Candida comes in. She has finished her household work and taken off the apron. She at once notices his dejected appearance, and posts herself quietly at the visitors' chair, looking down at him attentively. She says nothing.

MORELL [*looking up, but with his pen raised ready to resume his work*] Well? Where is Eugene?

CANDIDA. Washing his hands in the scullery under the tap. He will make an excellent cook if he can only get over his dread of Maria.

MORELL [*shortly*] Ha! No doubt. [*He begins writing again*].[113]

CANDIDA [*going nearer, and putting her hand down softly on his to stop him as she says*] Come here, dear. Let me look at you. [*He drops his pen and yields himself to her disposal. She makes him rise, and brings him a little away from the table, looking at him critically all the time*]. Turn your face to the light. [*She places him facing the window*]. My boy is not looking well. Has he been overworking?

MORELL. Nothing more than usual.

CANDIDA. He looks very pale, and grey, and wrinkled, and old. [*His melancholy deepens; and she attacks it with wilful gaiety*] Here: [*pulling him towards the easy chair*] youve done enough writing for today. Leave Prossy to finish it. Come and talk to me.

MORELL. But—

CANDIDA [*insisting*] Yes, I must be talked to. [*She makes him sit down, and seats herself on the carpet beside his knee*]. Now [*patting his hand*] youre beginning to look better already. Why must you go out every night lecturing and talking? I hardly have one evening a week with you. Of course what you say is all very true; but it does no good: they dont mind what you say to them one little bit. They think they agree with you; but whats the use of their agreeing with you if they go and do just the opposite of what you tell them the moment your back is turned? Look at our congregation at St Dominic's! Why do they come to hear you talking about Christianity every Sunday? Why, just because theyve been so full of business and money-making for six days that they want to forget all about it and have a rest on the seventh; so that they can go back fresh and make money harder than ever! You positively help them at it instead of hindering them.

MORELL [*with energetic seriousness*] You know very well, Candida, that I often blow them up soundly for that. And if there is nothing in their churchgoing but rest and diversion, why dont they try something more amusing? more self-indulging? There must be some good in the fact that they prefer St Dominic's to worse places on Sundays.

CANDIDA. Oh, the worse places arnt open; and even if they were, they darent be seen going to them. Besides, James dear, you preach so splendidly that it's as good as a play for them. Why do[114] you think the women are so enthusiastic?

MORELL [*shocked*] Candida!

CANDIDA. Oh, *I* know. You silly boy: you think it's your Socialism and your religion; but if it were that, theyd do what you tell them instead of only coming to look at you. They all have Prossy's complaint.

MORELL. Prossy's complaint! What do you mean, Candida?

CANDIDA. Yes, Prossy, and all the other secretaries you ever had. Why does Prossy condescend to wash up the things, and to peel potatoes and abase herself in all manner of ways for six shillings a week less than she used to get in a city office? She's in love with you, James: thats the reason. Theyre all in love with you. And you are in love with preaching because you do it so beautifully. And you think it's all enthusiasm for the kingdom of Heaven on earth; and so do they. You dear silly!

MORELL. Candida: what dreadful! what soul-destroying cynicism! Are you jesting? Or—can it be?—are you jealous?

CANDIDA [with curious thoughtfulness] Yes, I feel a little jealous sometimes.

MORELL [incredulously] Of Prossy?

CANDIDA [laughing] No, no, no, no. Not jealous of anybody. Jealous for somebody else, who is not loved as he ought to be.

MORELL. Me?

CANDIDA. You! Why, youre spoiled with love and worship: you get far more than is good for you. No: I mean Eugene.

MORELL [startled] Eugene!

CANDIDA. It seems unfair that all the love should go to you, and none to him; although he needs it so much more than you do. [A convulsive movement shakes him in spite of himself]. Whats the matter? Am I worrying you?

MORELL [hastily] Not at all. [Looking at her with troubled intensity] You know that I have perfect confidence in you, Candida.

CANDIDA. You vain thing! Are you so sure of your irresistible attractions?

MORELL. Candida: you are shocking me. I never thought of my[115] attractions. I thought of your goodness, of your purity. That is what I confide in.

CANDIDA. What a nasty uncomfortable thing to say to me! Oh, you are a clergyman, James: a thorough clergyman!

MORELL [turning away from her, heart-stricken] So Eugene says.

CANDIDA [with lively interest, leaning over to him with her arms on his knee] Eugene's always right. He's a wonderful boy: I have grown fonder and fonder of him all the time I was away. Do you know, James, that though he has not the least suspicion of it himself, he is ready to fall madly in love with me?

MORELL [*grimly*] Oh, he has no suspicion of it himself, hasnt he?

CANDIDA. Not a bit. [*She takes her arms from his knee, and turns thoughtfully, sinking into a more restful attitude with her hands in her lap*]. Some day he will know: when he is grown up and experienced, like you. And he will know that I must have known. I wonder what he will think of me then.

MORELL. No evil, Candida. I hope and trust, no evil.

CANDIDA [*dubiously*] That will depend.

MORELL [*bewildered*] Depend!

CANDIDA [*looking at him*] Yes: it will depend on what happens to him. [*He looks vacantly at her*]. Dont you see? It will depend on how he comes to learn what love really is. I mean on the sort of woman who will teach it to him.

MORELL [*quite at a loss*] Yes. No. I dont know what you mean.

CANDIDA [*explaining*] If he learns it from a good woman, then it will be all right: he will forgive me.

MORELL. Forgive?

CANDIDA. But suppose he learns it from a bad woman, as so many men do, especially poetic men, who imagine all women are angels! Suppose he only discovers the value of love when he has thrown it away and degraded himself in his ignorance! Will he forgive me then, do you think?

MORELL. Forgive you for what?

CANDIDA [*realizing how stupid he is, and a little disappointed, though quite tenderly so*] Dont you understand? [*He shakes his head.*[116] *She turns to him again, so as to explain with the fondest intimacy*]. I mean, will he forgive me for not teaching him myself? For abandoning him to the bad women for the sake of my goodness, of my purity, as you call it? Ah, James, how little you understand me, to talk of your confidence in my goodness and purity! I would give them both to poor Eugene as willingly as I would give my shawl to a beggar dying of cold, if there were nothing else to restrain me. Put your trust in my love for you, James; for if that went, I should care very little for your sermons: mere phrases that you cheat yourself and others with every day. [*She is about to rise*].

MORELL. His words!

CANDIDA [*checking herself quickly in the act of getting up*] Whose words?

MORELL. Eugene's.

CANDIDA [*delighted*] He is always right. He understands you; he understands me; he understands Prossy; and you, darling, you understand nothing. [*She laughs, and kisses him to console him. He recoils as if stabbed, and springs up*].

MORELL. How can you bear to do that when—Oh, Candida [*with anguish in his voice*] I had rather you had plunged a grappling iron into my heart than given me that kiss.

CANDIDA [*amazed*] My dear: whats the matter?

MORELL [*frantically waving her off*] Dont touch me.

CANDIDA. James!!!

They are interrupted by the entrance of Marchbanks with Burgess, who stop near the door, staring.

MARCHBANKS. Is anything the matter?

MORELL [*deadly white, putting an iron constraint on himself*] Nothing but this: that either you were right this morning, or Candida is mad.

BURGESS [*in loudest protest*] What! Candy mad too! Oh, come! come! come! [*He crosses the room to the fireplace, protesting as he goes, and knocks the ashes out of his pipe on the bars*].

Morell sits down at his table desperately, leaning forward to hide his face, and interlacing his fingers rigidly to keep them steady.[117]

CANDIDA [*to Morell, relieved and laughing*] Oh, youre only shocked! Is that all? How conventional all you unconventional people are! [*She sits gaily on the arm of the chair*].

BURGESS. Come: be'ave yourself, Candy. Whatll Mr Morchbanks think of you?

CANDIDA. This comes of James teaching me to think for myself, and never to hold back out of fear of what other people may think of me. It works beautifully as long as I think the same things as he does. But now! because I have just thought something different! look at him! Just look! [*She points to Morell, greatly amused*].

Eugene looks, and instantly presses his hand on his heart, as if some pain had shot through it. He sits down on the sofa like a man witnessing a tragedy.

BURGESS [*on the hearthrug*] Well, James, you certnly haint as himpressive lookin as usu'l.

MORELL [*with a laugh which is half a sob*] I suppose not. I beg all your pardons: I was not conscious of making a fuss. [*Pulling himself together*] Well, well, well, well, well! [*He sets to work at his papers again with resolute cheerfulness*].

CANDIDA [*going to the sofa and sitting beside Marchbanks, still in a bantering humor*] Well, Eugene: why are you so sad? Did the onions make you cry?

MARCHBANKS [*aside to her*] It is your cruelty. I hate cruelty. It is a horrible thing to see one person make another suffer.

CANDIDA [*petting him ironically*] Poor boy! have I been cruel? Did I make it slice nasty little red onions?

MARCHBANKS [*earnestly*] Oh, stop, stop: I dont mean myself. You have made him suffer frightfully. I feel his pain in my own heart. I know that it is not your fault: it is something that must happen; but dont make light of it. I shudder when you torture him and laugh.

CANDIDA [*incredulously*] *I* torture James! Nonsense, Eugene: how you exaggerate! Silly! [*She rises and goes to the table, a little troubled*]. Dont work any more, dear. Come and talk to us.

MORELL [*affectionately but bitterly*] Ah no: I cant talk. I can only[118] preach.

CANDIDA [*caressing his hand*] Well, come and preach.

BURGESS [*strongly remonstrating*] Aw no, Candy. Ang it all!

Lexy Mill comes in, anxious and important.

LEXY [*hastening to shake hands with Candida*] How do you do, Mrs Morell? So glad to see you back again.

CANDIDA. Thank you, Lexy. You know Eugene, dont you?

LEXY. Oh yes. How do you do, Marchbanks?

MARCHBANKS. Quite well, thanks.

LEXY [*to Morell*] Ive just come from the Guild of St Matthew. They are in the greatest consternation about your telegram.

CANDIDA. What did you telegraph about, James?

LEXY [*to Candida*] He was to have spoken for them tonight. Theyve taken the large hall in Mare Street and spent a lot of money on posters. Morell's telegram was to say he couldnt come. It came on them like a thunderbolt.

CANDIDA [*surprised, and beginning to suspect something wrong*] Given up an engagement to speak!

BURGESS. Fust time in his life, I'll bet. Ain it, Candy?

LEXY [*to Morell*] They decided to send an urgent telegram to

you asking whether you could not change your mind. Have you received it?

MORELL [*with restrained impatience*] Yes, yes: I got it.

LEXY. It was reply paid.

MORELL. Yes, I know. I answered it. I cant go.

CANDIDA. But why, James?

MORELL [*almost fiercely*] Because I dont choose. These people
forget that I am a man: they think I am a talking machine to be turned
on for their pleasure every evening of my life. May I not have one
night at home, with my wife and my friends?

*They are all amazed at this outburst, except Eugene. His expres-
sion remains unchanged.*

CANDIDA. Oh, James, you musnt mind what I said about that. And
if you dont go youll have an attack of bad conscience tomorrow.

LEXY [*intimidated, but urgent*] I know, of course, that they[119]
make the most unreasonable demands on you. But they have been
telegraphing all over the place for another speaker; and they can get
nobody but the President of the Agnostic League.

MORELL [*promptly*] Well, an excellent man. What better do they
want?

LEXY. But he always insists so powerfully on the divorce of Socialism from Christianity. He will undo all the good we have been doing.
Of course you know best; but—[*he shrugs his shoulders and wanders
to the hearth beside Burgess*].

CANDIDA [*coaxingly*] Oh, do go, James. We'll all go.

BURGESS [*grumblingly*] Look ere, Candy! I say! Lets stay at home
by the fire, comfortable. He wont need to be more'n a couple-o-hour
away.

CANDIDA. Youll be just as comfortable at the meeting. We'll all
sit on the platform and be great people.

EUGENE [*terrified*] Oh please dont let us go on the platform. No:
everyone will stare at us: I couldnt. I'll sit at the back of the room.

CANDIDA. Dont be afraid. Theyll be too busy looking at James to
notice you.

MORELL. Prossy's complaint, Candida! Eh?

CANDIDA [*gaily*] Yes: Prossy's complaint.

BURGESS [*mystified*] Prossy's complaint! What are you talkin
about, James?

MORELL [*not heeding him, rises; goes to the door; and holds it open, calling in a commanding tone*] Miss Garnett.

PROSERPINE [*in the distance*] Yes, Mr Morell. Coming.

They all wait, except Burgess, who turns stealthily to Lexy.

BURGESS. Listen ere, Mr Mill. Whats Prossy's complaint? Whats wrong with er?

LEXY [*confidentially*] Well, I dont exactly know; but she spoke very strangely to me this morning. I'm afraid she's a little out of her mind sometimes.

BURGESS [*overwhelmed*] Why, it must be catchin! Four in the same ouse!

PROSERPINE [*appearing on the threshold*] What is it, Mr Morell?[120]

MORELL. Telegraph to the Guild of St Matthew that I am coming.

PROSERPINE [*surprised*] Dont they expect you?

MORELL [*peremptorily*] Do as I tell you.

Proserpine, frightened, sits down at her typewriter, and obeys. Morell, now unaccountably resolute and forceful, goes across to Burgess. Candida watches his movements with growing wonder and misgiving.

MORELL. Burgess: you dont want to come.

BURGESS. Oh, dont put it like that, James. It's only that it aint Sunday, you know.

MORELL. I'm sorry. I thought you might like to be introduced to the chairman. He's on the Works Committee of the County Council, and has some influence in the matter of contracts. [*Burgess wakes up at once*]. Youll come?

BURGESS [*with enthusiasm*] Cawrse I'll come, James. Aint it awlus a pleasure to ear you!

MORELL [*turning to Prossy*] I shall want you to take some notes at the meeting, Miss Garnett, if you have no other engagement. [*She nods, afraid to speak*]. You are coming, Lexy, I suppose?

LEXY. Certainly.

CANDIDA. We're all coming, James.

MORELL. No: you are not coming; and Eugene is not coming. You will stay here and entertain him—to celebrate your return home. [*Eugene rises, breathless*].

CANDIDA. But, James—

MORELL [*authoritatively*] I insist. You do not want to come; and he does not want to come. [*Candida is about to protest*]. Oh, dont concern yourselves: I shall have plenty of people without you: your chairs will be wanted by unconverted people who have never heard me before.

CANDIDA [*troubled*] Eugene: wouldnt you like to come?

MORELL. I should be afraid to let myself go before Eugene: he is so critical of sermons. [*Looking at him*] He knows I am afraid of him: he told me as much this morning. Well, I shall shew him how much afraid I am by leaving him here in your custody,[121] Candida.

MARCHBANKS [*to himself, with vivid feeling*] Thats brave. Thats beautiful.

CANDIDA [*with anxious misgiving*] But—but—Is anything the matter, James? [*Greatly troubled*] I cant understand—

MORELL [*taking her tenderly in his arms and kissing her on the forehead*] Ah, I thought it was *I* who couldnt understand, dear.[122]

ACT III

Past ten in the evening. The curtains are drawn, and the lamps lighted. The typewriter is in its case: the large table has been cleared and tidied: everything indicates that the day's work is over.

Candida and Marchbanks are sitting by the fire. The reading lamp is on the mantelshelf above Marchbanks, who is in the small chair, reading aloud. A little pile of manuscripts and a couple of volumes of poetry are on the carpet beside him. Candida is in the easy chair. The poker, a light brass one, is upright in her hand. Leaning back and looking intently at the point of it, with her feet stretched towards the blaze, she is in a waking dream, miles away from her surroundings and completely oblivious of Eugene.

MARCHBANKS [*breaking off in his recitation*] Every poet that ever lived has put that thought into a sonnet. He must: he cant help it. [*He looks to her for assent, and notices her absorption in the poker*]. Havnt you been listening? [*No response*]. Mrs Morell!

CANDIDA [*starting*] Eh?

MARCHBANKS. Havnt you been listening?

CANDIDA [*with a guilty excess of politeness*] Oh yes. It's very nice. Go on, Eugene. I'm longing to hear what happens to the angel.

MARCHBANKS [*letting the manuscript drop from his hand to the floor*] I beg your pardon for boring you.

CANDIDA. But you are not boring me, I assure you. Please go on. Do, Eugene.

MARCHBANKS. I finished the poem about the angel quarter of an hour ago. Ive read you several things since.

CANDIDA [*remorsefully*] I'm so sorry, Eugene. I think the poker must have hypnotized me. [*She puts it down*].

MARCHBANKS. It made me horribly uneasy.

CANDIDA. Why didnt you tell me? I'd have put it down at once.

MARCHBANKS. I was afraid of making you uneasy too. It looked as if it were a weapon. If I were a hero of old I should have laid my drawn sword between us. If Morell had come in he would[123] have thought you had taken up the poker because there was no sword between us.

CANDIDA [*wondering*] What? [*With a puzzled glance at him*] I cant quite follow that. Those sonnets of yours have perfectly addled me. Why should there be a sword between us?

MARCHBANKS [*evasively*] Oh, never mind. [*He stoops to pick up the manuscript*].

CANDIDA. Put that down again, Eugene. There are limits to my appetite for poetry: even your poetry. Youve been reading to me for more than two hours, ever since James went out. I want to talk.

MARCHBANKS [*rising, scared*] No: I mustnt talk. [*He looks round him in his lost way, and adds, suddenly*] I think I'll go out and take a walk in the park. [*He makes for the door*].

CANDIDA. Nonsense: it's closed long ago. Come and sit down on the hearth-rug, and talk moonshine as you usually do. I want to be amused. Dont you want to?

MARCHBANKS [*half in terror, half enraptured*] Yes.

CANDIDA. Then come along. [*She moves her chair back a little to make room*].

He hesitates; then timidly stretches on the hearth-rug, face upwards, and throws back his head across her knees, looking up at her.

MARCHBANKS. Oh, I've been so miserable all the evening, because I was doing right. Now I'm doing wrong; and I'm happy.

CANDIDA [*tenderly amused at him*] Yes: I'm sure you feel a great grown-up wicked deceiver. Quite proud of yourself, arnt you?

MARCHBANKS [*raising his head quickly and turning a little to look round at her*] Take care. I'm ever so much older than you, if you only knew. [*He turns quite over on his knees, with his hands clasped and his arms on her lap, and speaks with growing impulse, his blood beginning to stir*]. May I say some wicked things to you?

CANDIDA [*without the least fear or coldness, and with perfect respect for his passion, but with a touch of her wise-hearted maternal humor*] No. But you may say anything you really and truly feel. Anything at all, no matter what it is. I am not afraid, so long as it is your real self that speaks, and not a mere attitude: a gallant[124] attitude, or a wicked attitude, or even a poetic attitude. I put you on your honor and truth. Now say whatever you want to.

MARCHBANKS [*the eager expression vanishing utterly from his lips and nostrils as his eyes light up with pathetic spirituality*] Oh, now I cant say anything: all the words I know belong to some attitude or other—all except one.

CANDIDA. What one is that?

MARCHBANKS [*softly, losing himself in the music of the name*] Candida, Candida, Candida, Candida, Candida. I must say that now, because you have put me on my honor and truth; and I never think or feel Mrs Morell: it is always Candida.

CANDIDA. Of course. And what have you to say to Candida?

MARCHBANKS. Nothing but to repeat your name a thousand times. Dont you feel that every time is a prayer to you?

CANDIDA. Doesnt it make you happy to be able to pray?

MARCHBANKS. Yes, very happy.

CANDIDA. Well, that happiness is the answer to your prayer. Do you want anything more?

MARCHBANKS. No: I have come into heaven, where want is unknown.

Morell comes in. He halts on the threshold, and takes in the scene at a glance.

MORELL [*grave and self-contained*] I hope I dont disturb you.

Candida starts up violently, but without the smallest embarrassment, laughing at herself. Eugene, capsized by her sudden movement, recovers himself without rising, and sits on the rug hugging his ankles, also quite unembarrassed.

CANDIDA. Oh, James, how you startled me! I was so taken up with

Eugene that I didn't hear your latchkey. How did the meeting go off? Did you speak well?

MORELL. I have never spoken better in my life.

CANDIDA. That was first rate! How much was the collection?

MORELL. I forgot to ask.

CANDIDA [*to Eugene*] He must have spoken splendidly, or he would never have forgotten that. [*To Morell*] Where are all the others? [125]

MORELL. They left long before I could get away: I thought I should never escape. I believe they are having supper somewhere.

CANDIDA [*in her domestic business tone*] Oh, in that case, Maria may go to bed. I'll tell her. [*She goes out to the kitchen*].

MORELL [*looking sternly down at Marchbanks*] Well?

MARCHBANKS [*squatting grotesquely on the hearth-rug, and actually at ease with Morell: even impishly humorous*] Well?

MORELL. Have you anything to tell me?

MARCHBANKS. Only that I have been making a fool of myself here in private whilst you have been making a fool of yourself in public.

MORELL. Hardly in the same way, I think.

MARCHBANKS [*eagerly, scrambling up*] The very, very, very same way. I have been playing the Good Man. Just like you. When you began your heroics about leaving me here with Candida—

MORELL [*involuntarily*] Candida!

MARCHBANKS. Oh yes: Ive got that far. But dont be afraid. Heroics are infectious: I caught the disease from you. I swore not to say a word in your absence that I would not have said a month ago in your presence.

MORELL. Did you keep your oath?

MARCHBANKS [*suddenly perching himself on the back of the easy chair*] It kept itself somehow until about ten minutes ago. Up to that moment I went on desperately reading to her—reading my own poems —anybody's poems—to stave off a conversation. I was standing out-side the gate of Heaven, and refusing to go in. Oh, you cant think how heroic it was, and how uncomfortable! Then—

MORELL [*steadily controlling his suspense*] Then?

MARCHBANKS [*prosaically slipping down into a quite ordinary attitude on the seat of the chair*] Then she couldnt bear being read to any longer.

MORELL. And you approached the gate of Heaven at last?

MARCHBANKS. Yes.[126]

MORELL. Well? [*Fiercely*] Speak, man: have you no feeling for me?

MARCHBANKS [*softly and musically*] Then she became an angel; and there was a flaming sword that turned every way, so that I couldnt go in; for I saw that that gate was really the gate of Hell.

MORELL [*triumphantly*] She repulsed you!

MARCHBANKS [*rising in wild scorn*] No, you fool: if she had done that I should never have seen that I was in Heaven already. Repulsed me! You think that would have saved us! virtuous indignation! Oh, you are not worthy to live in the same world with her. [*He turns away contemptuously to the other side of the room*].

MORELL [*who has watched him quietly without changing his place*] Do you think you make yourself more worthy by reviling me, Eugene?

MARCHBANKS. Here endeth the thousand and first lesson. Morell: I dont think much of your preaching after all: I believe I could do it better myself. The man I want to meet is the man that Candida married.

MORELL. The man that—? Do you mean me?

MARCHBANKS. I dont mean the Reverend James Mavor Morell, moralist and windbag. I mean the real man that the Reverend James must have hidden somewhere inside his black coat: the man that Candida loved. You cant make a woman like Candida love you by merely buttoning your collar at the back instead of in front.

MORELL [*boldly and steadily*] When Candida promised to marry me, I was the same moralist and windbag you now see. I wore my black coat; and my collar was buttoned behind instead of in front. Do you think she would have loved me any the better for being insincere in my profession?

MARCHBANKS [*on the sofa, hugging his ankles*] Oh, she forgave you, just as she forgives me for being a coward, and a weakling, and what you call a snivelling little whelp and all the rest of it. [*Dreamily*] A woman like that has divine insight: she loves our souls, and not our follies and vanities and illusions, nor our[127] collars and coats, nor any other of the rags and tatters we are rolled up in. [*He reflects on this for an instant; then turns intently to question Morell*]. What I want to know is how you got past the flaming sword that stopped me.

MORELL. Perhaps because I was not interrupted at the end of ten minutes.

MARCHBANKS [*taken aback*] What!

MORELL. Man can climb to the highest summits; but he cannot dwell there long.

MARCHBANKS [*springing up*] It's false: there can he dwell for ever, and there only. It's in the other moments that he can find no rest, no sense of the silent glory of life. Where would you have me spend my moments, if not on the summits?

MORELL. In the scullery, slicing onions and filling lamps.

MARCHBANKS. Or in the pulpit, scrubbing cheap earthenware souls?

MORELL. Yes, that too. It was there that I earned my golden moment, and the right, in that moment, to ask her to love me. *I* did not take the moment on credit; nor did I use it to steal another man's happiness.

MARCHBANKS [*rather disgustedly, trotting back towards the fireplace*] I have no doubt you conducted the transaction as honestly as if you were buying a pound of cheese. [*He stops on the brink of the hearth-rug, and adds, thoughtfully, to himself, with his back turned to Morell*] I could only go to her as a beggar.

MORELL [*starting*] A beggar dying of cold! asking for her shawl!

MARCHBANKS [*turning, surprised*] Thank you for touching up my poetry. Yes, if you like: a beggar dying of cold, asking for her shawl.

MORELL [*excitedly*] And she refused. Shall I tell you why she refused? I can tell you, on her own authority. It was because of—

MARCHBANKS. She didnt refuse.

MORELL. Not!

MARCHBANKS. She offered me all I chose to ask for: her shawl, her wings, the wreath of stars on her head, the lilies in her hand, the crescent moon beneath her feet—[128]

MORELL [*seizing him*] Out with the truth, man: my wife is my wife: I want no more of your poetic fripperies. I know well that if I have lost her love and you have gained it, no law will bind her.

MARCHBANKS [*quaintly, without fear or resistance*] Catch me by the shirt collar, Morell: she will arrange it for me afterwards as she did this morning. [*With quiet rapture*] I shall feel her hands touch me.

MORELL. You young imp, do you know how dangerous it is to say that to me? Or [*with a sudden misgiving*] has something made you brave?

MARCHBANKS. I'm not afraid now. I disliked you before: that was why I shrank from your touch. But I saw today—when she tortured you—that you love her. Since then I have been your friend: you may strangle me if you like.

MORELL [*releasing him*] Eugene: if that is not a heartless lie—if you have a spark of human feeling left in you—will you tell me what has happened during my absence?

MARCHBANKS. What happened! Why, the flaming sword [*Morell stamps with impatience*]—Well, in plain prose, I loved her so exquisitely that I wanted nothing more than the happiness of being in such love. And before I had time to come down from the highest summits, you came in.

MORELL [*suffering deeply*] So it is still unsettled. Still the misery of doubt.

MARCHBANKS. Misery! I am the happiest of men. I desire nothing now but her happiness. [*In a passion of sentiment*] Oh, Morell, let us both give her up. Why should she have to choose between a wretched little nervous disease like me, and a pig-headed parson like you? Let us go on a pilgrimage, you to the east and I to the west, in search of a worthy lover for her: some beautiful archangel with purple wings—

MORELL. Some fiddlestick! Oh, if she is mad enough to leave me for you, who will protect her? who will help her? who will work for her? who will be a father to her children? [*He sits down distractedly on the sofa, with his elbows on his knees and his head propped on his clenched fists*].[129]

MARCHBANKS [*snapping his fingers wildly*] She does not ask those silly questions. It is she who wants somebody to protect, to help, to work for: somebody to give her children to protect, to help and to work for. Some grown up man who has become as a little child again. Oh, you fool, you fool, you fool, you triple fool! I am the man, Morell: I am the man. [*He dances about excitedly, crying*] You dont understand what a woman is. Send for her, Morell: send for her and let her choose between—[*The door opens and Candida enters. He stops as if petrified*].

CANDIDA [*amazed, on the threshold*] What on earth are you at, Eugene?

MARCHBANKS [*oddly*] James and I are having a preaching match; and he is getting the worst of it.

Candida looks quickly round at Morell. Seeing that he is distressed, she hurries down to him, greatly vexed.

CANDIDA. You have been annoying him. Now I wont have it, Eugene: do you hear? [*She puts her hand on Morell's shoulder, and quite forgets her wifely tact in her anger*]. My boy shall not be worried: I will protect him.

MORELL [*rising proudly*] Protect!

CANDIDA [*not heeding him: to Eugene*] What have you been say·ing?

MARCHBANKS [*appalled*] Nothing. I—

CANDIDA. Eugene! Nothing?

MARCHBANKS [*piteously*] I mean—I—I'm very sorry. I wont do it again: indeed I wont. I'll let him alone.

MORELL [*indignantly, with an aggressive movement towards Eugene*] Let me alone! You young—

CANDIDA [*stopping him*] Sh!—no: let me deal with him, James.

MARCHBANKS. Oh, youre not angry with me, are you?

CANDIDA [*severely*] Yes I am: very angry. I have a good mind to pack you out of the house.

MORELL [*taken aback by Candida's vigor, and by no means relishing the position of being rescued by her from another man*] Gently, Candida, gently. I am able to take care of myself.

CANDIDA [*petting him*] Yes, dear: of course you are. But you[130] mustnt be annoyed and made miserable.

MARCHBANKS [*almost in tears, turning to the door*] I'll go.

CANDIDA. Oh, you neednt go: I cant turn you out at this time of night. [*Vehemently*] Shame on you! For shame!

MARCHBANKS [*desperately*] But what have I done?

CANDIDA. I know what you have done: as well as if I had been here all the time. Oh, it was unworthy! You are like a child: you cannot hold your tongue.

MARCHBANKS. I would die ten times over sooner than give you a moment's pain.

CANDIDA [*with infinite contempt for this puerility*] Much good your dying would do me!

MORELL. Candida, my dear: this altercation is hardly quite

seemly. It is a matter between two men; and I am the right person to settle it.

CANDIDA. Two men! Do you call that a man? [*To Eugene*] You bad boy!

MARCHBANKS [*gathering a whimsically affectionate courage from the scolding*] If I am to be scolded like a boy, I must make a boy's excuse. He began it. And he's bigger than I am.

CANDIDA [*losing confidence a little as her concern for Morell's dignity takes the alarm*] That cant be true. [*To Morell*] You didnt begin it, James, did you?

MORELL [*contemptuously*] No.

MARCHBANKS [*indignant*] Oh!

MORELL [*to Eugene*] You began it: this morning. [*Candida, instantly connecting this with his mysterious allusion in the afternoon to something told him by Eugene in the morning, looks at him with quick suspicion. Morell proceeds, with the emphasis of offended superiority*] But your other point is true. I am certainly the bigger of the two, and, I hope, the stronger, Candida. So you had better leave the matter in my hands.

CANDIDA [*again soothing him*] Yes, dear; but—[*troubled*] I dont understand about this morning.

MORELL [*gently snubbing her*] You need not understand, my dear.[131]

CANDIDA. But James, I [*the street bell rings*]—Oh bother! Here they all come. [*She goes out to let them in*].

MARCHBANKS [*running to Morell*] Oh, Morell, isnt it dreadful? She's angry with us: she hates me. What shall I do?

MORELL [*with quaint desperation, walking up and down the middle of the room*] Eugene: my head is spinning round. I shall begin to laugh presently.

MARCHBANKS [*following him anxiously*] No, no: she'll think Ive thrown you into hysterics. Dont laugh.

Boisterous voices and laughter are heard approaching. Lexy Mill, his eyes sparkling, and his bearing denoting unwonted elevation of spirit, enters with Burgess, who is greasy and self-complacent, but has all his wits about him. Miss Garnett, with her smartest hat and jacket on, follows them; but though her eyes are brighter than before, she is evidently a prey to misgiving. She places herself with her back to

*her typewriting table, with one hand on it to steady herself, passing
the other across her forehead as if she were a little tired and giddy.
Marchbanks relapses into shyness and edges away into the corner near
the window, where Morell's books are.*

LEXY [*exhilarated*] Morell: I must congratulate you. [*Grasping
his hand*] What a noble, splendid, inspired address you gave us! You
surpassed yourself.

BURGESS. So you did, James. It fair kep me awake to the lar's word.
Didnt it, Miss Gornett?

PROSERPINE [*worriedly*] Oh, I wasnt minding you: I was trying
to make notes. [*She takes out her note-book, and looks at her steno-
graphy, which nearly makes her cry*].

MORELL. Did I go too fast, Pross?

PROSERPINE. Much too fast. You know I cant do more than ninety
words a minute. [*She relieves her feelings by throwing her note-book
angrily beside her machine, ready for use next morning*].

MORELL [*soothingly*] Oh well, well, never mind, never mind,
never mind. Have you all had supper?

LEXY. Mr. Burgess has been kind enough to give us a really splendid supper at the Belgrave.

BURGESS [*with effusive magnanimity*] Dont mention it, Mr
Mill.[132] [*Modestly*] Youre arty welcome to my little treat.

PROSERPINE. We had champagne. I never tasted it before. I feel
quite giddy.

MORELL [*surprised*] A champagne supper! That was very handsome. Was it my eloquence that produced all this extravagance?

LEXY [*rhetorically*] Your eloquence, and Mr Burgess's goodness
of heart. [*With a fresh burst of exhilaration*] And what a very fine
fellow the chairman is, Morell! He came to supper with us.

MORELL [*with long drawn significance, looking at Burgess*]
O-o-o-h! the chairman. Now I understand.

*Burgess covers with a deprecatory cough a lively satisfaction with
his own diplomatic cunning. Lexy folds his arms and leans against the
head of the sofa in a high-spirited attitude after nearly losing his
balance. Candida comes in with glasses, lemons, and a jug of hot water
on a tray.*

CANDIDA. Who will have some lemonade? You know our rules:
total abstinence. [*She puts the tray on the table, and takes up the
lemon squeezer, looking enquiringly round at them*].

MORELL. No use, dear. Theyve all had champagne. Pross has broken her pledge.

CANDIDA [*to Proserpine*] You dont mean to say youve been drinking champagne!

PROSERPINE [*stubbornly*] Yes I do. I'm only a beer teetotaller, not a champagne teetotaller. I dont like beer. Are there any letters for me to answer, Mr Morell?

MORELL. No more to-night.

PROSERPINE. Very well. Goodnight, everybody.

LEXY [*gallantly*] Had I not better see you home, Miss Garnett?

PROSERPINE. No thank you. I shant trust myself with anybody to-night. I wish I hadnt taken any of that stuff. [*She takes uncertain aim at the door; dashes at it; and barely escapes without disaster*].

BURGESS [*indignantly*] Stuff indeed! That gurl dunno what champagne is! Pommery and Greeno at twelve and six a bottle. She took two glasses amost straight horff.

MORELL [*anxious about her*] Go and look after her, Lexy.

LEXY [*alarmed*] But if she should really be— Suppose she[133] began to sing in the street, or anything of that sort.

MORELL. Just so: she may. Thats why youd better see her safely home.

CANDIDA. Do, Lexy: theres a good fellow. [*She shakes his hand and pushes him gently to the door*].

LEXY. It's evidently my duty to go. I hope it may not be necessary. Goodnight, Mrs Morell. [*To the rest*] Goodnight. [*He goes. Candida shuts the door*].

BURGESS. He was gushin with hextra piety hisself arter two sips. People carnt drink like they huster. [*Bustling across to the hearth*] Well, James: it's time to lock up. Mr Morchbanks: shall I ave the pleasure of your company for a bit o the way ome?

MARCHBANKS [*affrightedly*] Yes: I'd better go. [*He hurries towards the door; but Candida places herself before it, barring his way*].

CANDIDA [*with quiet authority*] You sit down. Youre not going yet.

MARCHBANKS [*quailing*] No: I—I didnt mean to. [*He sits down abjectly on the sofa*].

CANDIDA. Mr Marchbanks will stay the night with us, papa.

BURGESS. Oh well, I'll say goodnight. So long, James. [*He shakes hands with Morell, and goes over to Eugene*]. Make em give you a nightlight by your bed, Mr Morchbanks: itll comfort you if you wake up in the night with a touch of that complaint of yores. Goodnight.

MARCHBANKS. Thank you: I will. Goodnight, Mr Burgess. [*They shake hands. Burgess goes to the door*].

CANDIDA [*intercepting Morell, who is following Burgess*] Stay here, dear: I'll put on papa's coat for him [*She goes out with Burgess*].

MARCHBANKS [*rising and stealing over to Morell*] Morell: theres going to be a terrible scene. Arnt you afraid?

MORELL. Not in the least.

MARCHBANKS. I never envied you your courage before. [*He puts his hand appealingly on Morell's forearm*]. Stand by me, wont you?

MORELL [*casting him off resolutely*] Each for himself, Eugene.[134] She must choose between us now.

Candida returns. Eugene creeps back to the sofa like a guilty schoolboy.

CANDIDA [*between them, addressing Eugene*] Are you sorry?

MARCHBANKS [*earnestly*] Yes. Heartbroken.

CANDIDA. Well then, you are forgiven. Now go off to bed like a good little boy: I want to talk to James about you.

MARCHBANKS [*rising in great consternation*] Oh, I cant do that, Morell. I must be here. I'll not go away. Tell her.

CANDIDA [*her suspicions confirmed*] Tell me what? [*His eyes avoid hers furtively. She turns and mutely transfers the question to Morell*].

MORELL [*bracing himself for the catastrophe*] I have nothing to tell her, except [*here his voice deepens to a measured and mournful tenderness*] that she is my greatest treasure on earth—if she is really mine.

CANDIDA [*coldly, offended by his yielding to his orator's instinct and treating her as if she were the audience at the Guild of St Matthew*] I am sure Eugene can say no less, if that is all.

MARCHBANKS [*discouraged*] Morell: she's laughing at us.

MORELL [*with a quick touch of temper*] There is nothing to laugh at. Are you laughing at us, Candida?

CANDIDA [*with quiet anger*] Eugene is very quick-witted, James. I hope I am going to laugh; but I am not sure that I am not going to be very angry. [*She goes to the fireplace, and stands there leaning with her arm on the mantelpiece, and her foot on the fender, whilst Eugene steals to Morell and plucks him by the sleeve*].

MARCHBANKS [*whispering*] Stop, Morell. Dont let us say anything.

MORELL [*pushing Eugene away without deigning to look at him*] I hope you dont mean that as a threat, Candida.

CANDIDA [*with emphatic warning*] Take care, James. Eugene: I asked you to go. Are you going?

MORELL [*putting his foot down*] He shall not go. I wish him to remain.

MARCHBANKS. I'll go. I'll do whatever you want. [*He turns to*[135] *the door*].

CANDIDA. Stop! [*He obeys*]. Didnt you hear James say he wished you to stay? James is master here. Dont you know that?

MARCHBANKS [*flushing with a young poet's rage against tyranny*] By what right is he master?

CANDIDA [*quietly*] Tell him, James.

MORELL [*taken aback*] My dear: I dont know of any right that makes me master. I assert no such right.

CANDIDA [*with infinite reproach*] You dont know! Oh, James! James! [*To Eugene, musingly*] I wonder do you understand, Eugene! [*He shakes his head helplessly, not daring to look at her.*] No: youre too young. Well, I give you leave to stay: to stay and learn. [*She comes away from the hearth and places herself between them*]. Now, James! whats the matter? Come: tell me.

MARCHBANKS [*whispering tremulously across to him*] Dont.

CANDIDA. Come. Out with it!

MORELL [*slowly*] I meant to prepare your mind carefully, Candida, so as to prevent misunderstanding.

CANDIDA. Yes, dear: I am sure you did. But never mind: I shant misunderstand.

MORELL. Well—er— [*he hesitates, unable to find the long explanation which he supposed to be available*].

CANDIDA. Well?

MORELL [*blurting it out badly*] Eugene declares that you are in love with him.

MARCHBANKS [*frantically*] No, no, no, no, never. I did not, Mrs Morell: it's not true. I said I loved you. I said I understood you, and that he couldnt. And it was not after what passed there before the fire that I spoke: it was not, on my word. It was this morning.

CANDIDA [*enlightened*] This morning!

MARCHBANKS. Yes. [*He looks at her, pleading for credence, and then adds simply*] That was what was the matter with my collar.

CANDIDA. Your collar? [*Suddenly taking in his meaning she turns to Morell, shocked*]. Oh, James: did you— [*she stops*]?

MORELL [*ashamed*] You know, Candida, that I have a temper[136] to struggle with. And he said [*shuddering*] that you despised me in your heart.

CANDIDA [*turning quickly on Eugene*] Did you say that?

MARCHBANKS [*terrified*] No.

CANDIDA [*almost fiercely*] Then James has just told me a falsehood. Is that what you mean?

MARCHBANKS. No, no: I—I—[*desperately*] it was David's wife. And it wasnt at home: it was when she saw him dancing before all the people.

MORELL [*taking the cue wtih a debater's adroitness*] Dancing before all the people, Candida; and thinking he was moving their hearts by his mission when they were only suffering from—Prossy's complaint. [*She is about to protest: he raises his hand to silence her*]. Dont try to look indignant, Candida—

CANDIDA. Try!

MORELL [*continuing*] Eugene was right. As you told me a few hours after, he is always right. He said nothing you did not say far better yourself. He is the poet, who sees everything; and I am the poor parson, who understands nothing.

CANDIDA [*remorsefully*] Do you mind what is said by a foolish boy, because I said something like it in jest?

MORELL. That foolish boy can speak with the inspiration of a child and the cunning of a serpent. He has claimed that you belong to him and not to me; and, rightly or wrongly, I have come to fear that it may be true. I will not go about tortured with doubts and suspicions. I will not live with you and keep a secret from you. I will not suffer the intolerable degradation of jealousy. We have agreed—he and I—that you shall choose between us now. I await your decision.

CANDIDA [*slowly recoiling a step, her heart hardened by his rhetoric in spite of the sincere feeling behind it*] Oh! I am to choose am I? I suppose it is quite settled that I must belong to one or the other.

MORELL [*firmly*] Quite. You must choose definitely.

MARCHBANKS [*anxiously*] Morell: you dont understand. She means that she belongs to herself.[137]

CANDIDA [*turning on him*] I mean that, and a good deal more, Master Eugene, as you will both find out presently. And pray, my lords and masters, what have you to offer for my choice? I am up for auction, it seems. What do you bid, James?

MORELL [*reproachfully*] Cand— [*He breaks down: his eyes and throat filled with tears: the orator becomes a wounded animal*]. I cant speak—

CANDIDA [*impulsively going to him*] Ah, dearest—

MARCHBANKS [*in wild alarm*] Stop: it's not fair. You musnt shew her that you suffer, Morell. I am on the rack too; but I am not crying.

MORELL [*rallying all his forces*] Yes: you are right. It is not for pity that I am bidding. [*He disengages himself from Candida*].

CANDIDA [*retreating, chilled*] I beg your pardon, James: I did not mean to touch you. I am waiting to hear your bid.

MORELL [*with proud humility*] I have nothing to offer you but my strength for your defence, my honesty for your surety, my ability and industry for your livelihood, and my authority and position for your dignity. That is all it becomes a man to offer to a woman.

CANDIDA [*quite quietly*] And you, Eugene? What do you offer?

MARCHBANKS. My weakness. My desolation. My heart's need.

CANDIDA [*impressed*] Thats a good bid, Eugene. Now I know how to make my choice.

She pauses and looks curiously from one to the other, as if weighing them. Morell, whose lofty confidence has changed into heartbreaking dread at Eugene's bid, loses all power of concealing his anxiety. Eugene, strung to the highest tension, does not move a muscle.

MORELL [*in a suffocated voice: the appeal bursting from the depths of his anguish*] Candida!

MARCHBANKS [*aside, in a flash of contempt*] Coward!

CANDIDA [*significantly*] I give myself to the weaker of the two.

Eugene divines her meaning at once: his face whitens like steel in a furnace.

MORELL [*bowing his head with the calm of collapse*] I accept
your sentence, Candida.[138]

CANDIDA. Do you understand, Eugene?

MARCHBANKS. Oh, I feel I'm lost. He cannot bear the burden.

MORELL [*incredulously, raising his head and voice with comic
abruptness*] Do you mean me, Candida?

CANDIDA [*smiling a little*] Let us sit and talk comfortably over it
like three friends. [*To Morell*] Sit down, dear. [*Morell, quite lost,
takes the chair from the fireside: the children's chair*]. Bring me that
chair, Eugene. [*She indicates the easy chair. He fetches it silently,
even with something like cold strength, and places it next Morell, a
little behind him. She sits down. He takes the visitor's chair himself,
and sits, inscrutable. When they are all settled she begins, throwing a
spell of quietness on them by her calm, tender tone*]. You remember what you told me about yourself, Eugene: how nobody has
cared for you since your old nurse died: how those clever fashionable
sisters and successful brothers of yours were your mother's and
father's pets: how miserable you were at Eton: how your father is
trying to starve you into returning to Oxford: how you have had to
live without comfort or welcome or refuge: always lonely, and nearly
always disliked and misunderstood, poor boy!

MARCHBANKS [*faithful to the nobility of his lot*] I had my books.
I had Nature. And at last I met you.

CANDIDA. Never mind that just at present. Now I want you to
look at this other boy here: my boy! spoiled from his cradle. We go
once a fortnight to see his parents. You should come with us, Eugene,
to see the pictures of the hero of that household. James as a baby! the
most wonderful of all babies. James holding his first school prize, won
at the ripe age of eight! James as the captain of his eleven! James in
his first frock coat! James under all sorts of glorious circumstances!
You know how strong he is (I hope he didnt hurt you): how clever
he is: how happy. [*With deepening gravity*] Ask James's mother and
his three sisters what it cost to save James the trouble of doing anything but be strong and clever and happy. Ask me what it costs to be
James's mother and three sisters and wife and mother to his children
all in one. Ask Prossy and Maria how troublesome the house is even
when[139] we have no visitors to help us to slice the onions. Ask the
tradesmen who want to worry James and spoil his beautiful sermons
who it is that puts them off. When there is money to give, he gives it:

when there is money to refuse, I refuse it. I build a castle of comfort and indulgence and love for him, and stand sentinel always to keep little vulgar cares out. I make him master here, though he does not know it, and could not tell you a moment ago how it came to be so. [*With sweet irony*] And when he thought I might go away with you, his only anxiety was—what should become of me! And to tempt me to stay he offered me [*leaning forward to stroke his hair caressingly at each phrase*] his strength for my defence! his industry for my livelihood! his dignity for my position! his— [*relenting*] ah, I am mixing up your beautiful cadences and spoiling them, am I not, darling? [*She lays her cheek fondly against his*].

MORELL [*quite overcome, kneeling beside her chair and embracing her with boyish ingenuousness*] It's all true, every word. What I am you have made me with the labor of your hands and the love of your heart. You are my wife, my mother, my sisters: you are the sum of all loving care to me.

CANDIDA [*in his arms, smiling, to Eugene*] Am I your mother and sisters to you, Eugene?

MARCHBANKS [*rising with a fierce gesture of disgust*] Ah, never. Out, then, into the night with me!

CANDIDA [*rising quickly*] You are not going like that, Eugene?

MARCHBANKS [*with the ring of a man's voice—no longer a boy's—in the words*] I know the hour when it strikes. I am impatient to do what must be done.

MORELL [*who has also risen*] Candida: dont let him do anything rash.

CANDIDA [*confident, smiling at Eugene*] Oh, there is no fear. He has learnt to live without happiness.

MARCHBANKS. I no longer desire happiness: life is nobler than that. Parson James: I give you my happiness with both hands: I love you because you have filled the heart of the woman I loved. Goodbye. [*He goes towards the door*].[140]

CANDIDA. One last word. [*He stops, but without turning to her. She goes to him*]. How old are you, Eugene?

MARCHBANKS. As old as the world now. This morning I was eighteen.

CANDIDA. Eighteen! Will you, for my sake, make a little poem out of the two sentences I am going to say to you? And will you promise to repeat it to yourself whenever you think of me?

MARCHBANKS [*without moving*] Say the sentences.

CANDIDA. When I am thirty, she will be forty-five. When I am sixty, she will be seventy-five.

MARCHBANKS [*turning to her*] In a hundred years, we shall be the same age. But I have a better secret than that in my heart. Let me go now. The night outside grows impatient.

CANDIDA. Goodbye. [*She takes his face in her hands; and as he divines her intention and falls on his knees, she kisses his forehead. Then he flies out into the night. She turns to Morell, holding out her arms to him*]. Ah, James!

They embrace. But they do not know the secret in the poet's heart.[141]

From "'Candida' Accepted, Rejected"

ARCHIBALD HENDERSON

Not until July 30, 1897, did *Candida* see the footlights, and then only in a single performance. This was a production by the Independent Theatre Company at Her Majesty's Theatre, Aberdeen.[1] On its propagandist tour of the provinces with *A Doll's House, Candida* was added to its repertory, "to the great astonishment of its audiences." In the spring of 1898, *Candida* was given at a few places by the Independent Theatre's Manchester Branch, the title rôle being taken by that most remarkable among English interpreters of modern *révoltées,* Janet Achurch. The performance at Manchester took place at the Gentleman's Concert Hall on March 14, 1898. A review of that performance by Oliver Elton serves as an index of the estimation in which this play was held in the provinces at this time.[2]

The conception of a childlike creature, a poet, a boy of eighteen, got up to look like Shelley, and not yet a man; femininely hectic and timid and fierce, the real chorus in the play and the final judge or searcher of hearts of his fellow puppets—this conception is hazardous, but it prevailed

---

[1] The copyright performance of *Candida* was given at the Theatre Royal, South Shields, March 30, 1895. The leading parts were taken as follows: George Young (Morell); A. E. Drinkwater (Eugene); Ethel Verne (Proserpine); Lillian Revell (Candida). The name of the poet was spelled on the program "Marjoribanks." See *Ellen Terry and Bernard Shaw: A Correspondence,* ed. Christopher St. John (New York: G. P. Putnam's Sons, 1932), pp. 259–60. Shaw described the review in the *Daily News* (London) as a "horribly garbled account." The cast of the characters in the Aberdeen performance is found in R. Mander and J. Mitchenson, *Theatrical Companion to Shaw* (London: Rockliff Publishing Corporation, 1954), p. 42.

[2] "Mr. and Mrs. Charrington (Miss Janet Achurch) in *Candida,*" the *Manchester Guardian,* March 15, 1898. [A longer portion of this review is reprinted in this book on pp. 175–77.]

From *George Bernard Shaw: Man of the Century* (New York: Appleton-Century-Crofts, Inc., 1956), pp. 443–44. Reprinted by permission of Appleton-Century-Crofts Trade Book Division. Copyright 1932 by D. Appleton & Co. Copyright 1956 by Archibald Henderson.

and triumphed. Mr. Courtenay Thorpe need not have come on at first with a stiff and lackadaisical stare, and he sometimes overplayed. But he understood the part, and gradually the audience felt that he could not properly look otherwise if he would realize it. Mr. Thorpe's voice and intelligence are very good; he had to act the real hero of the play. . . . Mr. Charles Charrington has worked well with Mr. Shaw in making the character of Morell very complete and formidably hopeless. We have never seen so persuasive a figuring of a hollow soul, ready with fresh and ever-fresh reserves of phrasing drawn up from its wells. The accent, posture, and amphitheatrical manner in the crises of private life were all masterly; so was the sincerity of his bewildered rage, and his bitter clinging to his position as apostle and master. . . . Miss Janet Achurch played the difficult and somewhat indistinct part of Candida very well, and in the only possible spirit, that of a serene,[443] *clairvoyante*, mistress of the whole position, disposing of a couple of children whose nature she explains to themselves and to each other. . . . Miss Achurch went through this piquant and abnormal situation (the "auction") with perfect naturalness and with an incisive deliverance of the points. . . . The three leading personages were therefore very well played. So, in their degrees, were the others. Burgess, Candida's father, was admirably acted by Mr. J. H. Atkinson. Mr. H. T. Bagnall did quite well as a curate and Miss Edith Craig as a typist. . . . *Candida* has been already played elsewhere in the provinces, though not often. It has yet to be heard in London, where it deserves no mean reception, especially if it is represented by the present company. . . . Last evening's performance we can only wish to applaud and celebrate.[3]

On one occasion, Janet Achurch said in Shaw's presence, after reading *Candida:* "I could be that woman—for two hours." Shaw forthwith promised to save the part for her; and actually held out against the temptation of filling the rôle with Elizabeth Robins, Mrs. Patrick Campbell, and Sybil Thorndike, then a slip of a girl. When he finally saw Janet in the part of Candida, his comment was: "She did not play it: she kicked it around the stage. But she was wonderful in the second act." He thought Sybil Thorndike also too strong for the part. His favorite Candida was Phyllis Neilson Terry, perhaps because of her resemblance in it to his old love, her aunt Ellen.

It was in 1898 that William Archer wrote: "The most significant event of the theatrical season did not occur in the theatre, but in the book-market—the appearance of Mr. Bernard Shaw's *Candida*. The

---

[3] It is worthy of note that Mr. Courtenay Thorpe gave the first production of Ibsen's *Ghosts* in the United States, at the Berkeley Lyceum, New York, January 5, 1894, he himself playing the part of Oswald.

fact that this play and *The Devil's Disciple* still await production in London shows that the conditions of the theatre are hostile to originality; but the existence of such originality is the main thing; it must, in the long run, make its own conditions."[4] Sorma in Berlin, Salbach in Dresden, and Petri in Vienna later gave noteworthy interpretations of the character of Candida; Arnold Daly in New York rose to prominence and something like fame through his denotement of the poet Marchbanks.[444]

[4] William Archer, *Study and Stage* (London, 1899), "French and English."

From "Arnold Daly Startles Broadway"

ARCHIBALD HENDERSON

Early in the autumn of 1903, Daly was playing the part of the faithful servant in Fitch's *Major André;* later, he was in the cast of *The Girl from Dixie,* which failed to achieve the success anticipated. He feared that he might soon be without an engagement; so on a capital of just $350, he and his partner, Winchell Smith, engaged a suitable cast, and on Tuesday, December 8, 1903, produced *Candida* at a sort of "trial" matinée at the Princess Theatre, New York. The play created quite a stir, and was favorably noticed by the critics; three matinées were then announced, these in turn being followed by another series of matinées. Place was made for the play at the Madison Square Theatre, where it crowded the house for weeks. But although Daly had raised the play from the "freak" class of "special matinée" to the dignity of a "regular attraction," his difficulties were not yet surmounted, for the play had to be moved next to the Bijou Theatre, and later to Carnegie Hall, the health authorities in each case causing the removal by condemning the theatre.[1] The Strollers Club

[1] This was immediately after the Chicago disaster, the burning of the Iroquois Theatre, which led to a much-needed overhauling of the New York playhouses.

From *George Bernard Shaw: Man of the Century* (New York: Appleton-Century Crofts, Inc., 1956), pp. 476–77. Reprinted by permission of Appleton-Century-Crofts Trade Book Division. Copyright 1932 by D. Appleton & Co. Copyright 1956 by Archibald Henderson.

on Madison Avenue for a time opened its doors to the successful comedy. *Candida* finally found a resting place at the Vaudeville Theatre, later known as the Berkeley Lyceum Theatre. The outcome fully repaid Daly for his strenuous and prolonged efforts. *Candida* proved to be the surprise, nay more, the event of the dramatic season. To re-apply Prossy's complaint, it was *Candida* here, *Candida* there, *Candida* everywhere. Instead of proving a fad of brief duration, the edifying comedy drew cultivated audiences, steadily increasing in size and enthusiasm. After *Candida* had proved an unqualified success in New York, Daly added *The Man of Destiny* to his repertory; subsequently these two plays were presented on the same evening until Daly broke down under the impossible task, and Shaw supplied *How He Lied to Her Husband* as a second piece. Daly's company might easily have played longer to crowded audiences in New York; but on April 23, 1904, after more[476] than a hundred and fifty performances in New York, the company went on tour, and elsewhere, notably in Boston, won its way to complete success.

As Marchbanks, Daly was moving and magnetic. With only one exception, he carried out the quaint stage directions, revealing the temperament of the neurotic and sensitive poet, with all its *gaucherie* and hysteria.[2] Although playing always with a pathetic sort of effeminacy, Daly succeeded nevertheless in imagining the rapt idealism of the visionary, the clairvoyance of the seer. Daly is not the actor that Shaw would have chosen to interpret Marchbanks; but in one noteworthy particular he achieved the ideal at which Shaw aims. Many of the audience went away with smiles on their lips, but in their eyes the tears that are "the natural expression in adult life of happiness"— the result Shaw seeks, in his comedies, to achieve. The Candida of Dorothy Donnelly, although better at the end than at the beginning of the evening, was not memorable, being marked as much by affectation as by engaging sweetness; there was no suggestion of the personification of the maternal instinct. The other members of the cast, Louise Closser (Prossy), Dodson Mitchell (Morell), John Findlay (Burgess), and Thomas Thorne (Mill), rose to the level of professional

---

[2] At a dinner party in February, 1904, Daly exclaimed, "I have acted out every one of Mr. Shaw's stage directions to the letter, as far as I am able, with one exception, and that is where Marchbanks goes 'trotting' across the stage to the fireplace. I'm too heavy to trot as Shaw meant. Three years ago I could have done it, and now perhaps I might do it three nights in six. But I don't dare risk it."

success. With the exception of Max Reinhardt's production of *Candida* at the Neues Theater, Berlin, on March 3, 1904, the performance of Daly and his New York company, in spite of a tinge of theatricality almost inseparable from the play itself, is certainly among the most memorable ever given of this play. Viewed in all aspects, Daly's feat of successfully producing *Candida* in New York at this time was a *tour de force* unexampled in the history of the Shavian movement.[477]

From "Playlets and Farces..."

ARCHIBALD HENDERSON

During the height of Arnold Daly's successful New York season[504] of Shaw plays, Shaw wrote a "comediettina" to eke out Daly's bill. "I began by asking Mr. Shaw to write me a play about Cromwell," Daly told a reporter. "The idea appealed to him in his own way. He said he thought it good, but then he raced on to suggest that we might have Charles the First come on with his head under his arm. I pointed out to Shaw that it would be highly inconvenient for a man to come on the stage with his head under his arm, even if he were an acrobat. Shaw, however, thought it could be done. In the end, he said he would compromise. 'Write the first thirty-five minutes of the play yourself,' said he, 'and let me write the last five minutes.' "[1] This is a perfect recipe for the concoction of Shaw's plays of anti-climax. Temperamentally like his master, Ibsen, Shaw reacts against being taken too seriously. *A Doll's House* and *Ghosts*, *An Enemy of the People* and *The Wild Duck*, are two pairs of companion pieces, the second a sort of obverse of the first. In a sardonic commentary on *Candida*, in a letter to the credulous Huneker, Shaw wrote: "The young things in

[1] Interview with Arnold Daly, *The Post-Express* (Rochester, New York), December 3, 1904.

From *Bernard Shaw: Playboy and Prophet* (New York: D. Appleton & Co., 1932), pp. 504–505. Reprinted by permission of Appleton-Century-Crofts Trade Book Division. Copyright 1932 by D. Appleton & Co.

front weep to see the poor boy [Marchbanks] going out lonely and broken-hearted in the cold night to save the proprieties of New England puritanism. . . ."[2] Shaw's "comediettina," *How He Lied to Her Husband,* was almost universally misjudged by the theatre critic penny-a-liners as a travesty on *Candida.* It is, of coures, after the Ibsen model, the obverse of Candida—in farce, not in tragi-comedy. This little topsy-turvy knockabout farce is the *reductio ad absurdum* of the Candidamaniacs. The persistent misinterpretation of the meaning and purpose of this little farce finally compelled Shaw to cable: "Need I say that anyone who imagines that How He Lied to Her Husband retracts Candida, or satirizes it, or travesties it, or belittles it in any way, understands neither the one nor the other?" The latest editions of the play omit all the references to *Candida,* as they were purely topical allusions to Daly's popularity as Marchbanks at the moment.[505]

[2] James Huneker, "The Truth about Candida," *Metropolitan Magazine,* XX (August 1904), 635. [This letter from Shaw is reprinted in this book on pp. 165–66.]

SHAW ON ART AND LIFE

From Love Among the Artists

"Listen to me," said Jack, after a pause, drawing his seat nearer to her, and watching her keenly. "You want to be romantic. You won't succeed. Look at the way we cling to the stage, to music and poetry, and so forth. Why do you think we do that? Just because we long to be romantic, and when we try it in real life, facts and duties baffle us at every turn. Men who write plays for you to act, cook up the facts and duties so as to heighten the romance; and so we all say 'How wonderfully true to nature!' and feel that the theatre is the happiest sphere for us all. Heroes and heroines are to be depended on: there is no more chance of their acting prosaically than there is of a picture in the Royal Academy having stains on its linen, or blacks in its sky. But in real life it is just the other way. The incompatibility is not in the world, but in ourselves. Your father is a romantic man; and so am I; but how much of our romance have we ever been able to put into practice?"

"More than you recollect, perhaps," said Madge, unmoved (for constant preoccupation with her own person had made her a bad listener], "but more than I shall ever forget. There has been one piece of romance in my life—a very practical piece. A perfect stranger once gave me, at my mere request, all the money he had in the world."

"Perhaps he fell in love with you at first sight. Or perhaps—which is much the same thing—he was a fool."

"Perhaps so. It occurred at Paddington Station some years ago."[427]

"Oh! Is that what you are thinking of! Well, that is a good illustration of what I am saying. Did any romance come out of that? In

From *Love Among the Artists* (1881) (Chicago: Herbert S. Stone & Company, 1900), pp. 427–29. Reprinted by permission of the Public Trustee and the Society of Authors (London).

three weeks time you were grubbing away at elocution with me at so much a lesson."

"I know that no romance came out of it—for you."

"So you think," said Jack complacently; "but romance comes out of everything for me. Where do you suppose I get the supplies for my music? And what passion there is in that!—what fire—what disregard of conventionality! In the music, you understand: not in my everyday life."

"Your art, then, is enough for you," said Madge, in a touching tone.

"I like to hear you speak," observed Jack: "you do it very well. Yes: my art is enough for me, more than I have time and energy for occasionally. However, I will tell you a little romance about myself which may do you some good. Eh? Have you the patience to listen?"

"Patience!" echoed Madge, in a low steady voice. "Try whether you can tire me."

"Very well: you shall hear. You must know that when, after a good many years of poverty and neglect, I found myself a known man, earning over a hundred a year, I felt for a while as if my house was built and I had no more to do than to put it in repair from time to time—much as you think you have mastered the art of acting, and need only learn a new part occasionally to keep your place on the stage. And so it came about that I—Owen Jack—began to languish in my solitude; to pine for a partner; and, in short, to suffer from all those symptoms which you so[428] admirably described just now." He gave this account of himself with a derision so uncouth that Madge lost for the moment her studied calm, and shrank back a little. "I was quite proud to think that I had the affections of a man as well as the inspiration of a musician; and I selected the lady; fell in love as hard as I could; and made my proposals in due form. I was luckier than I deserved to be. Her admiration of me was strictly impersonal; and she nearly had a fit at the idea of marrying me. She is now the wife of a city speculator; and I have gone back to my old profession of musical student, and quite renounced the dignity of past master of the art. I sometimes shudder when I think that I was once within an ace of getting a wife and family."

"And so your heart is dead?"

"No: it is marriage that kills the heart and keeps it dead. Better starve the heart than overfeed it. Better still to feed it only on fine food, like music.[429]

Two Chapters from
The Quintessence of Ibsenism

CHAPTER II. "IDEALS AND IDEALISTS"

We have seen that as Man grows through the ages, he finds himself bolder by the growth of his spirit (if I may so name the unknown) and dares more and more to love and trust instead of to fear and fight. But his courage has other effects: he also raises himself from mere consciousness to knowledge by daring more and more to face facts and tell himself the truth. For in his infancy of helplessness and terror he could not face the inexorable; and facts being of all things the most inexorable, he masked all the threatening ones as fast as he discovered them; so that now every mask requires a hero to tear it off. The king of terrors, Death, was the Arch-Inexorable: Man could not bear the dread of that thought. He must persuade himself that Death could be propitiated, circumvented, abolished. How he fixed the mask of immortality on the face of Death for this purpose we all know. And he did the like with all disagreeables as long as they remained[20] inevitable. Otherwise he must have gone mad with terror of the grim shapes around him, headed by the skeleton with the scythe and hourglass. The masks were his ideals, as he called them; and what, he would ask, would life be without ideals? Thus he became an idealist, and remained so until he dared to begin pulling the masks off and looking the spectres in the face—dared, that is, to be more and more a realist. But all men are not equally brave; and the greatest terror prevailed whenever some realist bolder than the rest laid hands on a mask which they did not yet dare to do without.

We have plenty of these masks around us still—some of them

From *The Quintessence of Ibsenism* (1891) (New York: Brentano's, 1905), pp. 20–47. Reprinted by permission of the Public Trustee and the Society of Authors (London).

more fantastic than any of the Sandwich Islanders' masks in the British Museum. In our novels and romances especially we see the most beautiful of all the masks—those devised to disguise the brutalities of the sexual instinct in the earlier stages of its development, and to soften the rigorous aspect of the iron laws by which Society regulates its gratification. When the social organism becomes bent on civilization, it has to force marriage and family life on the individual, because it can perpetuate itself in no other way whilst love is still known only by fitful glimpses, the basis of sexual relationship being in[21] the main mere physical appetite. Under these circumstances men try to graft pleasure on necessity by desperately pretending that the institution forced upon them is a congenial one, making it a point of public decency to assume always that men spontaneously love their kindred better than their chance acquaintances, and that the woman once desired is always desired: also that the family is woman's proper sphere, and that no really womanly woman ever forms an attachment, or even knows what it means, until she is requested to do so by a man. Now if anyone's childhood has been embittered by the dislike of his mother and the ill-temper of his father; if his wife has ceased to care for him and he is heartily tired of his wife; if his brother is going to law with him over the division of the family property, and his son acting in studied defiance of his plans and wishes, it is hard for him to persuade himself that passion is eternal and that blood is thicker than water. Yet if he tells himself the truth, all his life seems a waste and a failure by the light of it. It comes then to this, that his neighbors must either agree with him that the whole system is a mistake, and discard it for a new one, which cannot possibly happen until social organization so far outgrows the institution that Society can[22] perpetuate itself without it; or else they must keep him in countenance by resolutely making believe that all the illusions with which it has been masked are realities.

For the sake of precision, let us imagine a community of a thousand persons, organized for the perpetuation of the species on the basis of the British family as we know it at present. Seven hundred of them, we will suppose, find the British family arrangement quite good enough for them. Two hundred and ninety-nine find it a failure, but must put up with it since they are in a minority. The remaining person occupies a position to be explained presently. The 299 failures will not have the courage to face the fact that they are failures—irremediable failures, since they cannot prevent the 700 satisfied ones from coercing them into conformity with the marriage law. They will accordingly try to persuade themselves that, whatever their own particular domestic arrangements may be, the family is a beautiful and holy natural institution. For the fox not only declares that the grapes he cannot get are sour: he also insists that the sloes he *can* get are sweet. Now observe what has happened. The family as it really is is a conventional arrangement, legally enforced, which the majority, because it happens to suit them,[23] think good enough for the minority, whom it happens not to suit at all. The family as a beautiful and holy natural institution is only a fancy picture of what every family would have to be if everybody was to be suited, invented by the minority as a mask for the reality, which in its nakedness is intolerable to them. We call this sort of fancy picture an IDEAL; and the policy of forcing individuals to act on the assumption that all ideals are real, and to recognize and accept such action as standard moral conduct, absolutely valid under all circumstances, contrary conduct or any advocacy of it being discountenanced and punished as immoral, may therefore be described as the policy of IDEALISM. Our 299 domestic failures are therefore become idealists as to marriage; and in proclaiming the ideal in fiction, poetry, pulpit and platform oratory, and serious private conversation, they will far outdo the 700 who comfortably accept marriage as a matter of course, never dreaming of calling it an "institution," much less a holy and beautiful one, and being pretty plainly of opinion that idealism is a crackbrained fuss about nothing. The idealists, hurt by this, will retort by calling them Philistines. We then have our society classified as 700 Philistines and 299 idealists, leaving one man unclassified. He is the man who is[24] strong enough to face the truth that the idealists are shirking. He says flatly of marriage, "This thing is a failure for many of us. It is insufferable that two human beings, having entered into relations which only warm affection can render tolerable, should be forced to maintain them after such affections have ceased to exist, or in spite of the fact that they have never arisen. The alleged natural attractions and repulsions upon which the family ideal is based do not exist; and it is historically false that the family was founded for the purpose of satisfying them. Let us provide otherwise for the social ends which the family subserves, and then abolish its compulsory character altogether." What will be the attitude of the rest to this outspoken man? The Philistines will simply think him mad. But the idealists will be terrified beyond measure at the proclamation of their hidden thought—at the presence of the traitor among the conspirators of silence—at the rending of the beautiful veil they and their poets have woven to hide the unbearable face of the truth. They will crucify him, burn him, violate their own ideals of family affection by taking his children away from him, ostracize him, brand him as immoral, profligate, filthy, and appeal against him to the despised Philistines, specially idealized[25] for the occasion as SOCIETY. How far they will proceed against him depends on how far his courage exceeds theirs. At his worst, they call him cynic and paradoxer: at his best, they do their utmost to ruin him if not to take his life. Thus, purblindly courageous moralists like Mandeville and Larochefoucauld, who merely state unpleasant facts without denying the validity of current ideals, and who indeed depend on those ideals to make their statements piquant, get off with nothing worse than this name of cynic, the free use of which is a familiar mark of the zealous idealist. But take the case of the man who has already served us as an example—Shelley. The idealists did not call Shelley a cynic: they called him a fiend until they invented a new illusion to enable them to enjoy the beauty of his lyrics—said illusion being nothing less than the pretence that since he was at bottom an idealist himself, his ideals must be identical with those of Tennyson and Longfellow, neither of whom ever wrote a line in which some highly respectable ideal was not implicit.[1][26]

Here the admission that Shelley, the realist, was an idealist too, seems to spoil the whole argument. And it certainly spoils its verbal consistency. For we unfortunately use this word ideal indifferently to

---

[1] The following are examples of the two stages of Shelley criticism:

"We feel as if one of the darkest of the fiends had been clothed with a human body to enable him to gratify his enmity against the human race, and as if the supernatural atrocity of his hate were only heightened by his power to do injury. So strongly has this impression dwelt upon our minds that we absolutely asked a friend, who had seen this individual, to describe him to us—as if a cloven hoof, or horn, or flames from the mouth, must have marked the external appearance of so bitter an enemy of mankind." (*Literary Gazette*, 19th May, 1821.)

"A beautiful and ineffectual angel, beating in the void his luminous wings in vain." (MATTHEW ARNOLD, in his preface to the selection of poems by Byron, dated 1881.)

The 1881 opinion is much sillier than the 1821 opinion. Further samples will be found in the articles of Henry Salt, one of the few writers on Shelley who understand his true position as a social pioneer.

denote both the institution which the ideal masks and the mask itself, thereby producing desperate confusion of thought, since the institution may be an effete and poisonous one, whilst the mask may be, and indeed generally is, an image of what we would fain have in its place. If the existing facts, with their masks on, are to be called ideals, and the future possibilities which the masks depict are also to be called ideals—if, again, the man who is defending existing institutions by maintaining their identity with their masks is to be confounded under one name with the man who is striving to realize the future possibilities by tearing the mask and the thing masked asunder, then the position cannot be intelligibly[27] described by mortal pen: you and I, reader, will be at cross purposes at every sentence unless you allow me to distinguish pioneers like Shelley and Ibsen as realists from the idealists of my imaginary community of one thousand. If you ask why I have not allotted the terms the other way, and called Shelley and Ibsen idealists and the conventionalists realists, I reply that Ibsen himself, though he has not formally made the distinction, has so repeatedly harped on conventions and conventionalists as ideals and idealists that if I were now perversely to call them realities and realists, I should confuse readers of *The Wild Duck* and *Rosmersholm* more than I should help them. Doubtless I shall be reproached for puzzling people by thus limiting the meaning of the term ideal. But what, I ask, is that inevitable passing perplexity compared to the inextricable tangle I must produce if I follow the custom, and use the word indiscriminately in its two violently incompatible senses? If the term realist is objected to on account of some of its modern associations, I can only recommend you, if you must associate it with something else than my own description of its meaning (I do not deal in definitions), to associate it, not with Zola and Maupassant, but with Plato.

Now let us return to our community of 700[28] Philistines, 299 idealists, and 1 realist. The mere verbal ambiguity against which I have just provided is as nothing beside that which comes of any attempt to express the relations of these three sections, simple as they are, in terms of the ordinary systems of reason and duty. The idealist, higher in the ascent of evolution than the Philistine, yet hates the highest and strikes at him with a dread and rancor of which the easy-going Philistine is guiltless. The man who has risen above the danger and the fear that his acquisitiveness will lead him to theft, his temper to murder, and his affections to debauchery: this is he who is denounced as an arch-scoundrel and libertine, and thus confounded with the lowest because he is the highest. And it is not the ignorant and stupid who maintain this error, but the literate and the cultured. When the true prophet speaks, he is proved to be both rascal and idiot, not by those who have never read of how foolishly such learned demonstrations have come off in the past, but by those who have themselves written volumes on the crucifixions, the burnings, the stonings, the headings and hangings, the Siberia transportations, the calumny and ostracism which have been the lot of the pioneer as well as of the camp follower. It is from men of established[29] literary reputations that we learn that William Blake was mad, that Shelley was spoiled by living in a low set, that Robert Owen was a man who did not know the world, that Ruskin is incapable of comprehending political economy, that Zola is a mere blackguard, and that Ibsen is "a Zola with a wooden leg." The great musician, accepted by the unskilled listener, is vilified by his fellow-musicians: it was the musical culture of Europe that pronounced Wagner the inferior of Mendelssohn and Meyerbeer. The great artist finds his foes among the painters, and not among the men in the street: it is the Royal Academy which places Mr. Marcus Stone —not to mention Mr. Hodgson—above Mr. Burne Jones. It is not rational that it should be so; but it is so, for all that. The realist at last loses patience with ideals altogether, and sees in them only something to blind us, something to numb us, something to murder self in us, something whereby, instead of resisting death, we can disarm it by committing suicide. The idealist, who has taken refuge with the ideals because he hates himself and is ashamed of himself, thinks that all this is so much the better. The realist, who has come to have a deep respect for himself and faith in the validity of his own will, thinks it so much the worse. To[30] the one, human nature, naturally corrupt, is only held back from the excesses of the last years of the Roman empire by self-denying conformity to the ideals. To the other, these ideals are only swaddling-clothes which man has outgrown, and which insufferably impede his movements. No wonder the two cannot agree. The idealist says, "Realism means egotism; and egotism means depravity." The realist declares that when a man abnegates the will to live and be free in a world of the living and free, seeking only to conform to ideals for the sake of being, not himself, but "a good man," then he is morally dead and rotten, and must be left unheeded to abide his resurrection, if that by good luck arrive before his bodily death. Unfortunately, this is the sort of speech that nobody but a realist under-stands. It will be more amusing as well as more convincing to take an actual example of an idealist criticising a realist.[31]

CHAPTER III. "THE WOMANLY WOMAN"

Everybody remembers the "Diary of Marie Bashkirtseff." An outline of it, with a running commentary, was given in the *Review of Reviews* (June, 1890) by the editor, Mr. William Stead, a sort of modern Julian the Apostate, who, having gained an immense follow-ing by a public service in rendering which he had to perform a realistic feat of a somewhat scandalous character, entered upon a campaign with the object of establishing the ideal of sexual "purity" as a con-dition of public life. As he retains his best qualities—faith in himself, wilfulness, conscientious unscrupulousness—he can always make him-self heard. Prominent among his ideals is an ideal of womanliness. In support of that ideal he will, like all idealists, make and believe any statement, however obviously and grotesquely unreal. When he found Marie Bashkirtseff's account of herself utterly incompatible with the account of a woman's mind given to him by his ideal, he was confronted with the dilemma[32] that either Marie was not a woman or else his ideal did not correspond to nature. He actually accepted the former alternative. "Of the distinctively womanly," he says, "there is in her but little trace. She was the very antithesis of a true woman." Mr. Stead's next difficulty was, that self-control, being a leading quality in his ideal, could not have been possessed by Marie; other-wise she would have been more like his ideal. Nevertheless, he had to record that she, without any compulsion from circumstances, made herself a highly skilled artist by working ten hours a day for six years. Let any one who thinks that this is no evidence of self-control just try it for six months. Mr. Stead's verdict, nevertheless, was "No self-control." However, his fundamental quarrel with Marie came out in the following lines. "Marie," he said, "was artist, musician, wit, phi-losopher, student—anything you like but a natural woman with a heart to love, and a soul to find its supreme satisfaction in sacrifice for lover or for child." Now of all the idealist abominations that make society pestiferous, I doubt if there be any so mean as that of forcing self-sacrifice on a woman under pretence that she likes it; and, if she ventures to contradict the pretence, declaring her no true woman. In

India they carried this piece of[33] idealism to the length of declaring that a wife could not bear to survive her husband, but would be prompted by her own faithful, loving, beautiful nature to offer up her life on the pyre which consumed his dead body. The astonishing thing is that women, sooner than be branded as unsexed wretches, allowed themselves to be stupefied with drink, and in that unwomanly condition burnt alive. British Philistinism put down widow idealizing with a strong hand; and suttee is abolished in India. The English form of it still survives; and Mr. Stead, the rescuer of the children, is one of its high priests. Imagine his feelings on coming across this entry in a woman's diary, "I love myself." Or this, "I swear solemnly—by the Gospels, by the passion of Christ, by MYSELF—that in four years I will be famous." The young woman was positively proposing to exercise for her own sake all the powers that were given her, in Mr. Stead's opinion, solely that she might sacrifice them for her lover or child! No wonder he is driven to exclaim again, "She was very clever, no doubt; but woman she was not." Now observe this notable result. Marie Bashkirtseff, instead of being a less agreeable person than the ordinary female conformer to the ideal of womanliness, was conspicuously the reverse. Mr. Stead himself[34] wrote as one infatuated with her mere diary, and pleased himself by representing her as a person who fascinated everybody, and was a source of delight to all about her by the mere exhilaration and hope-giving atmosphere of her wilfulness. The truth is, that in real life a self-sacrificing woman, or, as Mr. Stead would put it, a womanly woman, is not only taken advantage of, but disliked as well for her pains. No *man* pretends that his soul finds its supreme satisfaction in self-sacrifice: such an affectation would stamp him as a coward and weakling; the manly man is he who takes the Bashkirtseff view of himself. But men are not the less loved on this account. No one ever feels helpless by the side of the self-helper; whilst the self-sacrificer is always a drag, a responsibility, a reproach, an everlasting and unnatural trouble with whom no really strong soul can live. Only those who have helped themselves know how to help others, and to respect their right to help themselves.

Although romantic idealists generally insist on self-surrender as an indispensable element in true womanly love, its repulsive effect is well known and feared in practice by both sexes. The extreme instance is the reckless self-abandonment seen in the infatuation of passionate sexual desire. Every[35] one who becomes the object of that infatuation shrinks from it instinctively. Love loses its charm when it is not free; and whether the compulsion is that of custom and law, or of infatuation, the effect is the same: it becomes valueless. The desire to give inspires no affection unless there is also the power to withhold; and the successful wooer, in both sexes alike, is the one who can stand out for honorable conditions, and, failing them, go without. Such conditions are evidently not offered to either sex by the legal marriage of to-day; for it is the intense repugnance inspired by the compulsory character of the legalized conjugal relation that leads, first to the idealization of marriage whilst it remains indispensable as a means of perpetuating society; then to its modification by divorce and by the abolition of penalties for refusal to comply with judicial orders for restitution of conjugal rights; and finally to its disuse and disappearance as the responsibility for the maintenance and education of the rising generation is shifted from the parent to the community.[2][36]

Although the growing repugnance to face the Church of England marriage service has led many celebrants to omit those passages which frankly explain the objects of the institution, we are not likely to dispense with legal ties and obligations, and trust wholly to the permanence of love, until the continuity of society no longer depends on the private nursery. Love, as a practical factor in society, is still a mere appetite. That higher development of it which Ibsen shows us occurring in the case of Rebecca West in *Rosmersholm* is only known to most of us by the descriptions of great poets, who themselves, as

---

[2] A dissertation on the anomalies and impossibilities of the marriage law at its present stage would be too far out of the main course of my argument to be introduced in the text above; but it may be well to point out in passing to those who regard marriage as an inviolable and inviolate institution, that necessity has already forced us to tamper with it to such an extent that at this moment the highest court in the kingdom is face to face with a husband and wife, the one demanding whether a woman may saddle him with all the responsibilities of a husband and then refuse to live with him, and the other asking whether the law allows her husband to commit abduction, imprisonment and rape upon her. If the court says Yes to the husband, marriage is made intolerable for men; if it says Yes to the wife, marriage is made intolerable for women; and as this exhausts the possible alternatives, it is clear that provision must be made for the dissolution of such marriages if the institution is to be maintained at all, which it must be until its social function is otherwise provided for. Marriage is thus, by force of circumstances, compelled to buy extension of life by extension of divorce, much as if a fugitive should try to delay a pursuing wolf by throwing portions of his own heart to it.

their biographies prove, have often known it, not by sustained experience, but only by brief glimpses. And it is never a first-fruit of their
love affairs. Tannhäuser may die in the conviction that one moment
of the emotion he felt with St. Elizabeth was fuller and[37] happier
than all the hours of passion he spent with Venus; but that does not
alter the fact that love began for him with Venus, and that its earlier
tentatives towards the final goal were attended with relapses. Now
Tannhäuser's passion for Venus is a development of the humdrum
fondness of the bourgeois Jack for his Gill, a development at once
higher and more dangerous, just as idealism is at once higher and
more dangerous than Philistinism. The fondness is the germ of the
passion: the passion is the germ of the more perfect love. When
Blake told men that through excess they would learn moderation,
he knew that the way for the present lay through the Venusberg,
and the race would assuredly not perish there as some individuals
have, and as the Puritan fears we all shall unless we find a way round.
Also he no doubt foresaw the time when our children would be
born on the other side of it, and so be spared that fiery purgation.

But the very fact that Blake is still commonly regarded as a crazy
visionary, and that the current criticism of *Rosmersholm* entirely fails
even to notice the evolution of Rebecca's passion for Rosmer into her
love for him, much more to credit the moral transfiguration which
accompanies it,[38] show how absurd it would be to pretend, for the
sake of edification, that the ordinary marriage of to-day is a union
between a William Blake and a Rebecca West, or that it would be
possible, even if it were enlightened policy, to deny the satisfaction
of the sexual appetite to persons who have not reached that stage. An
overwhelming majority of such marriages as are not purely *de conve-
nance*, are entered into for the gratification of that appetite either in
its crudest form or veiled only by those idealistic illusions which the
youthful imagination weaves so wonderfully under the stimulus of
desire, and which older people indulgently laugh at. This being so,
it is not surprising that our society, being directly dominated by men,
comes to regard Woman, not as an end in herself like Man, but solely
as a means of ministering to his appetite. The ideal wife is one who
does everything that the ideal husband likes, and nothing else. Now
to treat a person as a means instead of an end is to deny that person's
right to live. And to be treated as a means to such an end as sexual
intercourse with those who deny one's right to live is insufferable to

any human being. Woman, if she dares face the fact that she is
being so treated, must either loathe herself or[39] else rebel. As a rule,
when circumstances enable her to rebel successfully—for instance,
when the accident of genius enables her to "lose her character" without losing her employment or cutting herself off from the society she
values—she does rebel; but circumstances seldom do. Does she then
loathe herself? By no means: she deceives herself in the idealist fashion
by denying that the love which her suitor offers her is tainted with
sexual appetite at all. It is, she declares, a beautiful, disinterested, pure,
sublime devotion to another by which a man's life is exalted and
purified, and a woman's rendered blest. And of all the cynics, the
filthiest to her mind is the one who sees, in the man making honorable
proposals to his future wife, nothing but the human male seeking his
female. The man himself keeps her confirmed in her illusion; for the
truth is unbearable to him too: he wants to form an affectionate tie,
and not to drive a degrading bargain. After all, the germ of the highest
love is in them both, though as yet it is no more than the appetite they
are disguising so carefully from themselves. Consequently every
stockbroker who has just brought his business up to marrying point
woos in terms of the romantic illusion; and it is agreed between the
two that their marriage shall realize the[40] romantic ideal. Then comes
the breakdown of the plan. The young wife finds that her husband
is neglecting her for his business; that his interests, his activities, his
whole life except that one part of it to which only a cynic ever
referred before her marriage, lies away from home; and that her business is to sit there and mope until she is wanted. Then what can she
do? If she complains, he, the self-helper, can do without her; whilst she
is dependent on him for her position, her livelihood, her place in society, her home, her name, her very bread. All this is brought home
to her by the first burst of displeasure her complaints provoke. Fortunately, things do not remain forever at this point—perhaps the most
wretched in a woman's life. The self-respect she has lost as a wife she
regains as a mother, in which capacity her use and importance to the
community compare favorably with those of most men of business.
She is wanted in the house, wanted in the market, wanted by the children; and now, instead of weeping because her husband is away in
the city, thinking of stocks and shares instead of his ideal woman, she
would regard his presence in the house all day as an intolerable nuisance. And so, though she is completely disillusioned on the subject of

ideal love, yet, since it has not turned out so badly after[41] all, she countenances the illusion still from the point of view that it is a useful and harmless means of getting boys and girls to marry and settle down. And this conviction is the stronger in her because she feels that if she had known as much about marriage the day before her wedding as she did six months after, it would have been extremely hard to induce her to get married at all.

This prosaic solution is satisfactory only within certain limits. It depends altogether upon the accident of the woman having some natural vocation for domestic management and the care of children, as well as on the husband being fairly good-natured and livable-with. Hence arises the idealist illusion that a vocation for domestic management and the care of children is natural to women, and that women who lack them are not women at all, but members of the third, or Bashkirtseff sex. Even if this were true, it is obvious that if the Bashkirtseffs are to be allowed to live, they have a right to suitable institutions just as much as men and women. But it is not true. The domestic career is no more natural to all women than the military career is natural to all men; although it may be necessary that every able-bodied woman should be called on to risk her life in childbed just as it may be necessary that[42] every man should be called on to risk his life in the battlefield. It is of course quite true that the majority of women are kind to children and prefer their own to other people's. But exactly the same thing is true of the majority of men, who nevertheless do not consider that their proper sphere is the nursery. The case may be illustrated more grotesquely by the fact that the majority of women who have dogs are kind to them, and prefer their own dogs to other people's; yet it is not proposed that women should restrict their activities to the rearing of puppies. If we have come to think that the nursery and the kitchen are the natural sphere of a woman, we have done so exactly as English children come to think that a cage is the natural sphere of a parrot—because they have never seen one anywhere else. No doubt there are Philistine parrots who agree with their owners that it is better to be in a cage than out, so long as there is plenty of hempseed and Indian corn there. There may even be idealist parrots who persuade themselves that the mission of a parrot is to minister to the happiness of a private family by whistling and saying "Pretty Polly," and that it is in the sacrifice of its liberty to this altruistic pursuit that a true parrot finds the supreme satisfaction of its soul.

I will not go so far as to affirm that there[43] are theological parrots who are convinced that imprisonment is the will of God because it is unpleasant; but I am confident that there are rationalist parrots who can demonstrate that it would be a cruel kindness to let a parrot out to fall a prey to cats, or at least to forget its accomplishments and coarsen its naturally delicate fibres in an unprotected struggle for existence. Still, the only parrot a free-souled person can sympathize with is the one that insists on being let out as the first condition of its making itself agreeable. A selfish bird, you may say: one that puts its own gratification before that of the family which is so fond of it—before even the greatest happiness of the greatest number: one that, in aping the independent spirit of a man, has unparroted itself and become a creature that has neither the home-loving nature of a bird nor the strength and enterprise of a mastiff. All the same, you respect that parrot in spite of your conclusive reasoning; and if it persists, you will have either to let it out or kill it.

The sum of the matter is that unless Woman repudiates her womanliness, her duty to her husband, to her children, to society, to the law, and to everyone but herself, she cannot emancipate herself. But her duty to herself is no duty at[44] all, since a debt is cancelled when the debtor and creditor are the same person. Its payment is simply a fulfilment of the individual will, upon which all duty is a restriction, founded on the conception of the will as naturally malign and devilish. Therefore, Woman has to repudiate duty altogether. In that repudiation lies her freedom; for it is false to say that Woman is now directly the slave of Man: she is the immediate slave of duty; and as man's path to freedom is strewn with the wreckage of the duties and ideals he has trampled on, so must hers be. She may indeed mask her iconoclasm by proving in rationalist fashion, as Man has often done for the sake of a quiet life, that all these discarded idealist conceptions will be fortified instead of shattered by her emancipation. To a person with a turn for logic, such proofs are as easy as playing the piano is to Paderewski. But it will not be true. A whole basketful of ideals of the most sacred quality will be smashed by the achievement of equality for women and men. Those who shrink from such a clatter and breakage may comfort themselves with the reflection that the replacement of the broken goods will be prompt and certain. It is always a case of "The ideal is dead: long live the ideal!"[45] And the advantage of the work of destruction is, that every new ideal is less of an illusion than the one it has supplanted; so that the destroyer of ideals, though denounced as an enemy of society, is in fact sweeping the world clear of lies.

My digression is now over. Having traversed my loop as I promised, and come back to Man's repudiation of duty by way of Woman's, I may at last proceed to give some more particular account of Ibsen's work without further preoccupation with Mr. Clement Scott's protest, or the many others of which it is the type. For we now see that the pioneer must necessarily provoke such outcry as he repudiates duties, tramples on ideals, profanes what was sacred, sanctifies what was infamous, always driving his plough through gardens of pretty weeds in spite of the laws made against trespassers for the protection of the worms which feed on the roots, letting in light and air to hasten the putrefaction of decaying matter, and everywhere proclaiming that "the old beauty is no longer beautiful, the new truth no longer true." He can do no less; and what more and what else he does it is not given to all of his generation to understand. And if any man does[46] not understand, and cannot foresee the harvest, what can he do but cry out in all sincerity against such destruction, until at last we come to know the cry of the blind like any other street cry, and to bear with it as an honest cry, albeit a false alarm.[47]

On Shelley and Wagner

Taking it, then, as established that life is a curse to us unless it operates as pleasurable activity, and that as it becomes more intense with the upward evolution of the race it requires a degree of pleasure which cannot be extracted from the alimentary, predatory, and amatory instincts without ruinous perversions of them; seeing, also, that the alternative of "high thinking" is impossible until it is started

From "The Religion of the Pianoforte," *Fortnightly Review*, LXI (old series) (February, 1894), 264. Reprinted by permission of the Public Trustee and the Society of Authors (London). The title used here is the present editor's.

by "high feeling," to which we can only come through the education of the senses—are we to deliberately reverse our Puritan traditions and aim at becoming a nation of skilled voluptuaries? Certainly. It may require some reflection to see that high feeling brings high thinking; but we already know, without reflection, that high thinking brings what is called plain living. In this century the world has produced two men—Shelley and Wagner—in whom intense poetic feeling was the permanent state of their consciousness, and who were certainly not restrained by any religious, conventional, or prudential considerations from indulging themselves to the utmost of their opportunities. Far from being gluttonous, drunken, cruel, or debauched, they were apostles of vegetarianism and water-drinking; had an utter horror of violence and "sport"; were notable champions of the independence of women; and were, in short, driven into open revolution against the social evils which the average sensual man finds extremely suitable to him. So much is this the case that the practical doctrine of these two arch-voluptuaries always presents itself to ordinary persons as a saint-like asceticism.[264]

From Ellen Terry and Bernard Shaw: A Correspondence

FROM LETTER XII: G. B. S. TO E. T.

April 6, 1896

... You boast that you are a fool (it is at bottom, oh, such a tremendous boast: do you know that in Wagner's last drama, Parsifal, the redeemer is "der reine Thor," "the pure fool"?) but you have the wisdom of the heart, which makes it possible to say deep things to you. You say I'd be sick of you in a week; but this is another boast: it implies that you could entertain me for a whole week. Good heavens! with what? With art? with politics? with philosophy? or with any

From *Ellen Terry and Bernard Shaw: A Correspondence*, ed. Christopher St. John (New York: G. P. Putnam's Sons, 1932), pp. 23, 29–30, 31, 33–34, 80, 81, 181, and 248. Copyright 1931 by George Bernard Shaw and Elbridge L. Adams. Reprinted by permission of the Public Trustee and the Society of Authors (London).

other department of culture? I've written more about them all (for my living) than you ever thought about them. On that plane I would exhaust you before you began, and could bore you dead with my own views in two hours. But one does not get tired of adoring the Virgin Mother. Bless me! you will say, the man is a Roman Catholic. Not at all: the man is the author of Candida; and Candida, between you and me, is the Virgin Mother and nobody else. And my present difficulty is that I want to reincarnate her —to write another Candida play *for* you. Only, it wont come. . . .[23]

FROM LETTER XVII: G. B. S. TO E. T.

August, 1896

. . . It is all very well for you to say that you want a Mother Play; but why didnt you tell me that in time? I *have* written THE Mother Play—Candida—and I cannot repeat a masterpiece, nor can I take away Janet's one ewe lamb from her. She told me the other day that I had been consistently treacherous about it from the beginning, because I would not let the Independent Theatre produce it with a capital of £400! What[29] would she say if I handed it over to the most enviable and successful of her competitors—the only one, as she well knows, who has the secret of it in her nature? Besides, you probably wouldnt play it even if I did: you would rather trifle with your washerwomen and Nance Oldfields and Imogens and nonsense of that kind. I have no patience with this perverse world. . . .[30]

FROM LETTER XVIII: E. T. TO G. B. S.

August, 1896

. . . Thank you for your letter. Dont think that I want to hurt Janet. I would help her (I have tried). But Candida, a Mother! Attractive to me, very. I'm good at Mothers, and Janet can do the Loveresses. . . .[31]

FROM LETTER XIX: G. B. S. TO E. T.

August 28, 1896

Curiously—in view of Candida—you and Janet are the only women I ever met whose ideal of voluptuous delight was that life should be one long confinement from the cradle to the grave. If I make money out of my new play I will produce Candida at my own expense, and you and Janet shall play it on alternate nights. It must be a curious thing to be a mother. First the child is part of yourself; then it is *your* child; then it is its father's child; then it is the child of some remote ancestor; finally it is an independent human being whom you have been the mere instrument of bringing into the world, and whom perhaps you would never have thought of caring for if anyone else had performed that accidental service. It must be an odd sensation looking on at these young people and being out of it, staring at that amazing callousness, and being tolerated[33] and no doubt occasionally ridiculed by them before they have done anything whatsoever to justify them in presuming to the distinction of your friendship. Of the two lots, the woman's lot of perpetual motherhood, and the man's of perpetual babyhood, I prefer the man's I think. I dont hate successful people; just the contrary. But I dread success. To have succeeded is to have finished one's business on earth, like the male spider, who is killed by the female the moment he has succeeded in his courtship. I like a state of continual *becoming*, with a goal in front and not behind. Then too, I like fighting successful people; attacking them; rousing them; trying their mettle; kicking down their sand castles so as to make them build stone ones, and so on. It develops one's muscles. Besides, one learns from it: a man never tells you anything until you contradict him. I hate failure. Only, it must be real success: real skill, real ability, real power, not mere newspaper popularity and money, nor wicked frivolity. . . .[34]

LETTER LII: E. T. TO G. B. S.

October 19, 1896

I've cried my poor eyes out over your horrid play, your *heavenly* play. My dear, and now! How can I go out to dinner to-night? I must keep my blue glasses on all the while for my eyes are puffed up and burning. But I can scarce keep from reading it all over again. Henry would not care for that play, I think. I know he would laugh. And that sort of thing makes me hate him sometimes. He would not understand it, the dear, clever silly. *I* cant understand what *he* understands.

Janet would look, and be, that Candida beautifully, but I could help her I know, to a lot of bottom in it. I could do some of it much better than she. She could do most of it better than I. Oh dear me, I love you more every minute. I cant help it, and I guessed it would be like that! And so we wont meet. But write more plays, my *Dear*, and let me read them. It has touched me more than I could tell of.[80]

FROM LETTER LIII: E. T. TO G. B. S.

October 24, 1896

Your Mrs Webb is a dear (as well as all the other good things) I should say, but Candida "a sentimental prostitute"! *Well!* "Some said it thundered. Others that an Angel spake." You may wear your rue with a difference! . . .

Now I'm going to read Candida once more, and again Mrs Webb's explosion of opinion sets me a'thinking, and wondering whether—but there, you certainly will not benefit by knowing what I think. . . .[81]

FROM LETTER CLIII: E. T. TO G. B. S.

August 30, 1897

. . . Well, I've seen Candida, and it comes out on the stage even better than when one reads it. It is absorbingly interesting every second, and I long for it to be done in London. Even the audience understood it all. I dont see how anything so simple and direct could fail to be understood by the dullest. Only *one* thing struck me at the time as wrong. Towards quite the end of a play to say "Now let's sit down and talk the matter over." Several people took out their watches and some of them left to catch a train, or a drink! And it interrupted the attention of all of us who stayed. Of course you may think it unnecessary to mention such a trifle. . . .[181]

FROM LETTER CCXXV: G. B. S. TO E. T.[1]

August 8, 1899

. . . I try to shew you fearing nobody and managing them all as Daniel managed the lions, not by cunning—above all, not by even a momentary appeal to Cleopatra's stand-by, their passions—but by

---

[1] [Shaw's motive in writing is to get Ellen Terry to play Lady Cicely in *Captain Brassbound's Conversion.* See excerpt from this play on p. 94.]

simple moral superiority. It is a world-wide situation, and one totally incomprehensible to Cleopatras of all sorts and periods. . . . Here then is your portrait painted on a map of the world—and you prefer Sargent's Lady Macbeth! Here you get far beyond Candida, with her boy and her parson, and her suspicion of trading a little on the softness of her contours—and you want to get back to Cleopatra! . . . In every other play I have ever written—even in Candida—I have prostituted the actress more or less by making the interest in her partly a sexual interest: only the *man* in the Devil's Disciple draws clear of it. In Lady Cicely I have done without this, and gained a greater fascination by it. And you are disappointed. . . .[248]

From Preface to Pleasant Plays

In the autumn of 1894 I spent a few weeks in Florence, where I occupied myself with the religious art of the Middle Ages and[v] its destruction by the Renascence. From a former visit to Italy on the same business I had hurried back to Birmingham to discharge my duties as musical critic at the Festival there. On that occasion a very remarkable collection of the works of our British "pre-Raphaelite" painters was on view. I looked at these, and then went into the Birmingham churches to see the windows of William Morris and Burne-Jones. On the whole, Birmingham was more hopeful than the Italian cities; for the art it had to shew me was the work of living men, whereas modern Italy had, as far as I could see, no more connection with Giotto than Port Said has with Ptolemy. Now I am no believer in the worth of any mere taste for art that cannot produce what it professes to appreciate. When my subsequent visit to Italy found me practising the playwright's craft, the time was ripe for a modern pre-Raphaelite play. Religion was alive again, coming back upon men, even upon clergymen, with such power that not the Church of Eng-

From *Plays Pleasant and Unpleasant*, Standard Edition (London: Constable & Company, Ltd., 1952), II: *Pleasant Plays*, v–viii. Reprinted by permission of the Public Trustee and the Society of Authors (London). Preface first published in 1898.

land itself could keep it out. Here my activity as a Socialist had placed me on sure and familiar ground. To me the members of the Guild of St Matthew were no more "High Church clergymen," Dr Clifford no more "an eminent Nonconformist divine," than I was to them "an infidel." There is only one religion, though there are a hundred versions of it. We all had the same thing to say; and though some of us cleared our throats to say it by singing revolutionary lyrics and republican hymns, we thought nothing of singing them to the music of Sullivan's Onward Christian Soldiers or Haydn's God Preserve the Emperor.

Now unity, however desirable in political agitations, is fatal to drama; for every drama must present a conflict. The end may be reconciliation or destruction; or, as in life itself, there may be no end; but the conflict is indispensable: no conflict, no drama. Certainly it it easy to dramatize the prosaic conflict of Christian Socialism with vulgar Unsocialism: for instance, in Widowers' Houses, the clergyman, who does not appear on the stage at all, is the real antagonist of the slum landlord. But the obvious conflicts of unmistakeable good with unmistakeable evil can only supply the crude drama of villain and hero, in which some absolute[vi] point of view is taken, and the dissentients are treated by the dramatist as enemies to be piously glorified or indignantly vilified. In such cheap wares I do not deal. Even in my unpleasant propagandist plays I have allowed every person his or her own point of view, and have, I hope, to the full extent of my understanding of him, been as sympathetic with Sir George Crofts as with any of the more genial and popular characters in the present volume. To distil the quintessential drama from pre-Raphaelitism, medieval or modern, it must be shewn at its best in conflict with the first broken, nervous, stumbling attempts to formulate its own revolt against itself as it develops into something higher. A coherent explanation of any such revolt, addressed intelligibly and prosaically to the intellect, can only come when the work is done, and indeed *done with*: that is to say, when the development, accomplished, admitted, and assimilated, is a story of yesterday. Long before any such understanding can be reached, the eyes of men begin to turn towards the distant light of the new age. Discernible at first only by the eyes of the man of genius, it must be focussed by him on the speculum of a work of art, and flashed back from that into the eyes of the common man. Nay, the artist himself has no other way of making himself conscious of the ray: it is by a blind instinct that he keeps on building up his master-pieces until their pinnacles catch the glint of the unrisen sun. Ask him to explain himself prosaically, and you find that he "writes like an angel and talks like poor Poll," and is himself the first to make that epigram at his own expense. John Ruskin has told us clearly enough what is in the pictures of Carpaccio and Bellini: let him explain, if he can, where we shall be when the sun that is caught by the summits of the work of his favorite Tintoretto, of his aversion Rembrandt, of Mozart, of Beethoven and Wagner, of Blake and of Shelley, shall have reached the valleys. Let Ibsen explain, if he can, why the building of churches and happy homes is not the ultimate destiny of Man, and why, to thrill the unsatisfied younger generations, he must mount be-yond it to heights that now seem unspeakably giddy and dreadful to him, and from which the first climbers must fall and dash themselves to pieces.[vii] He cannot explain it: he can only shew it to you as a vision in the magic glass of his artwork; so that you may catch his presentiment and make what you can of it. And this is the function that raises dramatic art above imposture and pleasure hunting, and enables the playwright to be something more than a skilled liar and pandar.

Here, then, was the higher but vaguer and timider vision, the in-coherent, mischievous, and even ridiculous unpracticalness, which offered me a dramatic antagonist for the clear, bold, sure, sensible, benevolent, salutarily shortsighted Christian Socialist idealism. I availed myself of it in Candida, the drunken scene in which has been much appreciated, I am told, in Aberdeen. I purposely contrived the play in such a way as to make the expenses of representation insignif-icant; so that, without pretending that I could appeal to a very wide circle of playgoers, I could reasonably sound a few of our more en-lightened managers as to an experiment with half a dozen afternoon performances. They admired the play generously: indeed I think that if any of them had been young enough to play the poet, my proposal might have been acceded to, in spite of many incidental difficulties. Nay, if only I had made the poet a cripple, or at least blind, so as to combine an easier disguise with a larger claim for sympathy, some-thing might have been done. Richard Mansfield, who had, with ap-parent ease, made me quite famous in America by his productions of my plays, went so far as to put the play actually into rehearsal before he would confess himself beaten by the physical difficulties of the part. But they did beat him; and Candida did not see the footlights until my old ally the Independent Theatre, making a propagandist tour through the provinces with A Doll's House, added Candida to its repertory, to the great astonishment of its audiences.[viii]

From Captain Brassbound's Conversion[1]

LADY CICELY [*shaking her head*]: I have never been in love with any real person; and I never shall. How could I manage people if I had that mad little bit of self left in me? That's my secret.[686]

—ACT III

From "*Epistle Dedicatory*" *to* Man and Superman[2]

Among the friends to whom I have read this play in manuscript are some of our own sex who are shocked at the "unscrupulousness," meaning the utter disregard of masculine fastidiousness, with which the woman pursues her purpose. It does not occur to them that if women were as fastidious as men, morally or physically, there would be an end of the race. Is there anything meaner than to throw necessary work upon other people and then disparage it as unworthy and indelicate. We laugh at the haughty American nation because it makes the negro clean its boots and then proves the moral and physical in-- feriority of the negro by the fact that he is a shoeblack; but we our-

---

[1] From *Selected Plays by Bernard Shaw* (New York: Dodd, Mead and Company, 1948), p. 686. Reprinted by permission of the Public Trustee and the Society of Authors (London). *Captain Brassbound's Conversion* first published in 1899.

[2] From *Man and Superman: A Comedy and a Philosophy* (1903), Standard Edition (London: Constable & Company, Ltd., 1931), pp. xviii–xx. Reprinted by permission of the Public Trustee and the Society of Authors (London).

selves throw the whole drudgery of creation on one sex, and then imply[xviii] that no female of any womanliness or delicacy would initiate any effort in that direction. There are no limits to male hypocrisy in this matter. No doubt there are moments when man's sexual immunities are made acutely humiliating to him. When the terrible moment of birth arrives, its supreme importance and its superhuman effort and peril, in which the father has no part, dwarf him into the meanest insignificance: he slinks out of the way of the humblest petticoat, happy if he be poor enough to be pushed out of the house to outface his ignominy by drunken rejoicings. But when the crisis is over he takes his revenge, swaggering as the breadwinner, and speaking of Woman's "sphere" with condescension, even with chivalry, as if the kitchen and the nursery were less important than the office in the city. When his swagger is exhausted he drivels into erotic poetry or sentimental uxoriousness; and the Tennysonian King Arthur posing at Guinevere becomes Don Quixote grovelling before Dulcinea. You must admit that here Nature beats Comedy out of the field: the wildest hominist or feminist farce is insipid after the most commonplace "slice of life." The pretence that women do not take the initiative is part of the farce. Why, the whole world is strewn with snares, traps, gins, and pitfalls for the capture of men by women. Give women the vote, and in five years there will be a crushing tax on bachelors. Men, on the other hand, attach penalties to marriage, depriving women of property, of the franchise, of the free use of their limbs, of that ancient symbol of immortality, the right to make oneself at home in the house of God by taking off the hat, of everything that he can force Woman to dispense with without compelling himself to dispense with her. All in vain. Woman must marry because the race must perish without her travail: if the risk of death and the certainty of pain, danger, and unutterable discomforts cannot deter her, slavery and swaddled ankles will not. And yet we assume that the force that carries women through all these perils and hardships, stops abashed before the primnesses of our behavior for young ladies. It is assumed that the woman must wait, motionless, until she is wooed. Nay, she often does wait motionless. That is how[xix] the spider waits for the fly. But the spider spins her web. And if the fly, like my hero, shews a strength that promises to extricate him, how swiftly does she abandon her pretence of passiveness, and openly fling coil after coil about him until he is secured for ever!

If the really impressive books and other art-works of the world were produced by ordinary men, they would express more fear of women's pursuit than love of their illusory beauty. But ordinary men cannot produce really impressive art-works. Those who can are men of genius: that is, men selected by Nature to carry on the work of building up an intellectual consciousness of her own instinctive purpose. Accordingly, we observe in the man of genius all the unscrupulousness and all the "self-sacrifice" (the two things are the same) of Woman. He will risk the stake and the cross; starve, when necessary, in a garret all his life; study women and live on their work and care as Darwin studied worms and lived upon sheep; work his nerves into rags without payment, a sublime altruist in his disregard of himself, an atrocious egotist in his disregard of others. Here Woman meets a purpose as impersonal, as irresistible as her own; and the clash is sometimes tragic. When it is complicated by the genius being a woman, then the game is one for a king of critics: your George Sand becomes a mother to gain experience for the novelist and to develop her, and gobbles up men of genius, Chopins, Mussets and the like, as mere hors d'œuvres.[xx]

Heaven, Hell, and Woman

As this scene may prove puzzling at a first hearing, to those who are not to some extent skilled in modern theology, the Management have asked the Author to offer the Court audience the same assistance that concert-goers are accustomed to receive in the form of an analytical programme.

. . . . .

The scene, an abysmal void, represents hell; and the persons of the drama speak of hell, heaven and earth, as if they were separate

From printed program composed by Shaw to accompany a performance of "Don Juan in Hell" (Act III of *Man and Superman*) at the Court Theatre, London, on June 4, 1907. Reprinted by permission of the Public Trustee and the Society of Authors (London). The title used here is the present editor's.

localities, like "the heavens above, the earth beneath, and the waters under the earth." It must be remembered that such localizations are purely figurative, like our fashion of calling a treble voice "high" and the bass voice "low." Modern theology conceives heaven and hell, not as places, but as states of the soul; and by the soul it means, not an organ like the liver, but the divine element common to all life, which causes us "to do the will of God" in addition to looking after our individual interests, and to honour one another solely for our divine activities and not at all for our selfish activities.

Hell is popularly conceived not only as a place, but as a place of cruelty and punishment, and heaven as a paradise of idle pleasure. These legends are discarded by the higher theology, which holds that this world, or any other, may be made a hell by a society in a state of damnation: that is, a society so lacking in the highest orders of energy that it is given wholly to the pursuit of immediate individual pleasure, and cannot even conceive the passion of the divine will. Also that any world can be made a heaven by a society of persons in whom that passion is the master passion—a "communion of saints" in fact.

In the scene represented to-day hell is this state of damnation. It is personified in the traditional manner by the devil, who differs from the modern plutocratic voluptuary only in being "true to himself"; that is, he does not disguise his damnation either from himself or others, but boldly embraces it as the true law of life, and organizes his kingdom frankly on a basis of idle pleasure seeking, and worships love, beauty, sentiment, youth, romance, etc., etc.

Upon this conception of heaven and hell the author has fantastically grafted the seventeenth century legend of Don Juan Tenorio, Don Gonzalo, of Ulloa, Commandant of Calatrava, and the Commandant's daughter, Dona Ana, as told in the famous drama by Tirso de Molina and in Mozart's opera. Don Gonzalo, having, as he says, "always done what it was customary for a gentleman to do," until he died defending his daughter's honour, went to heaven. Don Juan, having slain him, and become infamous by his failure to find any permanent satisfaction in his love affairs, was cast into hell by the ghost of Don Gonzalo, whose statue he had whimsically invited to supper.

The ancient melodrama becomes the philosophic comedy presented to-day, by postulating that Don Gonzalo was a simple-minded officer and gentleman who cared for nothing but fashionable amusement, whilst Don Juan was consumed with a passion for divine contemplation and creative activity, this being the secret of the failure of love to interest him permanently. Consequently we find Don Gonzalo, unable to share the divine ecstasy, bored to distraction in heaven; and Don Juan suffering amid the pleasures of hell an agony of tedium.

At last Don Gonzalo, after paying several reconnoitring visits to hell under colour of urging Don Juan to repent, determines to settle there permanently. At this moment his daughter, Ana, now full of years, piety, and worldly honours, dies, and finds herself with Don Juan in hell, where she is presently the amazed witness of the arrival of her sainted father. The devil hastens to welcome both to his realm. As Ana is no theologian, and believes the popular legends as to heaven and hell, all this bewilders her extremely.

The devil, eager as ever to reinforce his kingdom by adding souls to it, is delighted at the accession of Don Gonzalo, and desirous to retain Dona Ana. But he is equally ready to get rid of Don Juan, with whom he is on terms of forced civility, the antipathy between them being fundamental. A discussion arises between them as to the merits of the heavenly and hellish states, and the future of the world. The discussion lasts more than an hour, as the parties, with eternity before them, are in no hurry. Finally, Don Juan shakes the dust of hell from his feet, and goes to heaven.

Dona Ana, being a woman, is incapable both of the devil's utter damnation and of Don Juan's complete supersensuality. As the mother of many children, she has shared in the divine travail, and with care and labour and suffering renewed the harvest of eternal life; but the honour and divinity of her work have been jealously hidden from her by man, who, dreading her domination, has offered her for reward only the satisfaction of her senses and affections. She cannot, like the male devil, use love as mere sentiment and pleasure; nor can she, like the male saint, put love aside when it has once done its work as a developing and enlightening experience. Love is neither her pleasure nor her study: it is her business. So she, in the end, neither goes with Don Juan to heaven nor with the devil and her father to the palace of pleasure, but declares that her work is not yet finished. For though by her death she is done with the bearing of men to mortal fathers, she may yet, as Woman immortal, bear the Superman to the Eternal Father.

From Preface to Androcles and the Lion[1]

When reproached, as Bunyan was, for resorting to the art of fiction when teaching in parables, [Jesus] justifies himself on the ground that art is the only way in which the people can be taught. He is, in short, what we should call an artist and a Bohemian in his manner of life.[769]

—[from "The Savage John and the Civilized Jesus"]

From Preface to Pygmalion

[*Pygmalion*] is so intensely and deliberately didactic . . . that I delight in throwing it at the heads of the wiseacres who repeat the parrot cry that art should never be didactic. It goes to prove my contention that art should never be anything else.[194]

Miscellaneous Critiques[2]

Artistic Creation

The great man leads his inspiration, makes its course for it, removes obstacles, holds it from gadding erratically after this or that passing fancy, thinks for it, and finally produces with it an admirable whole, the full appreciation of which keeps every faculty on the alert from the beginning to the end.[318]

---

[1] The two selections which follow are reprinted, by permission of the Public Trustee and the Society of Authors (London), from *Selected Plays by Bernard Shaw* (New York: Dodd, Mead and Company, 1948), pp. 769 and 194, respectively. First published in 1915 and 1912, respectively.

[2] From musical and dramatic critiques of Shaw recorded in R. F. Rattray, *Bernard Shaw: A Chronicle* (Luton, England: The Leagrave Press Ltd., 1951), Appendix I: pp. 318, 319–20; Appendix II: p. 327. Reprinted by kind

Neglected Art

... It is by offering the citizen every possible inducement not to be a man of genius that we keep him to safe,[319] everyday work; and this system is so completely successful that we may confidently boast that we never waste a man on high art unless he is so obsessed with it as to be fit for nothing else.[320]

Hell and Heaven in Life

... For the most part they [the public] never enjoy anything: they are always craving for stimulants, whereas the essence of art is re-creation. . . . Torment is the public's natural element: it is only the saint who has any capacity for happiness. There is no greater mistake in theology than to suppose that it is necesasry to lock people into hell or out of heaven.[3] . . . The artist's rule must be Cromwell's: "Not what they want but what is good for them." That rule, carried out in a kindly and sociable way, is the secret of success in the long run in the theatre as elsewhere.[327]

---

permission of the Public Trustee and the Society of Authors (London), the publishers, and the author. The title used here is the present editor's.

[3] [Compare *Man and Superman*, Act III, and *John Bull's Other Island, sub fin.*]

SOME OF SHAW'S SOURCES

From "The Pains of Opium"

THOMAS DE QUINCEY

"When I began writing the part of the young poet, I had in mind De Quincey's account of his adolescence in his Confessions. . . ."[1]

June 1819.—I have had occasion to remark, at various periods of my life, that the death of those whom we love,[443] and, indeed, the contemplation of death generally, is (*cæteris paribus*) more affecting in summer than in any other season of the year. And the reasons are these three, I think: first, that the visible heavens in summer appear far higher, more distant, and (if such a solecism may be excused) more infinite; the clouds by which chiefly the eye expounds the distance of the blue pavilion stretched over our heads are in summer more voluminous, more massed, and are accumulated in far grander and more towering piles; secondly, the light and the appearances of the declining and the setting sun are much more fitted to be types and characters of the infinite; and, thirdly (which is the main reason), the exuberant and riotous prodigality of life naturally forces the mind more powerfully upon the antagonist thought of death, and the wintery sterility of the grave. For it may be observed generally, that wherever two thoughts stand related to each other by a law of antagonism, and exist, as it were, by mutual repulsion, they are apt to suggest each other. On these accounts it is that I find it impossible to

---

[1] From George Bernard Shaw, "Candida Was Not Ellen Terry," *Evening Standard* (London), November 30, 1944. Reprinted by permission of the Public Trustee and the Society of Authors (London) and the *Evening Standard*. A longer selection from this letter is reprinted on pp. 158–59.

From *Confessions of an English Opium-Eater* (1821). The selection that follows is from Part III, "The Pains of Opium," and is reprinted from *The Collected Writings of Thomas De Quincey*, ed. David Masson (Edinburgh: Adam and Charles Black, 1890), III, 443–47.

banish the thought of death when I am walking alone in the endless days of summer; and any particular death, if not actually more affecting, at least haunts my mind more obstinately and besiegingly, in that season. Perhaps this cause, and a slight incident which I omit, might have been the immediate occasions of the following dream, to which, however, a predisposition must always have existed in my mind; but, having been once roused, it never left me, and split into a thousand fantastic variations, which often suddenly re-combined; locked back into startling unity, and restored the original dream.

I thought that it was a Sunday morning in May; that it was Easter Sunday, and as yet very early in the morning. I was standing, as it seemed to me, at the door of my own cottage. Right before me lay the very scene which could really be commanded from that situation, but exalted, as was usual, solemnised by the power of dreams. There were the same mountains, and the same lovely valley at their feet; but the mountains were raised to more than Alpine height, and there was interspace far larger between them of savannahs and forest lawns; the hedges were rich with[444] white roses; and no living creature was to be seen, excepting that in the green churchyard there were cattle tranquilly reposing upon the verdant graves, and particularly round about the grave of a child whom I had once tenderly loved, just as I had really beheld them, a little before sunrise, in the same summer when that child died. I gazed upon the well-known scene, and I said to myself, 'It yet wants much of sunrise; and it is Easter Sunday; and that is the day on which they celebrate the first-fruits of Resurrection. I will walk abroad; old griefs shall be forgotten to-day: for the air is cool and still, and the hills are high, and stretch away to heaven; and the churchyard is as verdant as the forest lawns, and the forest lawns are as quiet as the churchyard; and with the dew I can wash the fever from my forehead; and then I shall be unhappy no longer.' I turned, as if to open my garden gate, and immediately I saw upon the left a scene far different; but which yet the power of dreams had reconciled into harmony. The scene was an oriental one; and there also it was Easter Sunday, and very early in the morning. And at a vast distance were visible, as a stain upon the horizon, the domes and cupolas of a great city—an image or faint abstraction, caught perhaps in childhood from some picture of Jerusalem. And not a bow-shot from me, upon a stone, shaded by Judean palms, there sat a woman; and I looked, and it was—Ann! She fixed her eyes upon me earnestly; and

I said to her at length, 'So, then, I have found you at last.' I waited; but she answered me not a word. Her face was the same as when I saw it last; the same, and yet, again, how different! Seventeen years ago, when the lamp-light of mighty London fell upon her face, as for the last time I kissed her lips (lips, Ann, that to me were not polluted!), her eyes were streaming with tears. The tears were now no longer seen. Sometimes she seemed altered; yet again sometimes *not* altered; and hardly older. Her looks were tranquil, but with unusual solemnity of expression, and I now gazed upon her with some awe. Suddenly her countenance grew dim; and, turning to the mountains, I perceived vapours rolling between us; in a moment all had vanished; thick darkness came on; and in the twinkling of an eye I was far away from mountains, and by [445] lamp-light in London, walking again with Ann—just as we had walked, when both children, eighteen years before, along the endless terraces of Oxford Street.

Then suddenly would come a dream of far different character—a tumultuous dream—commencing with a music such as now I often heard in sleep—music of preparation and of awakening suspense. The undulations of fast-gathering tumults were like the opening of the Coronation Anthem; and, like *that*, gave the feeling of a multitudinous movement, of infinite cavalcades filing off, and the tread of innumerable armies. The morning was come of a mighty day—a day of crisis and of ultimate hope for human nature, then suffering mysterious eclipse, and labouring in some dread extremity. Somewhere, but I knew not where—somehow, but I knew not how—by some beings, but I knew not by whom—a battle, a strife, an agony, was travelling through all its stages—was evolving itself, like the catastrophe of some mighty drama, with which my sympathy was the more insupportable, from deepening confusion as to its local scene, its cause, its nature, and its undecipherable issue. I (as is usual in dreams where, of necessity, we make ourselves central to every movement) had the power, and yet had not the power, to decide it. I had the power, if I could raise myself to will it; and yet again had not the power, for the weight of twenty Atlantics was upon me, or the oppression of inexpiable guilt. 'Deeper than ever plummet sounded,' I lay inactive. Then, like a chorus, the passion deepened. Some greater interest was at stake, some mightier cause, than ever yet the sword had pleaded, or trumpet had proclaimed. Then came sudden alarms; hurryings to and fro; trepidations of innumerable fugitives, I knew not whether from the good cause or the bad; darkness and lights; tempest and human faces; and at last, with the sense that all was lost, female forms, and the features that were worth all the world to me; and but a moment allowed—and clasped hands, with heart-breaking partings, and then—everlasting farewells! and, with a sigh such as the caves of hell sighed when the incestuous mother uttered the abhorred name of Death, the sound was reverberated—everlasting farewells! and again, and yet again reverberated—everlasting farewells! [446]

And I awoke in struggles, and cried aloud, 'I will sleep no more!'[447]

From "The Everlasting Yea"

THOMAS CARLYLE

'But the whim we have of Happiness is somewhat thus. By certain valuations, and averages, of our own striking, we come upon some sort of average terrestrial lot; this we fancy belongs to us by nature, and of indefeasible right. It is simple payment of our wages, of our deserts, requires neither thanks nor complaint; only such *overplus* as there may be do we account Happiness; any *deficit* again is Misery. Now consider that we have the valuation of our own deserts ourselves, and what a fund of Self-conceit there is in each of us,—do you wonder that the balance should so often dip the wrong way, and many a Blockhead cry: See there, what a payment; was ever worthy gentleman so used!—I tell thee, Blockhead, it all comes of thy Vanity; of what thou *fanciest* those same deserts of thine to be. Fancy that thou deservest to be hanged (as is most likely), thou wilt feel it happiness to be only shot: fancy that thou deservest to be hanged in a hair-halter, it will be a luxury to die in hemp.

From *Sartor Resartus: The Life and Opinions of Herr Teufelsdröckh* (1834), Centenary Edition, ed. H. D. Traill (London: Chapman and Hall, Ltd., 1896), Bk. II, Chap. IX, pp. 152–54, 156–57. The explanatory footnotes have been adapted from various editions of Carlyle's text by the present editor. *Sartor Resartus* means the tailor re-tailored.

'So true is it, what I then said, that *the Fraction of Life can be increased in value not so much by increasing your*[152] *Numerator as by lessening your Denominator.* Nay, unless my Algebra deceive me, *Unity* itself divided by *Zero* will give *Infinity.* Make thy claim of wages a zero, then; thou hast the world under thy feet. Well did the Wisest of our time write: "It is only with Renunciation (*Entsagen*) that Life, properly speaking, can be said to begin."[1]

'I asked myself: What is this that, ever since earliest years, thou hast been fretting and fuming, and lamenting and self-tormenting, on account of? Say it in a word: is it not because thou art not HAPPY? Because the THOU (sweet gentleman) is not sufficiently honoured, nourished, soft-bedded, and lovingly cared-for? Foolish soul! What Act of Legislature was there that *thou* shouldst be Happy? A little while ago thou hadst no right to *be* at all. What if thou wert born and predestined not to be Happy, but to be Unhappy! Art thou nothing other than a Vulture, then, that fliest through the Universe seeking after somewhat to *eat;* and shrieking dolefully because carrion enough is not given thee? Close thy *Byron;* open thy *Goethe.*'[2]

'*Es leuchtet mir ein,*[3] I see a glimpse of it!' cries he elsewhere: 'there is in man a HIGHER than Love of Happiness: he can do without Happiness, and instead thereof find Blessedness![4] Was it not to preach-forth this same HIGHER that sages and martyrs, the Poet and the Priest, in all times, have spoken and suffered; bearing testimony, through life and through death, of the Godlike that is in Man, and how in the Godlike only has he Strength and Freedom? Which God-inspired Doctrine art thou also honoured to be taught; O Heavens! and broken with manifold merciful Afflictions, even till thou become contrite, and

[1] Carlyle, as was his habit, adapts a passage from German thought (Goethe's *Wilhelm Meister*), but gives renunciation a Calvinistic interpretation: a forsaking of worldly pleasures (fame, honor, wealth, respectability). See Carlyle's translation of *Wilhelm Meister's Travels* in his *Translations from the German* (London: Chapman and Hall, 1893), II, 278. Future references will be to this edition.

[2] *Wilhelm Meister* symbolized for Carlyle the new practical idealism which was replacing the strongly individualistic romanticism of Byronic literature.

[3] Meister so exclaims when he penetrates the mystery of the "Three Reverences." See *Travels*, II, 221.

[4] The disregard of moral values in favor of purely natural impulses is the subject of "The Everlasting No," *Sartor Resartus*, Bk. II, Chap. VII. Carlyle believed such "happiness" leads to eventual despair and spiritual decay. "The Everlasting Yea" teaches just the opposite and stresses Victorian obedience to duty (originally a Kantian principle).

learn it! O, thank thy Destiny for these; thankfully bear what yet remain: thou hadst need of them; the Self in thee needed to be annihilated. By benignant fever-paroxysms is Life rooting out the deepseated chronic Disease, and triumphs over Death. On the roaring billows of Time, thou art not engulfed, but borne aloft into the azure of Eternity. Love not Pleasure; love God.[5] This is the[153] EVERLASTING YEA, wherein all contradiction is solved: wherein whoso walks and works, it is well with him.'[154]

. . . . .

'But indeed Conviction, were it never so excellent, is worthless till it convert itself into Conduct. Nay properly Conviction is not possible till then; inasmuch as all Speculation is by nature endless, formless, a vortex amid vortices:[6] only by a felt indubitable certainty of Experience does it find any centre to revolve round, and so fashion itself into a system. Most true is it, as a wise man teaches us, that "Doubt of any sort cannot be removed except by Action."[7] On which ground, too, let him who gropes painfully in darkness or uncertain light, and prays vehemently that the dawn may ripen into day, lay this other precept well to heart, which to me was of invaluable service: *"Do the Duty which lies nearest thee,"*[8] which thou knowest to be a Duty! Thy second Duty will already have become clearer.

'May we not say, however, that the hour of Spiritual Enfranchisement is even this: When your Ideal World, wherein the whole man has been dimly struggling and inexpressibly languishing to work, becomes revealed, and thrown open; and you discover, with amazement enough, like the Lothario in *Wilhelm Meister*, that your "America is here or nowhere"?[9] The Situation that has not its Duty, its Ideal, was never yet occupied by man. Yes here, in this poor, miserable, ham-

[5] Adapted from II Tim. 3:4.
[6] That is, the deepest knowledge is intuitively, rather than logically or metaphysically, acquired.
[7] From Carlyle's translation of *Wilhelm Meister's Apprenticeship* in *Translations from the German*, I, Bk. VI.
[8] *Ibid.*, II, 2. "The safe plan is, always simply to do the task that lies nearest us . . . ."
[9] *Ibid.*, II, 9–10. "In America [observed Lothario], I fancied I might accomplish something . . . if any task was not begirt with a thousand dangers, I considered it trivial . . . . How differently do matters now appear! How precious, how important seems the duty which is nearest me . . . ." "I recollect the letter which you sent me from the Western world," said Jarno: "it contained the words: 'I will return, and . . . I will say: *Here or nowhere is America!*' "

pered, despicable Actual,[10] wherein thou even now standest, here or
nowhere is thy Ideal: work it out therefrom; and working, believe,
live, be free. Fool! the Ideal is in thyself, the impediment too is in
thyself: thy Condition is but the stuff thou art to shape that same Ideal
out of: what matters whether such stuff be of this sort or that, so the
Form thou give it be heroic, be poetic? O thou that pinest in the
imprisonment of the Actual, and criest bitterly to the gods for a
kingdom wherein to rule and create,[156] know this of a truth: the
thing thou seekest is already with thee, "here or nowhere," couldst
thou only see!

'But it is with man's Soul as it was with Nature: the beginning of
Creation is—Light.[11] Till the eye have vision, the whole members are
in bonds.[12] Divine moment, when over the tempest-tossed Soul, as once
over the wild-weltering Chaos, it is spoken: Let there be Light! Ever
to the greatest that has felt such moment, is it not miraculous and God-
announcing;[13] even as, under simpler figures, to the simplest and least.
The mad primeval Discord is hushed; the rudely-jumbled conflicting
elements bind themselves into separate Firmaments: deep silent rock-
foundations are built beneath; and the skyey vault with its everlasting
Luminaries above: instead of a dark wasteful Chaos, we have a bloom-
ing, fertile, heaven-encompassed World.

'I too could now say to myself: Be no longer a Chaos, but a World,
or even Worldkin. Produce! Produce! Were it but the pitifullest in-
finitesimal fraction of a Product, produce it, in God's name! 'Tis the
utmost thou hast in thee: out with it, then. Up, up! Whatsoever thy
hand findeth to do, do it with thy whole might. Work while it is called
Today; for the Night cometh, wherein no man can work.'[14] [157]

---

[10] In *Sartor Resartus*, Bk. II, Chap. IV, Carlyle says, "Our whole terrestrial
being is based on Time . . . . O Time-Spirit, how hast thou environed and im-
prisoned us, and sunk us so deep in thy troublous dim Time-Element, that only
in lucid moments can so much as glimpses of our upper Azure Home be revealed
to us!"

The reader should understand that the lesson of all these sentences climaxes
the long series of disillusionments experienced by Herr Teufelsdröckh, eccentric
old professor of Things in General at Weissnichtwo (Know Not Where). To be
a great lover, scholar, and man of worldly accomplishments (i.e., society's
conception of a happy man) his sensitive, impetuous temperament has hardly
fitted him.

[11] See Gen. 1:3.   [12] Based on Matt. 6.22–23.
[13] See Novalis, *Werke*, III, 183.
[14] Adapted from Eccles. 9:10, and John 9:4.

From "The Mystery of Life and Its Arts"

JOHN RUSKIN

127. And now, returning to the broader question, what these arts and labours of life have to teach us of its mystery, this is the first of their lessons—that the more beautiful the art, the more it is essentially the work of people who *feel themselves wrong;*—who are striving for the fulfilment of a law, and the grasp of a loveliness, which they have not yet attained, which they feel even farther and farther from attaining the more they strive for it. And yet, in still deeper sense, it is the work of people who know also that they are right. The very sense of inevitable error from their purpose marks the perfectness of that purpose, and the continued sense of failure arises from the continued opening of the eyes more clearly to all the sacredest laws of truth.

128. This is one lesson. The second is a very plain, and greatly precious one: namely—that whenever the arts and labours of life are fulfilled in this spirit of striving against misrule, and doing whatever we have to do, honourably and perfectly, they invariably bring happiness, as much as seems possible to the nature of man. In all other paths by which that happiness is pursued there is disappointment, or destruction: for ambition and for passion there is no rest—no fruition; the fairest pleasures of youth perish in a darkness greater than their past light: and the loftiest and purest love too often does but inflame the cloud of life[174] with endless fire of pain. But, ascending from lowest to highest, through every scale of human industry, that industry worthily followed, gives peace. Ask the labourer in the field, at the forge, or in the mine; ask the patient, delicate-fingered artisan, or the strong-armed, fiery-hearted worker in bronze, and in marble, and with

From Third Lecture, *Sesame and Lilies* (1865), Library Edition, ed. E. T. Cook and Alexander Wedderburn (London: George Allen, 1905), XVIII, 174–75, 179–80.

the colours of light; and none of these, who are true workmen, will ever tell you, that they have found the law of heaven an unkind one—that in the sweat of their face they should eat bread, till they return to the ground; nor that they ever found it an unrewarded obedience, if, indeed, it was rendered faithfully to the command—"Whatsoever thy hand findeth to do—do it with thy might."

129. These are the two great and constant lessons which our labourers teach us of the mystery of life. But there is another, and a sadder one, which they cannot teach us, which we must read on their tombstones.

"Do it with thy might." There have been myriads upon myriads of human creatures who have obeyed this law—who have put every breath and nerve of their being into its toil—who have devoted every hour, and exhausted every faculty—who have bequeathed their unaccomplished thoughts at death—who, being dead, have yet spoken, by majesty of memory, and strength of example. And, at last, what has all this "Might" of humanity accomplished, in six thousand years of labour and sorrow? What has it *done?* ... [175]

.   .   .   .   .

133. *Does* [life] vanish then? Are you sure of that?—sure, that the nothingness of the grave will be a rest from this troubled nothingness; and that the coiling shadow, which disquiets itself in vain, cannot change into the smoke of the torment that ascends for ever? Will any answer that they *are* sure of it, and that there is no fear, nor hope, nor desire, nor labour, whither they go? Be it so: will you not, then, make as sure of the Life that now is, as you are of the Death that is to come? Your hearts are wholly in this world—will you not give them to it wisely, as well as perfectly? And see, first of all, that you *have* hearts, and sound hearts, too, to give. Because you have no heaven to look for, is that any reason that you should remain ignorant of this wonderful and infinite earth, which is firmly and instantly given you in possession? Although your days are numbered, and the following darkness sure, is it necessary that you should share the degradation of the brute, because you are condemned to its mortality; or live the life of the moth, and of the worm, because you[179] are to companion them in the dust? Not so; we may have but a few thousands of days to spend, perhaps hundreds only—perhaps tens; nay, the longest of our time and best, looked back on, will be but as a moment, as the twinkling of an

eye; still we are men, not insects; we are living spirits, not passing clouds. "He maketh the winds His messengers; the momentary fire, His minister;" and shall we do less than *these?* Let us do the work of men while we bear the form of them; and, as we snatch our narrow portion of time out of Eternity, snatch also our narrow inheritance of passion out of Immortality—even though our lives *be* as a vapour, that appeareth for a little time, and then vanisheth away.[180]

"Even Love Is Sold"

PERCY   BYSSHE   SHELLEY

Not even the intercourse of the sexes is exempt from the despotism of positive institution. Law pretends even[477] to govern the indisciplinable wanderings of passion, to put fetters on the clearest deductions of reason, and, by appeals to the will, to subdue the involuntary affections of our nature. Love is inevitably consequent upon the perception of loveliness. Love withers under constraint: its very essence is liberty: it is compatible neither with obedience, jealousy, nor fear: it is there most pure, perfect, and unlimited, where its votaries live in confidence, equality, and unreserve.

How long then ought the sexual connection to last? what law ought to specify the extent of the grievances which should limit its duration? A husband and wife ought to continue so long united as they love each other: any law which should bind them to cohabitation for one moment after the decay of their affection, would be a most intolerable tyranny, and the most unworthy of toleration. How odious an usurpation of the right of private judgment should that law be considered, which should make the ties of friendship indissoluble, in spite of the caprices, the inconstancy, the fallibility, and capacity for improvement of the human mind. And by so much would the fetters of love be heavier and more unendurable than those of friendship, as love is more vehement and capricious, more dependent on those delicate peculiarities of imagination, and less capable of reduction to the ostensible merits of the object.

The state of society in which we exist is a mixture of feudal savageness and imperfect civilization. The narrow and unenlightened

From Notes to *Queen Mab: A Philosophical Poem* (1813). The note entitled ' Even Love Is Sold" is reprinted here from *The Works of Percy Bysshe Shelley*, ed. H. B. Forman (London: Reeves and Turner, 1880), IV, 447–82. The quotation is from *Queen Mab*, Part V, line 189 (*Works*, IV, 426).

morality of the Christian religion is an aggravation of these evils. It is not even until lately that mankind have admitted that happiness is the sole end of the science of ethics, as of all other sciences; and that the fanatical idea of mortifying the flesh for the love of God has been discarded. I have heard, indeed, an[478] ignorant collegian adduce, in favour of Christianity, its hostility to every worldly feeling.[1]

But if happiness be the object of morality, of all human unions and disunions; if the worthiness of every action is to be estimated by the quantity of pleasurable sensation it is calculated to produce, then the connection of the sexes is so long sacred as it contributes to the comfort of the parties, and is naturally dissolved when its evils are greater than its benefits. There is nothing immoral in this separation. Constancy has nothing virtuous in itself, independently of the pleasure it confers, and partakes of the temporizing spirit of vice in proportion as it endures tamely moral defects of magnitude in the object of its indiscreet choice. Love is free: to promise for ever to love the same woman, is not less absurd than to promise to believe the same creed: such a vow, in both cases, excludes us from all enquiry. The language of the votarist is this: The woman I now love may be infinitely inferior to many others; the creed I now profess may be a mass of errors and absurdities; but I exclude myself from all future information as to the amiability of the one and the truth of the other, resolving blindly, and in spite of conviction, to adhere to them. Is this the language of delicacy and reason? Is the love of such a frigid heart of more worth than its belief?

The present system of constraint does no more, in the majority of instances, than make hypocrites or open enemies. Persons of delicacy and virtue, unhappily united[479] to one whom they find it impossible to love, spend the loveliest season of their life in unproductive efforts to appear otherwise than they are, for the sake of the feelings of their partner or the welfare of their mutual offspring: those of less generosity and refinement openly avow their disappointment, and linger out the remnant of that union, which only death can dissolve, in a

---

1 The first Christian emperor made a law by which seduction was punished with death: if the female pleaded her own consent, she also was punished with death; if the parents endeavoured to screen the criminals, they were banished and their estates were confiscated; the slaves who might be accessary were burned alive, or forced to swallow melted lead. The very offspring of an illegal love were involved in the consequences of the sentence.— *Gibbon's Decline and Fall*, II, 210. See also, for the hatred of the primitive Christians to love and even marriage, p. 269.

state of incurable bickering and hostility. The early education of their children takes its colour from the squabbles of the parents; they are nursed in a systematic school of ill humour, violence, and falsehood. Had they been suffered to part at the moment when indifference rendered their union irksome, they would have been spared many years of misery: they would have connected themselves more suitably, and would have found that happiness in the society of more congenial partners which is for ever denied them by the despotism of marriage. They would have been separately useful and happy members of society, who, whilst united, were miserable, and rendered misanthropical by misery. The conviction that wedlock is indissoluble holds out the strongest of all temptations to the perverse: they indulge without restraint in acrimony, and all the little tyrannies of domestic life, when they know that their victim is without appeal. If this connection were put on a rational basis, each would be assured that habitual ill temper would terminate in separation, and would check this vicious and dangerous propensity.

Prostitution is the legitimate offspring of marriage and its accompanying errors. Women, for no other crime than having followed the dictates of a natural appetite, are driven with fury from the comforts and sympathies of society. It is less venial than murder; and the punishment which is inflicted on her who destroys her child to escape reproach, is lighter than the life of agony[480] and disease to which the prostitute is irrecoverably doomed. Has a woman obeyed the impulse of unerring nature;—society declares war against her, pitiless and eternal war: she must be the tame slave, she must make no reprisals; theirs is the right of persecution, hers the duty of endurance. She lives a life of infamy: the loud and bitter laugh of scorn scares her from all return. She dies of long and lingering disease: yet *she* is in fault, *she* is the criminal, *she* the froward and untameable child,—and society, forsooth, the pure and virtuous matron, who casts her as an abortion from her undefiled bosom! Society avenges herself on the criminals of her own creation; she is employed in anathematizing the vice today, which yesterday she was the most zealous to teach. Thus is formed one tenth of the population of London: meanwhile the evil is twofold. Young men, excluded by the fanatical idea of chastity from the society of modest and accomplished women, associate with these vicious and miserable beings, destroying thereby all those exquisite and delicate sensibilities whose existence cold-hearted worldlings have denied; annihilating all genuine passion, and debasing that to a selfish feeling which is the excess of generosity and devotedness. Their body and mind alike crumble into a hideous wreck of humanity; idiotcy and disease become perpetuated in their miserable offspring, and distant generations suffer for the bigotted morality of their forefathers. Chastity is a monkish and evangelical superstition, a greater foe to natural temperance even than unintellectual sensuality; it strikes at the root of all domestic happiness, and consigns more than half of the human race to misery, that some few may monopolize according to law. A system could not well have been devised more studiously hostile to human happiness than marriage.[481]

I conceive that, from the abolition of marriage, the fit and natural arrangement of sexual connection would result. I by no means assert that the intercourse would be promiscuous: on the contrary; it appears, from the relation of parent to child, that this union is generally of long duration, and marked above all others with generosity and self-devotion. But this is a subject which it is perhaps premature to discuss. That which will result from the abolition of marriage, will be natural and right; because choice and change will be exempted from restraint.

In fact, religion and morality, as they now stand, compose a practical code of misery and servitude: the genius of human happiness must tear every leaf from the accursed book of God, ere man can read the inscription on his heart. How would morality, dressed up in stiff stays and finery, start from her own disgusting image, should she look in the mirror of nature![482]

From "On Women"

ARTHUR SCHOPENHAUER

. . . In their hearts women think that it is men's business to earn money and theirs to spend it—if possible during their husband's life, but, at any rate, after his death. The very fact that their husband hands

From *Essays in Pessimism* (1819), tr. T. Bailey Saunders (London: Swan, Sonnenschein and Company, Ltd., 1891), pp. 108–12.

them over his earnings for purposes of housekeeping, strengthens them in this belief.

However many disadvantages all this may involve, there is at least this to be said in its favour: that the woman lives more in the present than the man, and that, if the present is at all tolerable, she enjoys it more eagerly. This is the source of that cheerfulness which is peculiar to woman, fitting her to amuse man in his hours of recreation, and, in case of need, to console him when he is borne down by the weight of his cares.

It is by no means a bad plan to consult women in matters of difficulty, as the Germans used to do in ancient times; for their way of looking at things is quite different from ours, chiefly in the fact that they like to take the shortest way to their goal, and, in general, manage to fix their eyes upon what lies before them; while we, as a rule, see far beyond it, just because it is in front of our noses. In cases like this, we need to be brought back to the right standpoint, so as to recover the near and simple view.[108]

Then, again, women are decidedly more sober in their judgment than we are, so that they do not see more in things than is really there; whilst, if our passions are aroused, we are apt to see things in an exaggerated way, or imagine what does not exist.

The weakness of their reasoning faculty also explains why it is that women show more sympathy for the unfortunate than men do, and so treat them with more kindness and interest; and why it is that, on the contrary, they are inferior to men in point of justice, and less honourable and conscientious. For it is just because their reasoning power is weak that present circumstances have such a hold over them, and those concrete things which lie directly before their eyes exercise a power which is seldom counteracted to any extent by abstract principles of thought, by fixed rules of conduct, firm resolutions, or, in general, by consideration for the past and the future, or regard for what is absent and remote. Accordingly, they possess the first and main elements that go to make a virtuous character, but they are deficient in those secondary qualities which are often a necessary instrument in the formation of it.[1]

Hence it will be found that the fundamental fault of the female

---

[1] In this respect they may be compared to an animal organism which contains a liver but no gall-bladder. Here let me refer to what I have said in my treatise on *The Foundation of Morals*, § 17.

character is that it has *no sense of justice*. This is mainly due to the fact, already mentioned, that women are defective in the powers of reasoning and deliberation; but it is also traceable to[109] the position which Nature has assigned to them as the weaker sex. They are dependent, not upon strength, but upon craft; and hence their instinctive capacity for cunning, and their ineradicable tendency to say what is not true. For as lions are provided with claws and teeth, and elephants and boars with tusks, bulls with horns, and the cuttle fish with its cloud of inky fluid, so Nature has equipped woman, for her defence and protection, with the arts of dissimulation; and all the power which Nature has conferred upon man in the shape of physical strength and reason, has been bestowed upon women in this form. Hence dissimulation is innate in woman, and almost as much a quality of the stupid as of the clever. It is as natural for them to make use of it on every occasion as it is for those animals to employ their means of defence when they are attacked; they have a feeling that in doing so they are only within their rights. Therefore a woman who is perfectly truthful and not given to dissimulation is perhaps an impossibility, and for this very reason they are so quick at seeing through dissimulation in others that it is not a wise thing to attempt it with them. But this fundamental defect which I have stated, with all that it entails, gives rise to falsity, faithlessness, treachery, ingratitude, and so on. Perjury in a court of justice is more often committed by women than by men. It may, indeed, be generally questioned whether women ought to be sworn at all. From time to time one finds repeated cases everywhere of ladies, who want for nothing, taking things from shop-counters when no one is looking, and making off with them.[110]

Nature has appointed that the propagation of the species shall be the business of men who are young, strong and handsome; so that the race may not degenerate. This is the firm will and purpose of Nature in regard to the species, and it finds its expression in the passions of women. There is no law that is older or more powerful than this. Woe, then, to the man who sets up claims and interests that will conflict with it; whatever he may say and do, they will be unmercifully crushed at the first serious encounter. For the innate rule that governs women's conduct, though it is secret and unformulated, nay, unconscious in its working, is this: *We are justified in deceiving those who think they have acquired rights over the species by paying little attention to the individual, that is, to us. The constitution and, therefore, the welfare of the species have been placed in our hands and com-*

*mitted to our care, through the control we obtain over the next
generation, which proceeds from us; let us discharge our duties conscientiously.* But women have no abstract knowledge of this leading
principle; they are conscious of it only as a concrete fact; and they
have no other method of giving expression to it than the way in which
they act when the opportunity arrives. And then their conscience
does not trouble them so much as we fancy; for in the darkest recesses
of their heart, they are aware that in committing a breach of their
duty towards the individual, they have all the better fulfilled their
duty towards the species, which is infinitely greater.[2][111]

And since women exist in the main solely for the propagation of
the species, and are not destined for anything else, they live, as a rule,
more for the species than for the individual, and in their hearts take
the affairs of the species more seriously than those of the individual.
This gives their whole life and being a certain levity; the general bent
of their character is in a direction fundamentally different from that
of man; and it is this which produces that discord in married life which
is so frequent, and almost the normal state.[112]

From Thus Spake Zarathustra

FRIEDRICH NIETZSCHE

OF CHILD AND MARRIAGE

"I have a question for thee alone, my brother: like the lead I heave
that question over into thy soul that I may know how deep it is.

Thou art young and wishest for child and marriage. But I ask
thee: art thou a man who darest to wish for a child?

Art thou the victorious one, the self-subduer, the commander of
thy senses, the master of thy virtues? Thus I ask thee.

---

[2] A more detailed discussion of the matter in question may be found in my
chief work, *Die Welt als Wille und Vorstellung*, II, Chap. 44.

From *Thus Spake Zarathustra* (1883–1885), tr. Alexander Tille (New York:
The Macmillan Company, 1896), Part I: pp. 94–96; Part IV: pp. 418–20, 467–68,
475–76, 478–79.

Or, in thy wish, doth there speak the animal or necessity? Or solitude? Or discord with thyself?

I would that thy victory and freedom were longing for a child. Thou shalt build living monuments unto thy victory and liberation.

Thou shalt build beyond thyself. But first thou must be built thyself square in body and soul.

Thou shalt not only propagate thyself but propagate thyself upwards! Therefore the garden of marriage may help thee!

Thou shalt create a higher body, a prime motor, a wheel of self-rolling—thou shalt create a creator.

Marriage: thus I call the will of two to create that[94] one which is more than they who created it. I call marriage reverence unto each other as unto those who will such a will.

Let this be the significance and the truth of thy marriage. But that which the much-too-many call marriage, those superfluous—alas, what call I that?

Alas! that soul's poverty of two! Alas! that soul's dirt of two! Alas! that miserable ease of two!

Marriage they call that; and they say marriage is made in heaven.

Well, I like it not, that heaven of the superfluous! Nay, I like them not, those animals caught in heavenly nets!

Far from me also be the God who cometh halting to bless what he did not join together.

Laugh not at such marriages! What child hath not reason to weep over its parents!

Worthy and ripe for the significance of earth appeared this man unto me, but when I saw his wife earth seemed unto me a madhouse.

Yea, I wish the earth would tremble in convulsions whenever a saint and a goose couple.

This one went out for truths like a hero and at last he secured a little dressed-up lie. He calleth it his marriage.

That one was reserved in intercourse and chose fastidiously. But suddenly he for ever spoiled his company: he calleth this his marriage.[95]

A third one looked for a servant with an angel's virtues. But suddenly he became the servant of a woman, and now it would be well if in consequence he became an angel.

I found all buyers careful, having cunning eyes. But even the most cunning one buyeth his wife in a sack.

Many short follies—that is what ye call love. And your marriage maketh an end of many short follies—being one long stupidity.

Your love unto woman, and woman's love unto man: alas! would it were sympathy with suffering and veiled Gods! But generally two animals find each other out.

But even your best love is but an enraptured parable and a painful heat. It is a torch that is to beacon you unto higher ways.

One day ye shall love beyond yourselves! If so, first *learn* how to love. And hence ye have had to drink the bitter cup of your love.

Bitterness is in the cup even of the best love: thus it bringeth longing for beyond-man: thus it bringeth thirst unto thee, the creator!

Thirst unto the creator, an arrow and longing for beyond-man: say, my brother, is that thy will unto marriage?

Holy I call such a will and such a marriage."

Thus spake Zarathustra.[96]

FROM "OF HIGHER MAN"

1

"When, for the first time, I went unto men, I committed the hermit folly, the great folly. I stood in the marketplace.

And speaking unto all, I spake unto none. But in the evening, ropedancers were my companions, and corpses; and I myself was almost a corpse.

But with the new morning a new truth came unto me. Then I learned to say: 'What matter for me market and mob, and mob's noise and the mob's long ears!'

Ye higher men, learn this from me. In the market no one believeth in higher men. And if ye are going to speak there, it is well! But the mob blink: 'We are all equal!'

'Ye higher men,'—thus the mob blink—'there are no higher men; we are all equal; man is man; in the presence of God we are all equal!'

In the presence of God! But now that God hath died. But in the presence of the mob we do not wish to be equal. Ye higher men, depart from the market![418]

. . . . .

3

The most careful ask to-day: 'How is man preserved?' But Zarathustra asketh as the only and first one: 'How is man *surpassed?*'

Beyond-man is my care; with me, *he* and *not* man is the first and only thing. Not the neighbour, not the poorest one, not the greatest sufferer, not the best one.

O my brethren, what I can love in man, is that he is a transition and a destruction. And even in you there are many things which make me love and hope.[419]

That ye had scorn, ye higher men, that maketh me hope. For the great scorners are the great reverers.

That ye despaired, therein is much to honour. For ye did not learn how to give yourselves up; ye did not learn petty policies.

For to-day the petty folk have become master. They all preach submission and resignation and policy and diligence and regard and the long etcetera of petty virtues.

Whatever is of the women's tribe, whatever descendeth from the slaves' tribe, and especially from the mishmash of the mob—*these* will now become master of all human fate. Oh, loathing! loathing! loathing!

These ask and ask and weary not with asking! 'How doth man preserve himself best, longest, and most agreeably?' Thereby they are the masters of to-day.

Surpass these masters of to-day, O my brethren,—the petty folk. *They* are the greatest danger for beyond-man!

Surpass, ye higher men, the petty virtues, the petty policies, the grains-of-sand-regards, the swarming of ants, the miserable ease, the 'happiness of the greatest number!'

And rather despair than give in! And, verily, I love you for the very reason that ye know not how to live to-day, ye higher men! For thus *ye* live best![420]

FROM "THE DRUNKEN SONG"

3

Ye higher men, it is nigh unto midnight. Now I will say something into your ears, as that old bell telleth it into mine;

As familiarly, as terribly, as heartily, as speaketh unto me that midnight-bell which hath seen more than any man;

Which hath long ago counted the pulses of your fathers' heart-beat, and pain. Alas! alas! how it sigheth! how it laugheth in dream! the old, deep, deep midnight!

Hush! hush! Then many things are heard which are not permitted to become audible in daytime. But now, in the cool air, after even all noise of your hearts hath been stilled;

Now they speak, now they are heard, now they steal into night-like over-wakeful souls. Alas! alas! how midnight sigheth, how it laugheth in dream! [467]

Hearest thou not, how it familiarly, terribly, heartily speaketh unto *thee*—old, deep, deep midnight?

O man lose not sight! [468]

FROM "THE SIGN"

But the morning after that night Zarathustra jumped up from his couch, girded his loins, and stepped out of his cave, glowing and strong, like a morning sun coming from dark mountains.

"Thou great star," he said, as he had said once, "thou deep eye of happiness, what would be all thy happiness, if thou hadst not those for whom thou shinest!

And if they would remain in their chambers, while thou art awake and comest and givest and distributest, how angry would thy proud shame be at that!

Up! They sleep still, these higher men, whilst *I* am awake. *They* are not my proper companions! Not for them wait I here in my mountains.

Unto my work will I go, unto my day. But they understand not what are the signs of my morning. My step is for them not a call that awaketh them from sleep!

They sleep still in my cave. Their dream drinketh still at my drunken songs. The ear that hearkeneth for *me*, the *obeying* ear, is lacking in their limbs." [475]

This had Zarathustra said unto his heart, when the sun rose. Then he asking looked upward, for he heard above him the sharp cry of his eagle. "Up!" he shouted upward, "thus it pleaseth me and is due unto me. Mine animals are awake, for I am awake.

Mine eagle is awake and like me, honoureth the sun. With an eagle's claws he graspeth for the new light. Ye are my proper animals. I love you.

But my proper men are still lacking unto me!"

Thus spake Zarathustra. . . .[476]

. . . . .

And immediately his memory came back, and with one look he understood all that had happened between yesterday and to-day. "Here is the stone," he said and stroked his beard. "On *it* I sat yester-morning. And here the fortune-teller stepped unto me; and here for the first time I heard the cry I heard this moment, the great cry for help.

Oh, ye higher men, of *your* need it was that yester-morning that old fortune-teller told me his tale.

Unto your need he tried to seduce me and tempt me. 'O Zarathustra,' he said unto me, 'I come to seduce thee unto thy last sin.'

Unto my last sin?" cried Zarathustra, and angrily laughed at his own word. "*What* hath been reserved for me as my last sin?"[478]

And once more Zarathustra sank into himself and again sat down on the great stone and meditated. Suddenly he jumped up.

"*Pity! Pity for the higher man!*" he cried out, and his face turned into brass. "Up! *That* hath had its time!

My woe and my pity, what matter? Do I seek for *happiness?* I seek for my *work!*

Up! the lion hath come. My children are nigh. Zarathustra hath ripened. Mine hour hath come!

This is *my* morning. *My* day beginneth! *Come up, then, come up, thou great noon!*"

Thus spake Zarathustra and left his cave, glowing and strong, like a morning sun which cometh from dark mountains.[479]

From "What Do Ascetic Ideals Mean?"

FRIEDRICH NIETZSCHE

7

Let us guard ourselves from making gloomy faces at the mere sound of the word "torture!" For in this very case quite a number of

From Third Essay, *The Genealogy of Morals* (1887), tr. William A. Hausemann (New York: The Macmillan Company, 1897), pp. 142–51.

allowances and deductions can be made. There even remains something to laugh at. Let us, above all, not undervalue the fact that
Schopenhauer—who actually treated sensuality (including the tool of
sensuality, woman, this *instrumentum diaboli*) as his personal enemy—
stood in *need* of enemies, to keep him in good spirits;[142] that he loved
the grim-humoured, gally, black-browed words; that he frowned for
frowning's sake; from inclination; that he would have become sick,
become *pessimist*(—for pessimist he was not, much though he wished
to be so), but for his enemies, but for Hegel, for women, for sensuality,
and the whole will to life, the will to stay here. Had Schopenhauer
been a pessimist, he would not have *stayed* here, to be sure; he would
have run away. But his enemies held him fast; his enemies kept
seducing him to existence; his anger, quite as in the case of the ancient
cynics, constituted his comfort, his recreation, his reward, his *re-
medium* for surfeit, his *happiness*. So much in regard to that which is
specifically personal in the case of Schopenhauer! But on the other
hand his case presents also something typical,—and now only we come
back to our problem. Undoubtedly there exists, as long as philosophers
exist on earth, and wherever philosophers have existed (from India as
far as England—to take the opposite poles of philosophical ability), a
specific philosopher's sensitiveness and rancour against sensuality;
Schopenhauer being, in fact, only the most eloquent and, if we have
ears for such sounds, the most ravishing and rapturous outburst of it.
In the same manner there exists a singular philosopher's prepossessed-
ness and heartiness in favour of the whole ascetic ideal;—about which
and against which fact it will hardly do for us to[143] shut our eyes.
Both things are, as I said, essential to the type. If either be wanting in
a philosopher, then, we may be sure, he is always but a "so-called"
philosopher. What does that *mean?* For this fact must first be interpreted: *in itself* it stands stupid to all eternity, as every "thing in itself."
Every animal, and hence also *la bête philosophe*, instinctively strives
for an optimum of favourable conditions under which it is free to
discharge fully its power and attains its maximum consciousness of
power; every animal, quite as instinctively and with a keenness of scent
which "passeth all understanding," abhors every kind of disturber or
obstacle which obstructs or *could* obstruct his road to the optimum
(—it is *not* its road to "happiness," of which I am now speaking, but
its road to power, to action, to mightiest action, and, actually, in most
cases, its road to unhappiness). So, also, the philosopher abhors *wed-*

lock and all that would fain persuade to this state—as being an obstacle and fatality on his road to the optimum. Who among the great philosophers is known to have been married? Heraclitus, Plato, Descartes, Spinoza, Leibnitz, Kant, Schopenhauer—they were not; nay, we cannot even so much as *conceive* them as married. A married philosopher is a figure *of comedy*, this is my proposition; and that exception, Socrates, mischievous Socrates, married, it seems, *ironice*, with the express purpose of demonstrating *this very* proposition. Every[144] philosopher would say what Buddha said, when the birth of a son was announced to him: "Râhula is born unto me, a fetter is forged for me" (Râhula means here "a little demon"). For every "free spirit" a thoughtful hour would be bound to come (assuming, that before he had a thoughtless hour), as it came to the same Buddha! " 'Closely confined,' he thought within himself, 'is the life in the house, a place of impurity! Freedom is in the leaving of the house.' " "Because he thought in this wise, he left the house." In the ascetic ideal there are indicated so many bridges leading to *independence* that a philosopher will not be able to hear, without some inner chuckling and exultation, the story of all those resolute souls, who one day said No to all un-freedom and went into some *desert;* even assuming that they were nothing but mighty asses and the very counterparts of mighty spirits. What, then, does the ascetic ideal mean in the case of a philosopher? My answer is—as long ago will have been anticipated—: the aspect of the ascetic ideal draws from the lips of the philosopher a smile because he recognises in it an optimum of the conditions of highest and keenest spirituality. In so doing, he does *not* negate "existence," but rather asserts *his own* existence and *only* his own existence, and this perhaps so much so that the frivolous wish is not far from him: *pereat mundus, fiat philosophia, fiat philosophus, fiam!* . . . .[145]

8

These philosophers, we see, are anything but unbiassed witnesses and judges as to the *value* of the ascetic ideal! They think *of themselves* —what does "the Saint" concern them! In valuing the ascetic ideal, they think of that which is most indispensable to *them:* freedom from constraint, interference, noise, from business, duties, cares; they think of a clear head, of dancing, leaping, flying of thoughts; good air, thin, clear, free, dry mountain-air, spiritualising and lending wings to all animal being; peace in all souterrains; all dogs securely chained; no barking indicative of hostility or shaggy rancour; no gnaw-worms of thwarted ambition; modest and obsequious intestines, busy as mills, but absent; the heart distant, beyond, futurous, posthumous. All in all, the ascetic ideal suggests to them that aerial asceticism of some deified and newly fledged animal which more roves than rests aloof from life. It is known what are the three great show-words of the ascetic ideal: Poverty, Humility, Chastity. And now let people for once examine the lives of all great productive and inventive spirits: to a certain extent all three will be found again in them. Not at all as their "virtues." This kind of man, what has it to do with virtues! But as the most essential, most natural conditions of their *best* existence, of their *finest* productivity. And it is also quite possible that their[146] dominating spirituality had, first of all, to subdue an untamable and tender pride or an unruly sensuality; or that it found it rather difficult to keep up their will to the "desert" perhaps against a hankering for luxury and most exquisite things, as also against an extravagant liberality of heart and hand. But this spirituality prevailed, even by virtue of its function of *dominating* instinct which insisted on its postulates against all other instincts. This spirituality still does so; for if it did not, then it would not dominate. In this kind of abstinence, therefore, is anything but a "virtue." The *desert*, by the bye, of which even now I spoke, into which the strong and independently constituted spirits retire to be lonesome—oh, how different it looks from the desert, as our *"educated classes"* imagine it. For, as the case may be, they themselves are the desert, these educated classes. And certain it is that all stage players of the spirit have ever found it unbearable. For them it is not by far romantic enough, not Syrian enough, not stage-desert enough! Camels, it is true, are not absent from it; but this is the only respect in which it resembles a real desert. Perchance, that desert consists in a self-willed obscurity; in a going out of the way of one's self; in a horror of noise, honours, newspapers, influence; in a little office, an everyday, something which more hides than exposes; in an occasional intercourse with harmless, gladsome, little "foules and beastes," the sight of which refreshes; in[147] some mountains as one's company—yet not mountains dead, but provided with *eyes* (—with lakes, to wit); at times even in a room in some crowded everybody hotel where one is sure to be mistaken and may safely converse with everybody else. This is a "desert" in this sense. Oh, believe me, it is lonesome enough! If Hera-

clitus retired into the courtyards and colonnades of the gigantic
Artemis-temple, that "desert," I admit, was rather more dignified.
Why are such temples *wanting* to us? (Peradventure they are *not*
wanting to us: I am just thinking of my finest study, the *piazza di San
Marco;* spring presupposed, as also forenoon, the hours between ten
and twelve.) But that which Heraclitus fled, is even this which *we*
also flee: the hubbub and Democrat gossip of the Ephesians, their
politics, their news from the "empire" (Persia, you understand), their
market-truck of "to-day." For we philosophers must have rest from
one thing first of all, from every "to-day." We revere what is still, cold,
calm, distant, past, everything, in fact, the aspect of which does not
assault or freeze the soul,—something with which we may talk, without
talking *aloud*. Mark but the timbre which a spirit has when talking;
every spirit has his own timbre, loves his own timbre. Yonder man,
for instance, must, I think, be an agitator, say rather a hollow-head, a
hollow-pot. Whatsoever goes into him, is sure to reverberate, heavy
and hollow, laden with the echo of great emptiness. That one over[148]
there speaks rarely otherwise than with a hoarse voice. Has he *thought*
himself into hoarseness? Possible enough—one may ask physiologists;—
he, however, who thinks in *words*, thinks, not as thinker but as speaker.
(It shows that he thinks, at bottom, not of matters, not to the point, but
only in regard to matters; that he thinks, in reality, of *himself* and of
his listeners.) This third one, here, talks impertinently, his body rubs
against our own; his breath breathes upon us. Involuntarily we shut
our mouths, though it is a book through which he speaks to us. The
timbre of his style tells the reason why; that he has no time, he
has little faith in himself, that to-day or never he has a chance
to speak. But a spirit, convinced of himself, speaks softly; he
seeks retirement; he waits to be asked. It characterises the philosopher
that he avoids three showy and noisy things,—glory, princes and
women; whereby it is not meant to be said, however, that they should
not come to him. He shuns all too glaring brightness; hence he shuns
his own time and the "day" of it. In this respect he is like a shadow;
the farther the sun sinks, the bigger he grows. As regards his "humility," he will endure, even as he endures darkness, so also a certain
amount of dependence and obscurity; nay, he fears to be disturbed
by lightnings, he shrinks back from the unprotectedness of an all too
isolated and exposed tree against which every storm vents its temper,
and every temper vents[149] its storm. His "motherly" instinct, the

secret love for that which grows within him, consigns him to conditions in which he is freed from the duty of taking care *of himself;* in the same sense that the instinct of the *mother* in woman has so far maintained the dependent condition of woman in general. All in all, it is little enough they demand, these philosophers. Their motto is: "He who possesses, is possessed;" *not,* as again and again I must urge, from a virtue, or a meritorious will to simplicity and contentedness, but because their supreme lord demands it of them, demands it wisely and inexorably; which lord, has but one end in view and gathers and saves exclusively for it time, strength, love, interest, everything. Men of his kind like to be disturbed by enmities, as little as by amities: they are quick to forget, quick to despise. They deem it a poor taste to play the martyr. "To *suffer* for truth"—this they leave to the ambitious, the stage-heroes of the spirit and whoso has time enough for it. (They themselves, the philosophers, have *to do* something for truth.) They are niggard in the use of big words; we are told that they cannot brook to hear the word "truth;" they say, it sounds grandiloquent. . . . And finally, as regards the "chastity" of philosophers, the productivity of such spirits consists manifestly in something else than in children. Perhaps they also have somewhere else the continuance of their name, their little immortality. (Still more immodestly the [150] ancient Indian philosophers expressed themselves: "Wherefore posterity for him whose soul is the world?") Therein is nothing of chastity out of any ascetic scrupulosity or hatred of the senses; as little as it is chastity if an athlete or jockey abstains from woman. Rather, thus it is demanded by the dominating instinct of the philosopher, especially during the period of his great pregnancy. All artists know the injurious effects of sexual intercourse in times of great spiritual suspense and preparation; in the case of the most powerful among them, and those in whom the instinct operates with the greatest certainty, experience, fatal experience is not even necessary,—for in their case it is even their "motherly" instinct which, for the benefit of the work in preparation, will regardlessly dispose of all other supplies and advances of power,— of the *vigour* of animal life. In such cases the greater power will *absorb* the lesser. . . .[151]

Three Reviews

GEORGE BERNARD SHAW

"A DOLL'S HOUSE"

Unfortunately, *Pillars of Society*, as a propagandist play, is disabled by the circumstance that the hero, being a fraudulent hypocrite in the ordinary police-court sense of the phrase, is not accepted as a typical pillar of society by the class which he represents. Accordingly, Ibsen took care next time to make his idealist irreproachable from the standpoint of the ordinary idealist morality. In the famous *Doll's House*, the pillar of society who owns the doll is a model husband, father, and citizen. In his little household, with the three darling children and the affectionate little wife, all on the most loving terms with one another, we have the sweet home, the womanly woman, the happy family life of the idealist's dream. Mrs. Nora Helmer is happy in the belief that she has attained a valid realization of all these illusions—that she is an ideal wife and mother, and that Helmer is an ideal husband who would, if the necessity arose, give his life to save her reputation. A few simply contrived incidents disabuse her effectually on all these points. One of her earliest acts[82] of devotion to her husband has been the secret raising of a sum of money to enable him to make a tour which was necessary to restore his health. As he would have broken down sooner than go into debt, she has had to persuade him that the money was a gift from her father. It was really obtained from a moneylender, who refused to make her the loan unless she induced her father to endorse the promissory note. This being impossible, as her father was dying at the time, she took the shortest way out of the difficulty by writing the name herself, to the entire satisfaction of the moneylender, who, though not at all duped, knows that

From *The Quintessence of Ibsenism* (New York: Brentano's, 1905), pp. 82–86, 100–105, 114–17. Reprinted by permission of the Public Trustee and the Society of Authors (London).

forged bills are often the surest to be paid. Then she slaves in secret at scrivener's work until she has nearly paid off the debt. At this point Helmer is made manager of the bank in which he is employed; and the moneylender, wishing to obtain a post there, uses the forged bill to force Nora to exert her influence with Helmer on his behalf. But she, having a hearty contempt for the man, cannot be persuaded by him that there was any harm in putting her father's name on the bill, and ridicules the suggestion that the law would not recognize that she was right under the circumstances. It is her husband's own contemptuous denunciation of a forgery[83] formerly committed by the moneylender himself that destroys her self-satisfaction and opens her eyes to her ignorance of the serious business of the world to which her husband belongs—the world outside the home he shares with her. When he goes on to tell her that commercial dishonesty is generally to be traced to the influence of bad mothers, she begins to perceive that the happy way in which she plays with the children, and the care she takes to dress them nicely, are not sufficient to constitute her a fit person to train them. In order to redeem the forged bill, she resolves to borrow the balance due upon it from a friend of the family. She has learnt to coax her husband into giving her what she asks by appealing to his affection for her: that is, by playing all sorts of pretty tricks until he is wheedled into an amorous humor. This plan she has adopted without thinking about it, instinctively taking the line of least resistance with him. And now she naturally takes the same line with her husband's friend. An unexpected declaration of love from him is the result; and it at once explains to her the real nature of the domestic influence she has been so proud of. All her illusions about herself are now shattered; she sees herself as an ignorant and silly woman, a dangerous mother, and a wife[84] kept for her husband's pleasure merely; but she only clings the harder to her delusion about him: he is still the ideal husband who would make any sacrifice to rescue her from ruin. She resolves to kill herself rather than allow him to destroy his own career by taking the forgery on himself to save her reputation. The final disillusion comes when he, instead of at once proposing to pursue this ideal line of conduct when he hears of the forgery, naturally enough flies into a vulgar rage and heaps invectives on her for disgracing him. Then she sees that their whole family life has been a fiction—their home a mere doll's house in which they have been playing at ideal husband and father, wife and mother. So she leaves him then and there in order to find out the reality of things for herself, and to gain some position not fundamentally false, refusing to see her children again until she is fit to be in charge of them, or to live with him until she and he become capable of a more honorable relation to one another than that in which they have hitherto stood. He at first cannot understand what has happened, and flourishes the shattered ideals over her as if they were as potent as ever. He presents the course most agreeable to him—that of her staying at home and avoiding a scandal[85]—as her duty to her husband, to her children, and to her religion; but the magic of these disguises is gone; and at last even he understands what has really happened, and sits down alone to wonder whether that more honorable relation can ever come to pass between them.[86]

"THE WILD DUCK"

After *An Enemy of the People*, Ibsen, as I have said, left the vulgar ideals for dead, and set about the exposure of those of the choicer spirits,[100] beginning with the incorrigible idealists who had idealized his very self, and were becoming known as Ibsenites. His first move in this direction was such a tragi-comic slaughtering of sham Ibsenism that his astonished victims plaintively declared that *The Wild Duck*, as the new play was called, was a satire on his former works; whilst the pious, whom he had disappointed so severely by his interpretation of *Brand*, began to think that he had come back repentant to the fold. The household to which we are introduced in *The Wild Duck* is not, like Mrs. Alving's, a handsome one made miserable by superstitious illusions, but a shabby one made happy by romantic illusions. The only member of it who sees it as it really is, is the wife, a good-natured Philistine who desires nothing better. The husband, a vain, petted, spoilt dawdler, believes that he is a delicate and high-souled man, devoting his life to redeeming his old father's name from the disgrace brought on it by an imprisonment for breach of the forest laws. This redemption he proposes to effect by making himself famous as a great inventor some day when he has the necessary inspiration. Their daughter, a girl in her teens, believes intensely in her father and in the promised invention. The disgraced grandfather cheers himself by drink whenever he[101] can get it; but his chief resource is a wonderful garret full of rabbits and pigeons. The old man has procured a

number of second-hand Christmas trees; and with these he has turned
the garret into a sort of toy forest, in which he can play at bear hunting, which was one of the sports of his youth and prosperity. The
weapons employed in the hunting expeditions are a gun which will
not go off, and a pistol which occasionally brings down a rabbit or a
pigeon. A crowning touch is given to the illusion by a wild duck,
which, however, must not be shot, as it is the special property of the
girl, who reads and dreams whilst the woman cooks and washes, besides carrying on the photographic work which is supposed to be the
business of her husband. She does not appreciate his highly strung
sensitiveness of character, which is constantly suffering agonizing jars
from her vulgarity; but then she does not appreciate that other fact
that he is a lazy and idle impostor. Downstairs there is a disgraceful
clergyman named Molvik, a hopeless drunkard; but even he respects
himself and is tolerated because of a special illusion invented for him
by another lodger, a doctor—the now famous Dr. Relling—upon
whom the lesson of the household above has not been thrown away.
Molvik, says the doctor, must[102] break out into drinking fits because
he is daimonic, an interesting explanation which completely relieves
the reverend gentleman from the imputation of vulgar tippling.

Into this domestic circle there comes a new lodger, an idealist of
the most advanced type. He greedily swallows the daimonic theory
of the clergyman's drunkenness, and enthusiastically accepts the
photographer as the high-souled hero he supposes himself to be; but
he is troubled because the relations of the man and his wife do not
constitute an ideal marriage. He happens to know that the woman,
before her marriage, was the cast-off mistress of his own father; and
because she has not told her husband this, he conceives her life as
founded on a lie, like that of Bernick in *Pillars of Society*. He accordingly sets himself to work out the woman's salvation for her, and establish ideally frank relations between the pair, by simply blurting
out the truth, and then asking them, with fatuous self-satisfaction,
whether they do not feel much better for it. This wanton piece of
mischief has more serious results than a mere domestic scene. The
husband is too weak to act on his bluster about outraged honor and
the impossibility of his ever living with his wife again; and the woman
is merely annoyed with the idealist[103] for telling on her; but the girl
takes the matter to heart and shoots herself. The doubt cast on her
parentage, with her father's theatrical repudiation of her, destroy her

ideal place in the home, and make her a source of discord there; so
she sacrifices herself, thereby carrying out the teaching of the idealist
mischief-maker, who has talked a good deal to her about the duty and
beauty of self-sacrifice, without foreseeing that he might be taken in
mortal earnest. The busybody thus finds that people cannot be freed
from their failings from without. They must free themselves. When
Nora is strong enough to live out of the doll's house, she will go out
of it of her own accord if the door stands open; but if before that
period you take her by the scruff of the neck and thrust her out, she
will only take refuge in the next establishment of the kind that offers
to receive her. Woman has thus two enemies to deal with: the old-
fashioned one who wants to keep the door locked, and the new-
fashioned one who wants to thrust her into the street before she is
ready to go. In the cognate case of a hypocrite and liar like Bernick,
exposing him is a mere police measure: he is none the less a liar and
hypocrite when you have exposed him. If you want to make a sincere
and truthful man of him, all that you can do is to[104] remove what you
can of the external obstacles to his exposing himself, and then wait for
the operation of his internal impulse to confess. If he has no such impulse, then you must put up with him as he is. It is useless to make
claims on him which he is not yet prepared to meet. Whether, like
Brand, we make such claims because to refrain would be to compromise with evil, or, like Gregers Werle, because we think their
moral beauty must recommend them at sight to everyone, we shall
alike incur Relling's impatient assurance that "life would be quite
tolerable if we could only get rid of the confounded duns that keep
on pestering us in our poverty with the claims of the ideal."[105]

"THE LADY FROM THE SEA"

Ibsen's next play, though it deals with the old theme, does not insist on the power of ideals to kill, as the two previous plays do. It
rather deals with the origin of ideals in unhappiness—in dissatisfaction
with the real. The subject of *The Lady from the Sea* is the most poetic
fancy imaginable. A young woman, brought up on the sea-coast,
marries a respectable doctor, a widower, who idolizes her and places
her in his household with nothing to do but dream and be made much
of by everybody. Even the housekeeping is done by her stepdaughter:
she has no responsibility, no care, and no trouble. In other words, she

is an idle, helpless, utterly dependent article of luxury. A man turns red at the thought of being such a thing; but he thoughtlessly accepts a pretty and fragile-looking woman in the same position as a charming natural picture. The lady from the sea feels an indefinite want in her life. She reads her want into all other lives, and comes to the conclusion that man once had to[114] choose whether he would be a land animal or a creature of the sea; and that having chosen the land, he has carried about with him ever since a secret sorrow for the element he has forsaken. The dissatisfaction that gnaws her is, as she interprets it, this desperate longing for the sea. When her only child dies and leaves her without the work of a mother to give her a valid place in the world, she yields wholly to her longing, and no longer cares for her husband, who, like Rosmer, begins to fear that she is going mad. At last a seaman appears and claims her as his wife on the ground that they went years before through a rite which consisted of their marrying the sea by throwing their rings into it. This man, who had to fly from her in the old time because he killed his captain, and who fills her with a sense of dread and mystery, seems to her to embody the attraction which the sea has for her. She tells her husband that she must go away with the seaman. Naturally the doctor expostulates—declares that he cannot for her own sake let her do so mad a thing. She replies that he can only prevent her by locking her up, and asks him what satisfaction it will be to him to have her body under lock and key whilst her heart is with the other man. In vain he urges that he will only keep her under[115] restraint until the seaman goes—that he must not, dare not, allow her to ruin herself. Her argument remains unanswerable. The seaman openly declares that she will come; so that the distracted husband asks him does he suppose he can force her from her home. To this the seaman replies that, on the contrary, unless she comes of her own free will there is no satisfaction to him in her coming at all—the unanswerable argument again. She echoes it by demanding her freedom to choose. Her husband must cry off his law-made and Church-made bargain, renounce his claim to the fulfilment of her vows; and leave her free to go back to the sea with her old lover. Then the doctor, with a heavy heart, drops his prate about his heavy responsibility for her actions, and throws the responsibility on her by crying off as she demands. The moment she feels herself a free and responsible woman, all her childish fancies vanish: the seaman becomes simply an old acquaintance whom she no longer cares for;

and the doctor's affection produces its natural effect. In short, she says No to the seaman, and takes over the housekeeping keys from her stepdaughter without any further speculations concerning that secret sorrow for the abandoned sea.

It should be noted here that Ellida, the Lady[116] from the Sea, appears a much more fantastic person to English readers than to Norwegian ones. The same thing is true of many other characters drawn by Ibsen, notably Peer Gynt, who, if born in England, would certainly not have been a poet and metaphysician as well as a black-guard and a speculator. The extreme type of Norwegian, as depicted by Ibsen, imagines himself doing wonderful things, but does nothing. He dreams as no Englishman dreams, and drinks to make himself dream the more, until his effective will is destroyed, and he becomes a broken-down, disreputable sot, carrying about the tradition that he is a hero, and discussing himself on that assumption. Although the number of persons who dawdle their life away over fiction in England must be frightful, and is probably increasing, yet we have no Ulric Brendels, Rosmers, Ellidas, Peer Gynts, nor anything at all like them; and it is for this reason that I am disposed to fear that *Rosmersholm* and *The Lady from the Sea* will always be received much more in-credulously by English audiences than *A Doll's House* and the plays in which the leading figures are men and women of action.[117]

From The Art of Poetry[1]

QUINTUS HORATIUS FLACCUS (HORACE)

He who blends the useful [*utile*] with the merely pleasing [*dulci*] triumphs by delighting and at the same time enlightening the reader. That is the book to make money for the publisher, to travel the seven seas, and to make its author's fame endure.

Miscellaneous Critiques[2]

GEORGE BERNARD SHAW

DRAMA: The goodness of a "good acting play" consists in the skill with which it is constructed so as to require no acting for its successful performance.[320]

---

[1] From *The Art of Poetry* (c. 13 B.C.), tr. the present editor, lines 343–46.

[2] From musical critiques of George Bernard Shaw recorded in R. F. Rattray, *Bernard Shaw: A Chronicle* (Luton, England: The Leagrave Press, Ltd., 1951), Appendix I, p. 320. Reprinted by kind permission of the Public Trustee and the Society of Authors (London), the publishers, and the author. The title used here is the present editor's.

From The Twentieth Century Molière: Bernard Shaw

AUGUSTIN HAMON

FROM "EPISTLE DEDICATORY TO GEORGE BERNARD SHAW"

Paris followed the lead of Brussels, and in April and May 1908 *Candida* was played at the Théâtre des Arts. This introduction of the critics and of the Parisian public to your drama was unfortunate.[27] The company was a talented one, and their interpretation was painstaking, but it was completely falsified by the transformation of the Molièresque figure of Burgess into a wearisome "comic man." As you are aware, I was unable to prevent this vulgarization of your splendid *Candida*. With real distress I attended the final rehearsals, doing all that was possible to attenuate the clumsiness and stupidity of the crime that was being perpetrated against art. You know how painful I found the dress rehearsal and the first night. The result was what I had anticipated, and there came a moment when the actors, whose interpretation was in the vein of tragedy, could hardly go on, so harassed were they by the perpetual smiles and laughter of the audience. As for the critics, they completely lost their bearings. They felt, confusedly, that the interpretation was inadequate. They did not and they could not understand the play, because all its values had been falsified. The result was that some of the critics wrote unfavourably of *Candida*, while even those who liked the play, recognizing its poetic force, sensing its tragical greatness, and understanding some of its ideas and characters, yet failed to grasp the intense spirit of comedy which is as characteristic of *Candida* as of all of your other plays.

From *The Twentieth Century Molière: Bernard Shaw*, tr. Eden and Cedar Paul (London: George Allen and Unwin, Ltd., 1915), pp. 27–29, 182–88, 200–202, 205. Reprinted by permission of the publisher.

This unfortunate experience in Paris could not[28] fail to retard the appreciation of your drama, that drama which is destined in France to enjoy an enormous popular success, when it comes to be played in the comical, farcical, or Molièresque vein, for then all the wealth of its wit will be perceived. Yet out of evil came good.

This transmutation of the Shavian comedy into a wearisome, pseudo-psychological comedy, and its results in the interpretation of *Candida,* impressed me with the importance of the farcical element in the serious comedy that deals with ideas, characters, and customs. It enabled me to understand why Molière had been the leader of all writers of farce. I grasped why it was that Molière was a great writer and a profound philosopher without ever ceasing to make use of the methods of medieval farce and the tricks of a clown at the fair. It recalled to my mind the advice you had yourself given me to disregard all academic counsels on the construction of "well-written plays,"[1] and to learn my trade by going to the circus and studying the methods of the clown. The result was that I saw more clearly all the resemblances between your comedy and that of Molière.[29]

FROM "ANALYSIS OF BERNARD SHAW'S DRAMATIC METHOD"

It is a remarkable fact that *Candida,* one of the *Four Pleasant Plays,* whose meaning is so clear, has not been understood by the great majority of critics in England or elsewhere. This failure of understanding must depend on causes foreign to the play itself, for, let me repeat, the clarity of *Candida,* as of all Bernard Shaw's plays, is extreme. If it bears "a Mystery" as a subtitle, this is merely because at the end of the play the poet goes away with a secret which is a mystery for Candida[182] and her husband. But before we examine the reasons of the critics' failure to understand *Candida,* let us give the argument of this fine play.

The following ideas constitute the intellectual action. What binds a man and a woman together is not legal marriage, but love. Virtue and

---

1 [Hamon means the French "well-made" play, which depends for its effect almost entirely upon plot structure rather than upon character or theme. It has been a tremendously successful kind of drama, nevertheless, for over a century. For further information, consult my "Introduction to the Well-Made Play," in *Camille and Other Plays* (New York: Hill and Wang, Inc., 1957), pp. vii–xxxix. See also my essay, "Shaw's Debt to Scribe," included in this section.]

purity are conventions which do not arrest the play of the instincts, and to act according to our instincts is necessary. Moral force is greater than physical force. Woman dominates man, domesticates him. Woman's love is a love tinged by motherhood. The poet's mission is a more elevated one than the attainment of domestic happiness. The artist, the creator, is like woman, and cannot be domesticated. The Socialist ideal triumphs over the capitalist ideal. The poetic ideal is vaguer, more remote from realization, than the Socialist ideal, and if the former is in certain respects inferior to the latter it is also in certain respects superior; neither of these two ideals triumphs over the other. Woman, man's social equal, is her own mistress. No occupation is base or inferior *per se*. True strength is to be found in a clear view of the reality of things, after the veils of convention and prejudice have been stripped off. Lying is a cause of weakness. Love—that is to say, sexual attraction—is the universal desire. Youth is the future, it is life; old age is the past, it is death. Upon[183] those endowed with moral strength suffering has a fortifying influence. Wealth is based upon the exploitation of the workers. Justice and beauty—that is to say, the apostle and the poet—make the world greater, thanks to the help of woman.

Six characters represent these ideas. Candida, the heroine, thirty-three years of age, is commonplace from the intellectual point of view, but has a great soul, is eminently intuitive, reading others' minds, and seeing things naked, just as they are in their pure reality; she is absolutely emancipated from prejudices and conventions. Morell, Candida's husband, a man over forty, is of vigorous physique, intelligent, cultivated, lively, but not of particularly fine fibre either in body or in mind; he is comfortably established as incumbent of a large East End parish. Eugene Marchbanks, of a refined and delicate temperament, but nervous to the verge of the morbid, physically a weakling, but endowed with moral strength, intuitive because a poet, extremely timid, exhibiting a mingling of childlike and of serious or rather profound characteristics, is eighteen years old. Proserpine, an unmarried woman of about thirty, is Morell's typist; she is intelligent, brisk, and somewhat irritable. Lexy Mill, Morell's curate, has no marked character of his own, and models himself upon Morell. Last of all we have Burgess, Candida's father, a[184] bourgeois of sixty, a well-to-do man of business, coarse-minded, vulgar, and ignorant, vain of his wealth, which he has acquired as a contractor in municipal undertakings by the shameless exploitation of his workmen.

Among these characters conflicts arise. There is a struggle between Morell, who symbolizes Christian Socialist idealism, and is clear-sighted, bold, sure of himself, sensible, a man who takes short views; and Eugene, who symbolizes poetic idealism, and is lofty-spirited, a lover of beauty, but vague and confused in his mind. There is a struggle between Burgess, in whose personality we have a concrete representation of capitalism, of the bourgeois ideal of our time, a narrow-minded man, summing up everything in terms of money, thoroughly satisfied with the world as it is with all its social inequalities; and Morell, a concrete representation of the Socialist idealism which will be a reality tomorrow, a man of broad and elevated views, delighting in equality and justice. There is no struggle between Burgess and Eugene, for Burgess is quite incapable of understanding Eugene, who incorporates the poetic ideal. The two are so remote from one another that mutual comprehension is impossible.

The material action is simple. In the peaceful household of the Morells there is received as a[185] friend of the family a young poet, Eugene Marchbanks, no more than a big baby, so far does he live from the realities of life. Eugene loves Candida, and tells her husband so. Morell, after a preliminary impulse to turn Eugene out of the house, recognizing the uselessness of forcible methods, wishes Candida to make her choice between himself and Eugene. Candida chooses her husband, and Eugene goes out into the night. This extremely simple material action exhibits to us several kinds of love: Morell's love for Candida, egoistic, narrow, and sexual; Eugene's love for Candida, ideal, romantic, and ethereal, the love he feels for a visionary Candida rather than for the real Candida of flesh and blood; the love of Proserpine for Morell, a sexual adoration. These various kinds of love, as they develop and take definite shape, give rise to intense spiritual dramas. Morell, Marchbanks, and Proserpine suffer, and we witness their internal struggles. Candida's soul remains serene. In her there is no internal struggle.

Some . . . [186] . . . critics have been extremely pleased with the *dénouement*, gratified by the fact that Candida stays with her husband, obeying the voice of duty in an extremely moral manner. Here, they tell us, the traditional ideal, after all, proves victorious over the new ideal that is symbolized by Nora in *A Doll's House*.[2] It need hardly

---

[2] [See Maurice Muret's essay, "From Nora to Candida," reprinted in this book on pp. 171–74.]

be said that this view is totally wrong-headed. Candida does not stay with her husband in obedience to the voice of duty. She does not care a bit about the voice of duty, for she is a realist, without prejudices, and freed from all conventions. In her view, duty, purity, and virtue are prejudices. She stays with her husband because she loves him and not Eugene. She says this very clearly: "Put your trust in my love for you, James; for if that went, I should care very little for your sermons —mere phrases that you cheat yourself and others with every day."

Candida has been compared with Nora, and also with Ellida in *The Lady from the Sea*. This comparison, which arises solely from a similarity in external circumstances, in the act of choice, is really quite unmeaning. Candida is not in the least like one of Ibsen's heroines; she is not a woman trying to find herself, a woman seeking emancipation; she *is* an emancipated woman, one who *has* found herself. She does not, like Ellida, ask her husband[187] to set her free; and she has no need, like Nora, to go away in order to obtain freedom, for she has already freed herself, by discarding social conventions and religious, worldly, and other prejudices.[188]

. . . . .

With two or three exceptions, the French critics have not grasped the importance of Burgess. They have overlooked the struggle between Burgess and Morell. They have failed to understand that this character, who passes through the play without seeing anything of the spiritual crises in Morell and Eugene, who understands nothing in the actions[200] and the logical thoughts of Candida, Eugene, Morell, and Proserpine, and who therefore thinks them all mad, is extremely important. He is introduced, not only because he symbolizes the contemporary bourgeois who sees nothing but money, and who sets his face against Socialism with its ideals of justice and of equality, but also because he is the symbol of the bourgeois who is permeated with prejudices and blinded by conventions. It is inevitable that to him, in the exposition of motives, all sincerity and all frankness should appear insane, and this is why he explains that all the others are mad. By this assertion, not only does he create in the play an atmosphere of indulgence for the ultra-logical reasoners who are liberated from all tradition, but he also creates an atmosphere which illuminates by contrast those wiser than himself, whom he, coarse-grained, thick-headed, and common, calls mad. It is for this very reason that the character of Burgess must be made thoroughly coarse-grained, common, and thick-headed. It is for this very reason that he must exhibit these characteristics to a degree verging upon caricature. The more violent the contrast with the others, with those who are mad, the more will his character be in harmony with the intellectual action, for the more clearly will it appear that those whom he calls mad are truly wise. To make Burgess a cultured,[201] refined, and delicate-minded bourgeois, would be to sin against reason and good taste. In playing his part, care must be taken to avoid attenuating his characteristics, which have been deliberately accentuated by the author in conformity with a logical conception of the intellectual action of the play.[202]

. . . . .

It is possible that my analysis of *Candida* may have seemed unduly lengthy. I hope not, however, for in this chapter, in addition to giving brief analyses of the intellectual and material action of some of the other plays, I have been able, in my detailed analysis of Candida, to show the whole anatomy of the Shavian drama. By this process of dissection has been revealed the inmost essence of Shaw's dramatic works, which are magnificent because they are so extremely amusing and because at the same time they are so profound.[205]

Shaw on Shaw and Molière

GEORGE BERNARD SHAW

There is a difference between the satire of Molière and the criticism of Shaw.[1] Molière does not criticise his doctors: he guys them. He represents them as humbugs who discuss their professional expenses with one another when they are pretending to discuss their patients'

---

[1] [Shaw drafted these comments in the third person for Professor Henderson.]

From Archibald Henderson, *George Bernard Shaw: Man of the Century* (New York: Appleton-Century-Crofts, Inc., 1956), pp. 740–41. Reprinted by permission of Appleton-Century-Crofts Trade Book Division, and the Public Trustee and the Society of Authors (London). Copyright 1932 by D. Appleton & Co. Copyright 1956 by Archibald Henderson. The title used here is the present editor's.

symptoms. He makes them ridiculous by making one of them stammer. . . .

The tradition of satire which vilifies what it criticises lasted well up to Shaw's time. . . .

Shaw reverses the procedure. He strikes at Hector or Achilles, not at Thersites. Morell in *Candida*, though he is the butt of the piece, is "a first rate clergyman" without a single mean trait, who generously and affectionately owns up when he is convicted by his wife of being a little spoilt by his very pardonable masculine self-satisfaction. His gifts are genuine; and his character corresponds to them. . . .

Shaw is not really interested in villains and guys. They are to him pathological specimens; and he holds that disease is not dramatic. The late Sir George Alexander, the actor who kept a leading position on the London stage in his own theatre to the end by sheer good looks which no play-going woman could withstand, offered to produce *Candida* and play the part of Eugene Marchbanks if Shaw would ensure sympathy by making the poet blind. Shaw refused on the ground that it would, on the contrary, destroy all possibility of sympathy and substitute a mixture of curiosity and pity for a defect which would make almost everything said to him in the play appear brutal. "I have seen a man who had lost his arms and legs," he said, "but I shall not make him the hero of a play." Always Shaw makes the best of his[740] *bêtes noires*. . . .[741]

From "Shaw's Debt to Scribe"

STEPHEN S. STANTON

I

It is now generally known that Bernard Shaw had no love for Augustin-Eugène Scribe (1791–1861), father of the French "well-made" play, or Scribe's well-known disciple Victorien Sardou, whose

The following essay is taken from a much longer article, "Shaw's Debt to Scribe," *Publications of the Modern Language Association* (*PMLA*) (December, 1961), pp. 575–85. It has been revised for this reprinting.

technical bravura Shaw scornfully dubbed "Sardoodledom." [1] Perhaps his most outspoken recorded condemnation of the prolific playwright and his factory of collaborators is this (undated) outburst to his authorized biographer Archibald Henderson: "Why the devil should a man write like Scribe when he can write like Shakespeare or Molière, Aristophanes or Euripides? Who was Scribe that he should dictate to me or anyone else how a play should be written?"[2] . . .[575]

In view of all this, many students of the drama are startled to discover that not only did Shaw construct his plays upon the foundations of the well-made play, but he created several of his first successes as subtle and ironic variations on a situation dramatized in one of Scribe's best-known (and best-made) plays. In the early *Philanderer* and *Arms and the Man* Shaw had arranged comic inversions of Scribe and Ernest Legouvé's universally popular *Bataille de Dames* (1851).[3] More than once translated into English,[4] this highly entertaining romantic comedy was performed frequently in England and America throughout the latter half of the nineteenth century and established itself as a favorite among Scribe's many plays.[5] When

[1] *Saturday Review* (London), May 27, 1895; reprinted in Bernard Shaw, *Our Theatres in the Nineties*, Standard Edition (London, 1954), I, 133-40. In its original form the well-made play combined a complex plot with a maximum of theatrical ingenuity and a minimum of thought. Its principle traits are summarized later in this essay. For a more complete study of Scribe and the well-made play, the reader should consult my Introduction to *Camille and Other Plays*, Dramabook MD6 (New York: Hill and Wang, Inc., 1957), and my article, "Scribe's *Bertrand et Raton*: A Well-Made Play," *Tulane Drama Review*, II, No. 1 (November, 1957), 58-70.

[2] Henderson, *Bernard Shaw, Playboy and Prophet* (New York, 1932), p. 595. Henderson comments: "As a matter of fact Shaw was full of the great dramatists, knew nothing about Scribe, and cared less."

[3] I discuss the likeness of these two plays to *Bataille* in my "English Drama and the French Well-Made Play: 1815-1915" (unpubl. diss., Columbia Univ., 1955), in which my original demonstration of Shaw's use of Scribe's dramatic method appears. See also the Introduction to *Camille*.

[4] See Eric Bentley's "Homage to Scribe," a review of the 1955 Columbia University production of Scribe's play (in Maurice Valency's adaptation, *The Queen's Gambit*), in *What is Theatre?* (Boston, 1956), pp. 64-67. A translation by Charles Reade was first performed at the Olympic Theatre, London, on May 7, 1851; another by T. W. Robertson was produced at the Haymarket on November 18.

[5] See, for example, "The ever-delightful 'The Ladies' Battle,' played through the years by so many clever actresses, and, on this occasion, in the T. W. Robertson version, was the choice offering of April 16th and 17th" (1891 at Palmer's Theatre, New York), George C. D. Odell, *Annals of the New York Stage*, XIV (New York, 1945), 525.

Shaw was reluctantly forced to accept the fact that his first four plays[6] were failures in the commercial sense, he turned once more to the successful French theatrician and this time leaned even more heavily upon the lively and ingenious construction of *Bataille de Dames* as he wrote his first unqualified success—*Candida*. . . .[576]

II

Before the specifically "well-made" features of this drawing-room comedy of ideas are discussed, however, the prototypal characteristics of a well-made play should perhaps be briefly described.

A typical plot unfolds around a secret withheld from the central character or characters until the climax, at which point an unsympathetic character is unmasked and the hero restored to good fortune. The curtain rises upon a situation already nearing completion, for much of the action has occurred before the play opens. This late point in the action is known as the late point of attack.[7] The physical action of the play gathers momentum at an ever-increasing pace after one or more acts of expository dialogue. The mounting suspense is assisted by every possible trick known to the theatre: letters which miscarry, mistaken identity, calculated exits and entrances which appear to be natural, contrived groupings, contrasts or parallelisms to underscore situation, and *quiproquos,* or misunderstandings in which a word or a situation is interpreted differently by two or more characters, each assuming his interpretation to be that of everyone else.

The central movement of such a play involves a series of ups and downs, or gambits, between two central characters, the hero and his antagonist, who are locked in a deadly battle of wits, each seeking a victory at the expense of the other. Usually, as the play opens, the hero is dominated by his rival, but in the course of events he ends up the victor. After the contest has seesawed back and forth, the hero suffers a crushing defeat in a scene called the peripeteia, or reversal. Since, however, in nearly all well-made plays this shuttle of good and

---

[6] *Widowers' Houses* (1892), *The Philanderer* (1893), *Mrs. Warren's Profession* (1893), and *Arms and the Man* (1894).

[7] Most of the technical terms included in this essay are discussed in detail in William Archer's *Playmaking: A Manual of Craftsmanship* (New York, 1928), pp. 85–110, 225–259, 260–274.

bad fortunes for the hero must end in the latter's favor, the peripeteia is quickly followed by an "obligatory" scene or *scène à faire* (so termed by the critic Francisque Sarcey) which discloses the secret on which the entire situation has been based. This disclosure abruptly reverses the hero's and his antagonist's situation with the latter usually experiencing a humiliating and lasting defeat.

All the remaining loose ends of the plot are resolved in an extended "recognition" scene (or climax) which guarantees the hero's future good fortune by releasing additional information, such as some secret long obscured. Appropriate rewards are dispensed to the good and bad characters in the dénouement.

Each act of a well-made play is really a well-made play in miniature; that is, it passes from exposition to action, to seesaw and suspense, to reversal, *coup de théâtre*, and resolution much as does the whole play, in the manner just described.

Not infrequently the outcome of the hero's shifting fortunes partially depends upon a romantic triangle in which two women—one middle-aged, charming, and above all, worldly, the other young and pretty, but sometimes unbelievably naive—compete for his affections. In a series of rather artificially emotional scenes he vacillates between duty to the first and love for the second. The course of true love is never smooth, and after a number of ups and downs the older woman sportingly loses her lover to the more immediate attractions of the younger.[577]

Precise timing of the complex movements of the plot produces the excitement on which the well-made play depends. By planting clues to forthcoming events throughout the play, but especially in the first act, the playwright coaches the audience to anticipate these events, thereby creating suspense. He also creates it by withholding from certain characters information known to the audience. Trifling incidents, introduced casually or as if by accident, turn out to have in the *scène à faire* some vital significance.

. . . . .

III

While *Candida* is principally a play of ideas, it also represents Shaw's most thorough application to date of conventional dramaturgy. He had gradually come to see that any playwright with a mission to teach must rely upon such construction to project his dramas of ideas across the footlights. Not the least of his models had been the plays of Ibsen, who had at first rejected Scribe's theatrical bag of tricks, but later accepted it and drew extensively from it in his own influential plays. Since no thorough demonstration, to my knowledge, of Ibsen's or Shaw's use of the methods of Scribe has ever really been attempted (though it would not be difficult to show that Ibsen's familiarity with *Bataille de Dames* was considerable), I feel that *Candida* furnishes an excellent example of Shaw's use of Scribe, and I offer the following unusually detailed comparison of *Candida* and *Bataille de Dames* in an attempt to generally broaden the reader's understanding of Shaw's comedy and to increase his appreciation of Shaw's growing mastery of tight, economical play construction. He makes particular use, for example, of the suspense technique of the withheld secret, the *qui-proquo* or misunderstanding,[8] the triangle of hero and two rival women (here becoming heroine and two rival men), and the Scribean act structure.

Three-quarters of the way through Act I the poet Marchbanks quite understandably shocks the self-complacent Reverend Morell with four words, "I love your wife." The inevitable "secret" of all well-made plays (often a sexual indiscretion) thus emerges early and rather abruptly in this play. At first glance the early revelation of a secret involving adultery seems untypical of Scribe. In many of his plays the husband remains ignorant of his wife's infidelity (whether actual or potential) until the last act. The balloon once punctured, how is suspense to be maintained for another two acts? Slowly we come to realize that the exposure of this secret in *Candida* serves to motivate two further secrets which are resolved only in the *scène à faire* and the climax in Act III.

Morell's confidence in himself and in his wife's[578] love is badly shaken in Act II, and near the close of the act Candida discloses a secret about Morell's conception of their marriage: to him it is a smug, conventional, one might say commercial, affair, in which, because he is an authoritative, hearty, and vain example of muscular Christianity, he expects from her perfect goodness and purity and basks torpidly in the false light of his absolute confidence in her. For Morell duty is the keystone of marriage; Candida herself realizes that

---

[8] William Irvine, in *The Universe of G. B. S.* (New York, 1949), pp. 174–77, refers to this misunderstanding as "a very old dramatic device," but he does not mention the well-made play or its characteristics.

marriage is based upon love alone and not upon conventional principles. But for each the other's view has to this time been kept a secret, and for Morell it continues to remain one until after Candida has given herself to the weaker of the two (*scène à faire*: the "auction" scene). After she has chosen Morell and told him the true meaning of their union, his almost dead sense of values is at least partly rejuvenated.

The second secret is the one Candida gives to Marchbanks in the climax which follows the auction scene, though she herself catches a mere intuitive glimmer of its meaning ("He has learnt to do without happiness"); he is seen to have abruptly altered his view of human happiness after hearing her tell "what it costs to be James's mother and three sisters and wife and mother to his children all in one." His "I no longer desire happiness: life is nobler than that" is a far cry from "I am the happiest of mortals" (end of Act I) and from the dreamy rhapsody in Act II: ". . . a chariot! to carry us up into the sky, where the lamps are stars . . . to be beautiful and free and happy." In short, he has become convinced that marriage, the "greasy fool's paradise" (as Shaw termed it in the famous letter to James Huneker), is suited to the average man, but not to realists whose natural habitat is the realm of ideas, not onions and children, and to whom marriage means only submission of one's will to that of another.

Thus Shaw elevated the well-made secret, based upon mere incident or situation, to the plane of ideas. Structurally, *Candida* owes much to *Bataille de Dames*, but for Shaw the Scribean structure acted as a springboard from the entertainment level to the instructional level. Here is a synopsis of Scribe's play.

Act I: Henri (hero), an escaped political prisoner, has taken refuge on the estate of an adoring countess who has effected his escape. Disguised as "Charles," a groom (withheld secret), he anxiously awaits a pardon, now on the way (late point of attack). Léonie (heroine), the countess's niece, falls in love with Henri when he reveals his true identity to her. The countess prepares Henri (exposition) for the arrival of Montrichard, the new prefect of police (antagonist) who wants to arrest him and who is seeking revenge on the countess for having outsmarted him in the past (conflict of opponents). "Charles" resolves to fool Montrichard by joining in the search for Henri. The countess, recognizing the flighty Léonie as her rival, jealously vows she will win Henri by her more mature devotion and understanding (triangle of hero and two women).

Act II: Montrichard arrives (seesaw: down for hero) and bribes "Charles" to help look for Henri (up). The countess sustains the deception by scolding "Charles." Léonie, frightened, breaks down before Montrichard and confesses to having seen Henri (down). When Henri appears she screams (down). The prefect arrests all the servants for a closer inspection. The countess vows she will save Henri from the blunders of the silly Léonie (reversal of hero's fortunes).

Act III: The countess persuades her cowardly suitor De Grignon (who imagines himself a hero) to dress like "Charles" and allow himself to be arrested as Henri. He is arrested (up for hero; decoy permits hero's escape). Again Léonie nearly compromises Henri (down), but Montrichard is completely taken in by the trick. Laying a hand on De Grignon, he says "je l'ai découvert . . . je le tiens" (*qui-proquo*: he refers to De Grignon, but we think he knows all) (down). But the countess saves Henri again by another stratagem (up). The unsuspecting prefect hires "Charles" as messenger to carry the news of Henri's capture to the marshal (up). When brought to "trial," the gullible De Grignon nearly exposes the trick (growing suspense). The countess, imagining Henri to be safely out of reach, reveals her entire strategy to Montrichard (down), who vows revenge (obligatory scene: secret revealed to antagonist's disadvantage). Henri unexpectedly returns without delivering the message, to save De Grignon's life. Montrichard receives Henri's pardon, but pretends it is a warrant for his arrest. The countess realizes Henri loves Léonie (climax A), and sadly unites the lovers. To trap the hiding Henri, Montrichard suddenly announces he has the pardon. Henri appears! The prefect tries to arrest him, but the more quick-witted countess challenges him to show the despatch he has received (climax B: it is the pardon). The antagonist is defeated, the lovers are jubilant, and the countess is resigned (*dénouement*).

In this play the countess's disclosure of her secret (hiding the hero) to Montrichard in the *scène à faire* leads to two further discoveries (the[579] first in the *scène à faire* and the second in the climax): her aid in the hero's escape on the prefect's horse, and her foiling of Montrichard's trick of pretending that the pardon is a warrant for arrest. In *Candida*, too, the heroine helps to reveal three secrets, and the holder of the first secret (the poet) is in a sense defeated in the last act, as in *Bataille de Dames* and other well-made plays. This defeat supplies a *coup de théâtre* in the style of Scribe and Augier (who

uphold marriage at all costs). But in a larger sense the poet is trium-
phant, and thus we note Shaw's ironical use of Scribe. Because Shaw
dealt with ideas, however, he chose to make his plays turn upon discussion. The discussion in *Candida* had to bring about the tense
"auction" scene and the clergyman husband's and poet "lover's" consequent self-analysis. With a large firecracker—the anti-conventional
poet's confession early in Act I—Shaw ignited the powder keg of discussion which exploded this complacently stuffy Victorian marriage.
The spectators were thus jolted upright in their seats in the hope of
seeing a play about adultery.

In the last third of Act II a *quiproquo* is established, more intellectual than those found in Scribe, but of the same type. Candida and
Morell mean different things by marriage and consequently see their
own marital relationship from two conflicting points of view. Each
has been unaware of this conflict and has always assumed that a respectable institution like marriage could have but one meaning for
both. Only the audience is aware of the full extent of the misunderstanding and follows with growing suspense the intense situation involving husband, wife, and lover. Shaw employs every means at his
disposal to prolong this suspense till the last possible moment—Morell's
enlightenment after the auction scene.

When Candida leaves Marchbanks washing his hands in the kitchen she deliberately begins to tease her husband. It is immediately
obvious that they do not understand one another. She chaffs him
about the merits of his preaching: he merely amuses his congregations;
the women are so enthusiastic because they have "Prossy's complaint."
She is being cruel, perhaps in order to shake him up and also because
she sees their marriage from an objective point of view. Its foundation is simply love.

Up to this point Candida has not realized the greatness of the
gulf which separates her from Morell, who cannot view their marriage with her detachment. Her perception has been sharpened in
her recent talks with the poet (before the beginning of the play).
Her irritation that her husband is conventional rather than realistic
increases markedly from this point to the auction scene. It begins
with her simple incredulity that Morell can be so vain and so self-
satisfied as to say that he is not thinking of his attractions, but only
of her goodness and purity. CANDIDA: "What a nasty uncomfortable
thing to say to me! Oh, you are a clergyman, James: a thorough

clergyman!" (Act II). Morell feels he has earned Candida's love and
that it is no more than her due to give it. She, on the other hand, can
be detached even about Eugene. Suppose he learns about love from
the wrong woman. Will he forgive Candida? For what? asks Morell,
limited by his idealistic nature. For not teaching him herself, of course.
Then follows the famous "shawl" speech: ". . . Put your trust in my
love for you, James; for if that went. . . ." Morell's suffering shows
he believes that because his wife does not love him by his purely subjective standards, she cannot love him at all.

Thus though they are now both aware of the misunderstanding,
Morell is ignorant of its true cause, and Candida has only just begun
to see the limitations of her husband's mind. But here Shaw, in order
to delay Candida's full comprehension and to sustain his *quiproquo*
for nearly another act, has already had recourse to Scribean incident
and situation: in Act I he manipulates Candida off the stage while the
two men are quarreling so that she will be ignorant that the poet has
challenged Morell to let Candida choose between their ideas. As a result she displays proper confusion when Morell, recalling the earlier
conversation, significantly offers to leave the poet in her custody
while he goes to a meeting. It is only at the beginning of the auction
scene near the close of Act III that she is enlightened. The *quiproquo*
ends when Morell comes to understand, immediately after this scene,
the true nature of her love for him.

Shaw duplicated in reverse Scribe's usual triangle and centered
Candida between the rival men. In *Bataille de Dames* the hero loves and
marries the less intelligent but more naive and romantically acceptable
(because of her age) of the two women rivals, while the skillful
countess, who has made it all possible and has saved the hero's life,
goes unrewarded. Candida loves and stays married to Morell, the less
intelligent and more conventional of the two men in her life, while
the sharply perceptive poet, having probed to the heart of the Morell
marriage's weakness,[580] and having given the momentary impression
of being responsible for its continued felicity, goes out alone into the
night.

The attention of Shaw's audiences was caught by this well-
made triangle plot (the only type of plot which really appealed to
them at this time). But he was also reversing the customary protagonist and antagonist of well-made Victorian melodrama: the rejected
poet becomes the true hero, and the eminently respectable parson,

bitterly disillusioned about his marriage, is, from one point of view, ridiculed in the manner of Scribe's antagonists. Under cover of entertaining his public with routine fare, Shaw was didactically forcing them to scrutinize the complacency of their own lives.

One critic has demonstrated the basic similarity of the inner action in *Candida* and *The Devil's Disciple*.[9] Since Shaw was undoubtedly familiar with the most popular of Scribe's plays in English, it seems not impossible that he drew from *Bataille de Dames* his central situation in both plays: an idyllic relationship invaded by a stranger. The countess has rescued the hero from prison and hopes to win his love by hiding him on her estate. The presence of her attractive niece is an intrusion and soon distresses her, just as Marchbanks' presence disturbs Morell. Later she is disillusioned in love, as is Morell about his marriage. On a less pretentious scale than in Shaw, Léonie learns the virtue of poise and self-control, just as the poet learns that he can stand alone. Both characters "grow up." Henri serves in a sense as a catalyst, as does Candida. The protagonists are Henri and Candida, the antagonists Léonie and Marchbanks; the countess and Morell are victims of the conflict.

· · · · ·

The *coup de théâtre* in which Morell seems to have lost Candida but suddenly realizes he has won her (*scène à faire*) resembles almost identically (in abstract form) the climax of *Bataille de Dames* in which the countess, knowing that the secret papers are Henri's pardon and not a warrant for arrest, calls the police officer's bluff. Though Shaw condemned marriages based upon shortsighted idealism and empty convention and believed in a nobler ascetic life for the comparatively few great realists of the world, he seemed in the ending of *Candida* to support the theme of *Arms and the Man* and many of Scribe's plays: that for the average man the marriage of reason, common sense, and love (in the realistic sense) was best.

In the four plays which preceded *Candida* Shaw had bludgeoned his audiences in a heavy-handed attempt to reform them. In trying to emulate Ibsen, he had identified them with his villains—the corrupt capitalist, the insincere Victorian husband, the military hero basking in romantic self-glory. He had made his heroes[581] enemies of respect-

---

[9] Eric Bentley, *Bernard Shaw: 1856–1950*, amended edition (New York, 1957), p. 110.

able society and of those values which he was to castigate once and for all through the mouth of Don Juan (John Tanner) in Act III of *Man and Superman*: "Hell is the home of honor, duty, justice, and the rest of the seven deadly virtues." Now Scribe never committed such an error. In upholding conventionality he could not help but achieve great box-office success. Shaw had learned, by the time he wrote *Candida*, to trick his public into thinking that he might at least be on their side. This play achieved a belated success—Shaw's first in the theatre—because he pursued, again with the methods of Scribe, a subtler approach which seemed to flatter the West Endians.

The play on first hearing seems to champion an average marriage, since in the last scene the unprincipled intruder is sent packing with his inscrutable secret. Yet on closer consideration this "antagonist" appears, despite a certain incredible and inhuman quality, to have won a victory over that august leader of the community, the Reverend James Morell. Perhaps Morell's failure to win or lose decisively in his struggle with the poet is realistically inconclusive. Shaw tried to give psychological veracity to his characterization of a man caught in a marital dilemma, and the dilemma carries a certain true-to-life inconsistency. In addition, Shaw managed to shock his complacent Victorian audience with an ironic interchange of roles: the poet, weak and socially maladjusted, turns out to be strong; a prominent clergyman of confident Christian faith is seen to be weak because he is blind to the meaning of marriage.[582]

From "The Making of a Dramatist (1892–1903)"

ERIC BENTLEY

We know from the correspondence with Mrs. Pat Campbell that Shaw liked to play with fire. Even the correspondence with Ellen

From the Foreword to *Plays by George Bernard Shaw*, ed. Eric Bentley (New York: The New American Library of World Literature, Inc., 1960), pp. xx–xxiv. Copyright © 1960 by The New American Library of World Literature, Inc. and reprinted with their permission.

Terry entailed a playfulness not quite devoid of "danger." The boy Shaw had been witness to an odd household arrangement whereby his mother's music teacher contrived to be (it would seem) almost but not quite her lover. A slightly older Shaw has recently been portrayed as the intruder into a friend's marriage, like his own Eugene March-banks: this is speculation. Let us look at the play *Candida*, which is a fact.

It has a notable Big Scene at the end, which is characterized by an equally notable improbability. A comfortable,[xxi] sensible parson's wife doesn't let herself get jockeyed into "choosing" between her husband and an almost total stranger. People—such people at least—don't do such things. A respectable woman's choice was made before the banns were read.

Perhaps Candida is not really respectable? That is the line of interpretation taken by Beatrice Webb, who declared her a prostitute. Will the play, taken as a play, bear this interpretation out? A drama-tist's license to have the truth turn out different from the impression given to the audience is very limited, for it is to a large extent by giving impressions that he creates characters. Shaw has given the impression that Candida is *not* a prostitute.

Against this it can be urged that Shaw himself took Beatrice Webb's side and attacked Candida—in remarks he made about her in letters to James Huneker, Richard Burton, and others. True, but was that legitimate? He himself admitted that he had no more right to say what his plays meant than any other critic. One might add that he may have had less, for when an author intervenes to correct our im-pressions of his work, he is often intervening to change or misinterpret that work.

Outside the play, Shaw is against Candida. Inside it, he is both for and against her, but he is for her effectually, and against her ineffec-tually, because the direct impression is favorable, while it is only by throwing logic back into the story when it is over that you can reach an unfavorable judgment. This means, I should think, that though Shaw's intellect is against Candida, his emotions are for her.

What is it that this play has always projected in the theater, and can always be counted on to project again? The charm of Candida. This is a reality so immediate and all-pervasive that it is hard for any other element in the play to make headway against it. Leading actresses know this, and hearing their director speak of Candida's essential badness, can afford to smile a Candida smile, strong in the knowledge that there is nothing a director can do about this badness, once that smile has been displayed on stage as well as off.

I would say that it is a confused play but that the confusion goes unnoticed because of Candida's charm and may even be the cause of a degree of emotional tension unusual in a Shaw play. Candida is made out of a Shavian ambivalence: he would like to reject this kind of woman, but actually he dotes on her. One quickly senses that he *is*[xxii] Marchbanks. One also find he protests (too much) that he is *not* Marchbanks. "I had in mind De Quincey's account of his adolescence in his Confessions," he wrote. "I certainly never thought of myself as a model." From the empty pretence of being De Quincey, no doubt, comes the prodigious unreality of many of the lines. As a character, Marchbanks must be reckoned a failure. Shaw was hiding. What better image to hide behind than that of the kind of writer he himself was—a romantic poet? Especially if De Quincey would do the job for him?

It didn't work, of course, except as pure histrionics. (Marchbanks, though a poorly drawn character, is always an effective stage role, and still seems to correspond to the actors' idea of a poet.) But if no one in the play can reject Candida, there is a noteworthy niche in it for the man whom she will reject. This niche Marchbanks can fill nobly, and has his dramatic moment as he marches into it: his final exit is a magnificent piece of action. Possibly everything before that (in this role) is just an improvisation. Shaw could not make us believe in the poet's poetry, but he does make us believe in his pain and his nobility, for at these points he could identify himself with Eugene completely without having to "think of himself as a model."

Dramatists usually speak of their characters individually, and that could be regarded as strange, because the drama, all through the centuries, has done much less with separate persons than with relationships. The traditional characters are, if you will, simplified to the point of crudity. What is not crude, as treated by the old dramatists, is the interaction of these characters: the dynamics of human relations are fully rendered. If what you do not get is the detailed psychological biography, what you do get is the essence of such relations as parent and child, boy and girl, man and wife.

Now, modern playwrights, happily, have not departed from the classic patterns as much as they are supposed to have, and what rings

true, emotionally, in *Candida* corresponds to Shaw's ability to find and
re-create some of these elemental relationships. An inner obstacle, one
would judge, hampered him when he tried to "do" the Marchbanks-
Candida relationship, but the Morell-Candida relation is both clear and
challenging. It is, as Shaw himself said, the relationship of Nora and
Torvald Helmer turned around: in Shaw's play the man is the doll.
But where Ibsen tells the story of a doll who finally comes to life, Shaw
tells the story[xxiii] of a seemingly living person who turns out to have
been a doll all along. (In other words, the relation of Shaw to Ibsen,
instead of being as direct as it might seem, is an inverse one, exactly
like the relation of Shaw to other nineteenth-century drama.) Into
Morell Shaw can put that part of himself (a child) which finds Candida
irresistible, just as into Candida he can put that part of Woman which
he finds irresistible—the mother in her. One would have to be as naïve
a psychologist as Frank Harris to consider the mother-and-child relation less emotional than that of lovers.

Or less dramatic. Relationships become dramatic not in the degree
of their eroticism but to the extent that they contain conflict. Pure
love would not be a dramatic subject at all. Love becomes dramatic
when it is impure—when the loving element is submerged in a struggle
for power. The axis about which *Candida* revolves is that of strength
and weakness, not love and hate. And if one knows Shaw's views on
the topic of the "weaker sex" in general, the conclusion of *Candida*
follows naturally: instead of the little woman reaching up toward the
arms of the strong man, we have the strong woman reaching down to
pick up her child. It is remarkable how far Shaw's thought is from the
standard "advanced thinking" of his generation, with its prattle of
equality and comradeship. He is closer to Nietzsche.

Of the ending of *A Doll's House* it has been said: perhaps Nora
has walked out in a mere tantrum and will be back in the morning.
How much more savage is the ending of *Candida!* Only Strindberg
could have written a sequel to it. The cruelty of the heroine—merely
implicit in the present play—would have to come to the surface in any
continuation of the story. Candida has chosen to let her husband discover his shame: she, as well as he, will have to take the consequences.
Let the stage manager hold razors and strait jackets in readiness![xxiv]

MODELS FROM LIFE

From "Candida Was Not Ellen Terry"

GEORGE BERNARD SHAW

. . . Ellen Terry was a wise and good woman, considering the intense segregation in her time of the profession into which she was born! but having tried five husbands[1] and discarded them all without losing their friendship, she was hardly a model for Candida.

I knew practically all the leading Christian Socialist clergymen. The nearest to Morell was Stopford Brooke, with touches of Canon Shuttleworth and Fleming Williams.

I had no models for Candida. I borrowed her name from an Italian lady I never met: Candida Bartolucci, afterwards a British marchioness. Candida is entirely imagined; and the play is a counterblast to Ibsen's *Doll's House*, showing that in the real typical doll's house it is the man who is the doll.

[1] [Ellen Terry was legally married three times. Shaw expressed himself far more delicately and accurately on this subject in his Preface (1929) to *Ellen Terry and Bernard Shaw: A Correspondence,* pp. xii–xiii. In defending the reputation of the great lady of the stage who, of all the women in Shaw's life, inspired probably his most touching relationship, Shaw describes Ellen Terry's strong yet endearing character: her rare combination of virtue and social freedom which disregarded the Victorian proprieties. Two of her "five domestic partnerships" were not recognized by the English marriage law, a law which Shaw more than once denounced for its narrow-minded impracticability. In spite of her great generosity and loveableness, Ellen Terry could not and would not submit to the intolerable restrictions imposed upon duty-ridden and insensitive women in typical Victorian marriages. In summary, her motherliness, her "sensitive pity," and her independent spirit made her somewhat unusually vulnerable to emotional attachments.]

Part of a letter written by Shaw in reply to Beverley Baxter (MP) in the *Evening Standard* (London), November 30, 1944. Reprinted by permission of the Public Trustee, the Society of Authors (London), and the *Evening Standard.* Baxter had published (in a previous letter in the same newspaper) his view that the three main characters in *Candida* were modeled after Ellen Terry, Sir Henry Irving, and Shaw. Shaw called this "quite the worst shot ever made by a twentieth century critic," and retorted that Baxter's statement had given him a shock sufficient to "kill any other man of my age." (He was eighty-eight years old!)

When I began writing the part of the young poet, I had in mind
De Quincey's account of his adolescence in his *Confessions*. I certainly
never thought of myself as a model.

From "Bernard Shaw's Beginnings on the London Stage"

IRVING MC KEE

Janet Achurch, the evidence suggests, was by far the most important woman in Shaw's adult life before his marriage in 1898 at the
age of forty-one. . . . Miss Achurch's acting proved distinguished, far
more so than her second husband's. . . . The two produced Archer's
translation of Ibsen's *Doll's House* in London, 1889, with[474] Miss
Achurch as Nora Helmer, the "doll". . . . Not until [1926] did Shaw
feel free to hint, but only hint, to the world at large of his profound
devotion to Janet Achurch[1]. . . . The first of a series of unpublished
letters to the actress . . . is dated 6 January 1891. The situation is obviously similar to and just as platonic as the one in the play he was
to write almost four years later (it also resembles the plot of his *Unfinished Novel* of 1888, published seventy years subsequently)[2]—with
Janet as Candida, Charrington as Morell, and Shaw as Marchbanks. In
the first letter he acknowledges in mock-romantic terms a gift of her
photograph and avows that he cannot remember her countenance
[without imagining himself lost at sea at night, steering desperately
toward a lighthouse (Janet), etc.[3]].[475]

----

1 Ashley Dukes, *Who's Who in the Theatre*, 2nd ed. (London, 1916); Ernest
Short, *Sixty Years of Theatre* (London, 1951), p. 104; W. Davenport Adams,
Dictionary of the Drama, Vol. I, "A–G" (London, 1904)—but no more published.

2 (New York: Dodd, Mead, 1958.)

3 [This is a paraphrase from Shaw's unpublished letter, quoted in part in
Professor McKee's essay. The original manuscript is in the Hanley Collection,
University of Texas.]

From *Publications of the Modern Language Association (PMLA)*, LXXIV
(September, 1959), 474–75. Reprinted by permission.

From "The Life Force in Action"

WILLIAM IRVINE

Of course Shaw began, as usual, not with the physical but with the metaphysical. Some of his love affairs were hardly love affairs at all, and one of the earliest was so tenuously mystical that the lady—May Morris—seems not to have known that it occurred until many years later, when she asked Shaw to write a memoir of her father for the latter's collected works. Shaw, then aged and respectable, responded with a brief account of the poet and a lengthy account of a heavenly betrothal with his beautiful daughter. Her comment was simply, "Really, Shaw!" But she published the memoir.

As a socialist and a writer, Shaw was a frequent guest at the Morris house:

One Sunday evening after lecturing and supping, I was on the threshold of the Hammersmith house when I turned to make my farewell, and at this moment she came from the diningroom into the hall. I looked at her, rejoicing in her lovely dress and lovely self; and she looked at me very carefully and quite deliberately made a gesture of assent with her eyes. I was immediately conscious that a Mystic Betrothal was registered in heaven, to be fulfilled when all the material obstacles should melt away, and my own position rescued from the squalors of my poverty and unsuccess. . . . I did not think it necessary to say anything. To engage her in any way—to go to Morris and announce that I was taking advantage of the access granted to me as comrade-Communist to commit his beautiful daughter to a desperately insolvent marriage, did not occur to me as a socially possible proceeding. . . . I made no sign at all: I had no doubt that the thing was written on the skies for both of us.[1]

[1] George Bernard Shaw, *William Morris as I Knew Him* (New York: Dodd, Mead and Company, Inc., 1936), pp. 31–32.

From *The Universe of G. B. S.* (New York: McGraw-Hill Book Company, Inc., 1949), pp. 148–49. Copyright, 1949, by William Irvine. Reprinted with permission of McGraw-Hill Book Company, Inc.

Then the beautiful daughter stunned him by marrying another socialist. He leaped to the conclusion that the Mystical Betrothal had[148] been the figment of a very susceptible imagination. Not at all. Shortly after, he became ill with overwork and was invited to recuperate at the house of the young couple, completing thus an idyllic *ménage à trois*, which "was probably the happiest passage in our three lives":

But the violated Betrothal was avenging itself. It made me from the first the centre of the household; and when I had quite recovered and there was no longer any excuse for staying unless I proposed to do so permanently and parasitically, her legal marriage dissolved as all illusions do; and the mystic marriage asserted itself irresistibly. I had to consummate it or vanish.[2]

Shaw vanished. And of course May Morris never owned up to the Mystical Betrothal. Nevertheless, her husband's account of the *ménage à trois*, according to Mr. Pearson, bears out Shaw's, and he told Holbrook Jackson "that after completely captivating his wife Shaw suddenly disappeared, leaving behind him a desolated female who might have been an iceberg so far as her future relations with her husband went." The episode bears more than a casual resemblance to the plot of "Candida" and may have been an experience out of which two works of art were created.[149]

From "Pleasant Plays"

ARCHIBALD HENDERSON

Candida was drawn from life. And its author approved of it as a first-class type of play, because it "consisted of a situation lasting several hours." Candida was modeled after Kate Salt, a brilliant, fascinating woman. The model for Morell was Edward Carpenter, a

---

[2] *Ibid.*, p. 36.

From *George Bernard Shaw: Man of the Century* (New York: Appleton-Century-Crofts, Inc., 1956), p. 544. Reprinted by permission of Appleton-Century-Crofts Trade Book Division. Copyright 1932 by D. Appleton & Co.

Socialist, and for a time an Anglican priest. Shaw was the model for Marchbanks, although he vehemently denied his identity with the poet. Shaw frequently visited the modest home of Henry Salt, the humanitarian; and Shaw vied with Carpenter, who lived nearby, for Kate's favor. They termed themselves her "Sunday husbands." From this trio, Shaw created a sex-triangle play of normal individuals. Carpenter divined Shaw's inspiration at once; and, after a reading of the play by the author, said: "No, Shaw, it won't do." Shaw parried all attempts to discover the models for the principals; but did say once that, when writing the part of the "penny poet," he "had in mind De Quincey's account of his adolescence in his *Confessions*."[544]

INTERPRETATION OF "CANDIDA"

Letter to James Huneker

GEORGE BERNARD SHAW

Don't ask me conundrums about that very immoral female, Candida. Observe the entry of W. Burgess: "You're the lady as hused to typewrite for him." "No." "Naaaow: *she* was younger." And therefore Candida sacked her. Prossy is a very highly selected young person indeed, devoted to Morell to the extent of helping in the kitchen but to him the merest pet rabbit, unable to get the slightest hold on him. Candida is as unscrupulous as Siegfried: Morell himself sees that "no law will bind her." She seduces Eugene just exactly as far as it is worth her while to seduce him. She is a woman without "character" in the conventional sense. Without brains and strength of mind she would be a wretched slattern or voluptuary. She is straight for natural reasons, not for conventional ethical ones. Nothing can be more cold-bloodedly reasonable than her farewell to Eugene: "All very well, my lad; but I don't quite see myself at fifty with a husband of thirty-five." It is just this freedom from emotional slop, this unerring wisdom on the domestic plane, that makes her so completely mistress of the situation.

Then consider the poet. She makes a man of him finally by showing him his own strength—that David must do without poor Uriah's wife. And then she pitches in her picture of the home, the onions, and the tradesmen, and the cossetting of big baby Morell. The New York *hausfrau* thinks it a little paradise; but the poet rises up and says, "Out then, into the night with me"—Tristan's holy night. If this greasy fool's paradise is happiness, then I give it to you with both hands, "life is nobler than that." That is the "poet's secret." The young things in front weep to see the poor boy going out lonely and broken-

From James Huneker, "The Truth about *Candida*," *Metropolitan Magazine*, XX (August, 1904), 635. Reprinted by permission of the Public Trustee and the Society of Authors (London). Huneker reprinted this letter (dated April, 1904) in his chapter on Shaw in *Iconoclasts* (New York, 1905), a selection from which is reprinted in this book on pp. 197–201.

hearted in the cold night to save the proprieties of New England Puritanism; but he is really a god going back to his heaven, proud, unspeakably contemptuous of the "happiness" he envied in the days of his blindness, clearly seeing that he has higher business on hand than Candida. She has a little quaint intuition of the completeness of his cure; she says, "he has learnt to do without happiness."

As I should certainly be lynched by the infuriated Candidamaniacs if this view of the case were made known, I confide it to your discretion . . . I tell it to you because it is an interesting sample of the way in which a scene, which should be conceived and written only by transcending the ordinary notion of the relations between the persons, nevertheless stirs the ordinary emotions to a very high degree, all the more because the language of the poet, to those who have not the clew to it, is mysterious and bewildering and therefore worshipful. I divined it myself before I found out the whole truth about it.[635]

"The 'Candida' Secret"

GEORGE A. RIDING

No play of Shaw's has had a greater vogue, on stages both amateur and professional, than *Candida*. No one who has read it has failed to wonder, as the author undoubtedly intended, what was the secret in the heart of the poet Marchbanks, left with the reader at the end of the play—with the reader, for to read the play reveals a mystery not apparent as the curtain falls upon a stage performance.

Those who know the play will remember that with his concluding words the poet turns to Candida saying, "In a hundred years we shall be the same age. But I have a better secret than that in my heart. Let me go now. The night outside grows impatient." What follows is among the most moving and poignant play-endings of the English stage. Candida "takes his face in her hands," her husband the parson standing silent by; Marchbanks goes down on a knee and

From *The Spectator*, CLXXXV (November 17, 1950), 506. Reprinted by permission of the Public Trustee and the Society of Authors (London) and *The Spectator* (London).

Candida kisses his forehead. "Then he flies out into the night." Candida turns to the embrace of the weaker man, Morell her husband, and Shaw's final "stage direction," if that it can be called, is, *"But they do not know the secret in the poet's heart."*

In my younger days, when I was a master at Rugby, I had contacts with a literary society whose members were senior boys belonging to the School House. Early in 1920 they met to read *Candida*, and at the end of their reading they fell naturally to a discussion of the poet's secret. They decided, their protracted discussion having led to nothing but divergent views, to instruct their secretary to write to Shaw, asking him to divulge his version of "the secret." The name of the secretary I have withheld; he is now the head of an important firm of publishers.

The correspondence which followed, a copy of which I am privileged to possess, constitutes both a piece of interesting and valuable literary criticism and a self-portrait of G. B. S. in one of his most characteristic and likable moods. It is surely too good to be buried and lost in the minutes of a school literary society—minutes which by now may well have passed into eternity.

The boys led off as follows:—

School House, Rugby   Feb. 25th, 1920
Dear Mr. Bernard Shaw,

We are a play-reading society formed of members of this house for the purpose of reading good plays of all kinds, and have been reading *Candida* in the volume of *Plays Pleasant*. A discussion arose among the members as to what the secret was in the heart of the poet Marchbanks, which you mention at the end. None of the suggestions satisfied the society as a whole. We therefore decided to write and ask you to reveal the secret, should there be one. Apologising for wasting your time.

One of Shaw's postcards brought his reply:—

10 Adelphi Terrace, W.C.   Feb. 26th, 1920
I have my own opinion on the subject, but do not pretend to know more about it than anyone else. If you will send me a statement of the various guesses made at the discussion, I will tell you what I think of them.

G. BERNARD SHAW

On March 1st the following letter was written to Marchbanks's creator, after the various members of the society had been asked to put on record their different interpretations of the secret:—

Dear Mr. Bernard Shaw,

I enclose the various suggestions we have made with regard to the poet's secret, and am much obliged to you for your kindness in giving us your opinion on them. They are as follows:—

1. The poet Marchbanks was going to seek an end to his miserable existence, finding that the woman he loved most could not live with him.
2. The poet was after another lady whose heart he would try to win.
3. He never found another love, so that he lost for ever his happiness on this earth.
4. There is no secret, and it is only mentioned for the purpose of puzzling the reader.
5. Marchbanks will come back when Morell is dead.
6. Marchbanks knew that Candida loved him, and she knew it, but her duty to Morell kept her with him.
7. See J. Galsworthy's *Strife*, Act II, Scene II. '*David Roberts:* For all that Mr. Simon Harness says, for all that Thomas Rous, for all that any man present here can say—We've won the fight!'

Thanking you for your kind help in this matter.

Yours truly,

The last and most valuable letter is illuminating, pretendingly prickly, in parts lovely—and very human:—

10 Adelphi Terrace, W.C.   March 8th, 1920

Dear Sir,

What has happened to Rugby? Never could I have believed that it would produce such a brigade of sentimental blighters. They are all wrong; and the soulless wretch (No. 4) who thinks that the secret is a spoof secret is the only one whose opinion is not pure sob-stuff. To bring them to a proper state of mind I recommend, first, a course of the poets on the subject of Night. Begin with something simple, like Act V of *The Merchant of Venice*, and then work on, not forgetting Byron's 'She Walks in Beauty Like the Night' until you finish up with Wagner's *Tristan and Isolde*, where you will find the final and complete repudiation of the day and acceptance of the night as the true realm of the poet.

Then your fellows will understand what Eugene means when he turns so fiercely away from Candida's picture of a happy home in Victoria Park, and exclaims 'Ah, never. Out then into the night with me,' and later on, 'Let me go now. The night outside grows impatient.' What did you all make of, 'I no longer desire happiness; life is nobler than that'? And why does Eugene speak of Candida not as 'the woman I love,' but as 'the woman I loved'?

The secret is very obvious after all—provided you know what a poet is.

What business has a man with the great destiny of a poet with the small beer of domestic comfort and cuddling and petting at the apron-string of some dear nice woman? Morell cannot do without it: it is the making of him; without it he would be utterly miserable and perhaps go to the devil. To Eugene, the stronger of the two, the daily routine of it is nursery slavery swaddling clothes, mere happiness instead of exaltation—an atmosphere in which great poetry dies. To choose it would be like Swinburne choosing Putney. When Candida brings him squarely face to face with it, his heaven rolls up like a scroll; and he goes out proudly into the majestic and beautiful kingdom of the starry night. Read the scene over with that in your heads, and every word of it will come right. Read it under the sentimental delusion that the poet is going to drown himself because he cannot have the other fellow's wife, and every word will seem utter nonsense.

Mind, I have no doubt that Eugene found that though his head was in the stars he had to keep his feet on the ground as much as Morell, and that some enterprising woman married him and made him dress himself properly and take regular meals. But he did not steal her from a friend. I hope this explanation—penned rather hastily in a fast train—will give satisfaction. It is only my way of looking at it; everybody who buys the book may fit it with an ending to suit his own taste.

Faithfully,

G. BERNARD SHAW

Hats off to the young men of Rugby—1920 vintage—for having produced for lovers of *Candida* that piece of light and guidance from its "onlie begetter" ! [506]

Note to the Late Editor of
The Kansas City Star

GEORGE BERNARD SHAW

6 January, 1900
10 Adelphi Terrace
London, W. C.

Dear Sir:

In *Candida* the poet begins pursuing happiness with a beloved woman as the object of his life. When at last, under stress of a most

Reprinted in Richard Burton, *Bernard Shaw: The Man and the Mask* (New

moving situation, she paints for him a convincing picture of what
that happiness is, he sees at once that such happiness could never fulfill his destiny. "I no longer desire happiness . . . Life is nobler than
that. . . . Out, then, into the night with me." That is, out of this stuffy
little nest of happiness and sentiment into the grandeur, the majesty,
the holiness that night means to me, the poet. Candida and Morell do
not understand this. Neither did you, eh?—

G. BERNARD SHAW[231]

From "Biographers' Blunders Corrected"

GEORGE BERNARD SHAW

TO HENRY CHARLES DUFFIN

"The secret in the poet's heart" is the one you[158] describe as the
most probable: that is, that the domestic life is not a poet's destiny:
"Life is nobler than that." The starry night, and not the cosy room
with the paraffin lamp, is the place for him. Your alternative solution
that "sooner or later she will come to me after all" is wildly silly.[1] [159]

York: Henry Holt and Company, 1916), p. 231; reprinted again in "Random
Thoughts" (column by Henry J. Haskell, late editor), *The Kansas City Star*,
February 20, 1949. Reproduced here by permission of the Public Trustee and
the Society of Authors (London), and *The Kansas City Star*.

1 [A reply to Duffin's interpretation of the *Candida* "secret" in *The Quintessence of Bernard Shaw*, p. 106, which appears in this book on pp. 184–88.]

From *Sixteen Self Sketches* (New York: Dodd, Mead and Company, 1949),
pp. 158–59. Copyright 1949 by George Bernard Shaw. Reprinted by permission of
the Public Trustee and the Society of Authors (London), and Dodd, Mead and
Company.

From "The Dramatist Bernard Shaw"

GEORG BRANDES

Bernard Shaw wished to dig deepest, and with the greatest economy of materials, in *Candida*. Here the quiet action, working itself
out in the dialogue, reminds one of Ibsen. In the play we meet an
English minister of our time, his superb young wife and an eighteen-
year-old poet of noble blood, whom the minister has taken into his
home, and who has fallen in love with the lady of the house. In this
play there is great depth of thought and a knowledge of human character which penetrates far below the surface. The minister is a Christian Socialist who is always making speeches, always preaching—in
the rhetorical jargon of his subject—but a warmhearted, kind man and
of a serious cast of mind. His congregation pampers and deifies him,
but he retains a clear view of the worth of his wife, without whom he
cannot live, and in the end the feeling that she is indispensable to him
vanquishes his professional showmanship. The poet is an immature
boy: unsophisticated, unfinished, fearful, shy, reticent and imperti-
nent, conceited and genial—in one word, unbearable. When he sees
that the minister's wife loves her husband,[33] he withdraws with
manly strength of character. We feel that he will achieve something
in the world; and Shaw's play did not need to end with the parenthesis:
"(Candida and James embrace, but they do not know the secret in the
poet's heart.)"[34]

Translated by Rudolf B. Schmerl from "Der Dramatiker Bernard Shaw,"
Die Zukunft (Berlin), XLIII (April 4, 1903), 33–34. Reprinted by permission.

A Note on Candida[1]

HERMANN BAHR

In the Germanic world, the woman wields power over the man only so long as he feels her to be a higher being, almost a saint: so Candida is the transcendent, the immaculate, the pure—the heaven, the stars, the eternal light. And this Candida? There is no doubt that she is an angel. The only question is in which heaven she dwells. There is a first heaven, and a second heaven, and so on up to the seventh heaven. In the seventh heaven, as you well know, Shaw, dwell only the poets; and of the seventh heaven must the woman be, before the worshipful Marchbanks will once kneel to her, if, indeed, it can be said that a poet ever kneels. But your beloved Candida is of a lower heaven —a lesser alp, a thousand metres below, in the region of the respectable *bourgeoisie*. There is she the saint the Germanic mannikin needs. There she shines—shines for the Morells, the good people who inculcate virtue and solve social questions every Sunday. And it is there that she belongs.[353]

From "From Nora to Candida"[2]

MAURICE MURET

Must we consider Bernard Shaw's *Candida* (an English comedy just published and successfully played in London and[1216] Berlin),

---

[1] As recorded by Archibald Henderson in *George Bernard Shaw: His Life and Works* (Cincinnati: Stewart and Kidd Company, 1911), p. 353n. Reprinted by permission of Appleton-Century-Crofts Trade Book Division. Copyright 1911 by Stewart Kidd. Copyright 1939 by Archibald Henderson. The title used here is the present editor's.

[2] Translated by Stephen and Jane Stanton from *Journal des Débats*, June 24, 1904, pp. 1216–18.

along with the majority of the critics, as a premeditated refutation of
A Doll's House and *The Lady from the Sea*? It is certainly possible to
do so. Shaw has neglected to outline his intentions. He probably hesi-
tated to make any absolute affirmations. All that one can say is that
Candida arouses, by antithesis, our memory of the Noras and the
Ellidas. Placed in a situation analogous to that in which the Norwegian heroines whom we have just been mentioning are struggling,
the heroine of the English play observes a code which is radically
different. Whether this has been done intentionally or by chance is
unimportant. Candida is none the less a delightful woman, and the
comedy in which she plays deserves to be described in some detail.

Candida is thirty-three years old. She is well built and well
nourished, good, beautiful, and sweet, writes Shaw, and her usual and
characteristic expression consists of an air of amused maternal indulgence which captures all hearts. When she speaks it seems as
though her voice is a peaceful whisper betraying goodness and well-
being. In her bedroom above the fireplace hangs a reproduction of
Titian's Virgin of the Assumption. And Shaw has concluded from
this a moral relationship between the Virgin, the creation of the Vene-
tian painter, and his own Candida. She is married to the Reverend
James Morell, an eloquent and learned minister. . . . Undoubtedly he
tenderly loves his beautiful and charming wife, but he regards himself as very superior in his field. The crisis in which we are going to
participate is necessary in order that the weakness of this man may
be revealed.

. . . . .

The scene of Candida's choice takes place in the third act. It is a
pure literary jewel. Shaw follows his well-known leanings toward
the didactic. He argues, pleads, and reasons with the finesse of a good
lawyer, the precision of a mathematician, and the elegance of an artist.
Without doubt, it is a matter of a simple literary illusion. One would
seek for a long time in real life before encountering such personified
ideas, such purely intellectual people as those he puts on the stage.
But we must take this comedy of *Candida* for what it is: a philosophical dialogue full of grace and poetry. As such it can be admired without reserve. And the last act worthily crowns the whole work: "I
give myself to the weaker of the two!" declares Candida, after having
heard her husband and her poet passionately plead their respective
causes. Morell, at these words, believes himself defeated and bows his

head. But he is wrong. For he is the weaker of the two, the learned proud man of no particular time, the restless, subdued husband of to-day. Candida provides him with the proof of his weakness, and that is her unique revenge. Now an Ibsen heroine, when given a similar alternative, chose without any question the freedom of the matri-monial fireside. Candida chooses slavery and duty, showing by her example that there are for a woman other means of developing and affirming her individuality than in escaping the law or in rebellion. In resigning and sacrificing herself, Candida proves to her husband, who fails to appreciate her and who even scorns her a little, how superior she is to him: "I have built for him a castle of security and indulgence and love...."[1217] Moved by so much goodness, and at last discovering the truth, Morell kneels before Candida while Eugene miserably sneaks away. "All this is true!" cries the minister. "What I am you have made me with the labor of your hands ...." The reconciliation is perfect, and there is every reason to believe that the Reverend James Mavor Morell will henceforth preserve for Candida the place in his heart and in his life to which she is entitled.

From the mass of *femmes révoltées* who encumber the contem-porary drama, the figure of Candida stands out with fortunate dis-tinction. Feminist literature has produced no one who compares with this delightful character. It is surely a tardy, but brilliant revenge of the traditional ideal on the new ideal—this victory of the "Lady as Titian painted her" over the Scandinavian virago, this triumph of Candida over Nora.[1218]

From "Miss Janet Achurch and Mr. Charles Charrington in 'Candida'"

OLIVER ELTON

Last evening's presentation we can only wish to applaud and celebrate. . . . The conception of a child-like creature, a poet, a boy of eighteen, got up to look like Shelley, not a man, femininely hectic and timid and fierce, who is the real chorus in the play and the final judge or searcher of hearts of his fellow-puppets [—this conception] is hazardous; but it prevailed and triumphed. Mr. Courtenay Thorpe need not have come on at first with a stuck and lackadaisical stare, and he sometimes overplayed. But he understood the part, and gradually the audience felt that he could not look otherwise to realize it. Mr. Thorpe's voice and intelligence are very good; he had to act the real hero of the play. The Reverend James Morell is a philanthropic "Socialist" vicar, ever living up to his private picture of himself as melting a churchful of admirers with his eloquence. He is a variation of an Ibsen husband of the Helmer type. He arranges his household on theories of "helpfulness" and fraternal service, which end in others

From "Miss Janet Achurch and Mr. Charles Charrington in *Candida*," the *Manchester Guardian*, March 15, 1898. Spelling and punctuation in some instances have been modernized. This is a review of a performance given at the Gentleman's Concert Hall, Manchester, England, on March 14, 1898. At this time *Candida* had been seen only in the English provinces. The first professional London performance was staged on July 1, 1900 at the Strand Theatre, and the New York première took place at the Princess Theater on December 8, 1903.

Elton's early review is interesting as an indication of *Candida's* general misinterpretation until Shaw added two sentences at the end of the play before its publication in 1898. These were: "But I have a better secret than that in my heart" and the final stage direction: "But they do not know the secret in the poet's heart." See Irving McKee, "Bernard Shaw's Beginnings on the London Stage," *PMLA*, LXXIV (September, 1959), 477, an excerpt from which is included in this book on p. 159. Also worth noting is Elton's early association of *Candida* with Ibsen's iconoclastic plays.

doing most things for him. His curate, his typewriting lady secretary, and others are blindly in love with him. This is part of the system, though he does not see it. . . . Mr. Charles Charrington has worked well with Mr. Shaw in making the character of Morell very complete and formidably hopeless. We have never seen so persuasive a figuring of a hollow soul, ready with fresh and ever fresh reserves of phrasing drawn up from its wells. The accent, posture, and amphitheatrical manner in the crises of private life were all masterly; so was the sincerity of his bewildered rage, and his bitter clinging to his position as apostle and master. . . . All this part of the play was full of sallies and fitful side-intentions that make it hard to follow when heard, and therefore untheatrical. Once, when a red-hot poker in some way served as a symbol of chaste separation, a wild humour was half apparent. The end, after various hesitations, approaches when the two men invite Candida to "choose between them." Here is the crucial part; the playwright has landed himself in a kind of stalemate. He gets out of it by a device that nearly reminds us of the remark made in the play, "How conventional you unconventional people are!" But it is convention at two removes. The obvious Adelphi plan would be for Candida to stick to her husband because she had promised in church to do so. The older romantic plan would be to assert her inner soul and go forth with the one man that can see into it, Eugene. One more double is requisite and sufficient for Mr. Shaw. Its sentimental and dubious character is concealed by the ingenious conduct of the dialogue. She says, "I choose the weaker." Superficially this is the feckless boy and vagabond Eugene, and Morell, histrionic to the last, "accepts" her judgment. She then explains that the "weaker" is Morell himself, whom she sees as he really is, but still, in a sort of maternal compassion, adopts. Eugene has understood; he rushes forth, "the night is impatient" for him. She lets him go with a cruel text for him to remember: that she is fifteen years older then he, and that this difference will increase in meaning with time. "When we are a hundred years older we shall be the same age" is the substance of his last retort. Then Morell embraces her, and the curtain descends. This whole passage, we have said, strikes us as sentiment wrapped up in ingenuities, and it is some strain on belief that even Morell should welcome his reward with such rapture when receiving it as the corollary of his weakness from his direst critic, who has upset his whole theory of himself. Perhaps the playwright tugged impatiently at his motley and intricate knot. It has to be said, however, that Miss Janet Achurch played the difficult and sometimes indistinct part of Candida very well and in the only possible spirit: that of a serene clairvoyant, mistress of the whole position, disposing of a couple of children whose natures she explains to themselves and to each other. She has no passion for either, no commonplace conflict of love and duty. When they ask her to "choose," she asks them to "bid," as if in auction, what they can give her. She then makes her choice on the subtle principle described. Miss Achurch went through this piquant and abnormal situation with perfect naturalness and with an incisive deliverance of the points. A plainer and stronger part in a modern play of this type would be easily within her compass, and indeed has, by her performance of Ibsen's Nora, often been proved to be her forte.

From "Candida"

A. B. WALKLEY

Fantasy has its place in the theatre, as well as realism, and that is one reason why the theatre has room for Mr. Bernard Shaw. His method of travestying life is to eliminate from it everything but the pure intelligence. Just as Mr. H. G. Wells amuses us by supposing a world where the laws of gravity are suspended, or where there is no such thing as time, or where space is of x dimensions, so Mr. Shaw amuses us by representing a world where conduct is regulated by thought, and men love women, as the civil servant in *Pickwick* ate crumpets, on principle. There are, no doubt, such people in real life, people who choose their diet, their clothes, and their wives on principle; people, even, who in flat defiance of Scripture do by taking thought add a cubit to their stature. I forget how many millions of inhabitants there are on the Planet Terra, but evidently there are quite enough to realise all thinkable things in actual facts. If you will only

From *Drama and Life* (London: Methuen and Company, Ltd., 1907), pp. 214–18. Reprinted by permission of Methuen and Company, Ltd. Review of matinée at the Royal Court Theatre, London, on April 26 or 29, 1904, with Harley Granville-Barker in the role of Marchbanks.

go on dealing for ever, you are bound one day to hold thirteen trumps. All the same, if you choose that day for the "period" of a whist-drama, you will present fantasy, not realism. So it is with ideas. Ideas count for next to nothing in the fundamental human[214] relationships. Our little exploits in coherent thought are mere bobbing corks on the great stream of life. Ideas, like dukes in Mr. Gilbert's opera, are two a penny. We are such stuff as dreams, not manuals of logic, are made of. "Why did I love my friend?" asks Montaigne, and gives the only true answer: "Because it was he, because it was I." By systematically ignoring this all-important side of life, all its subconscious and unconscious elements, by representing life in general and love in particular as based upon ratiocination, Mr. Shaw obtains most amusing results.

Thus in *Candida* he takes the familiar dramatic situation of a woman between two men, but his peculiar treatment makes the familiar situation something quite new and strange and diverting. The lady is beloved by her clerical husband, who has a clergyman's ideas, and also by a young poet, who has a poet's ideas. At a given moment the clergyman takes the poet by the coat-collar and gives him a good shaking. The poet, so soon as he has recovered his breath, shouts out: "I'm not afraid of a clergyman's ideas. I'll fight your ideas. I'll rescue her [Candida, the parson's wife] from her slavery to them; I'll pit my own ideas against them. You are driving me out of the house because you daren't let her choose between your ideas and mine." In an ordinary play, of course, in a representation of life, this would merely be a speech "in character"—the speech of a man who, being hit, cannot hit back with his fists, but hits back with his rhetoric. But Mr. Shaw actually means it; it is the very thesis of his play. The parson's ideas *do* waver, break, and flee before the poet's ideas; the lady *is* asked to choose between the[215] two sets of ideas, and gravely, without irony, makes her choice accordingly. It is an amusing game, worked out with the "elegance" of a mathematical demonstration.

To crown the joke, Mr. Shaw takes care to give his fantasy a certain admixture of reality. While his dramatic conflict is a conflict of pure ideas, it is ostensibly carried out by people who are, externally at any rate, familiar types in the world around us. We know the East End parson, a "muscular Christian," a bit of a socialist, a "strenuous" worker of good works. We know the poet, with some traits borrowed from Shelley and others from De Quincey. As for Candida herself, we know her only too well. She is the managing, mothering, thoroughly competent woman, who carries about innumerable bags and parcels, with an aggressive air of brisk usefulness, and cannot talk to a man without patting him on the back, or retying his cravat, or picking bits of cotton off his coat. In real life she is what American slang calls a "holy terror." In Mr. Shaw's fantasy she attracts the love and admiration of every man who comes near her. She is the star and they are the moths. Whole sets of ideas—parsonical ideas and poetical ideas—gyrate furiously around her. That is part of Mr. Shaw's fun, but this time it is not intentional fun. As a rule, he keeps his sympathies well in hand. He treats both parson and poet calmly and dispassionately. But he cannot conceal his conviction that the Candidas of this world are angels in petticoats.

There is nothing in all this that one could not have told from the printed play. What further impressions do we get from the acted play? Mainly a heightening of the fun, a sharper sense of the incongruity between the external reality of the people[216] and the internal fantasy of their actions. We *see* Candida flicking the cotton off the gentleman's coat and carrying the little parcels and bags, we *hear* her gravely "opting" between parson and poet: "I give myself to the weaker of the two." And the minor characters, who are unalloyed reality—the parson's typist and his curate and his father-in-law—become, of course, more solidly real on the stage, present a more startling contrast to the essentially fantastic protagonists. Further, we have the pleasure of an actual performance, the pleasure of seeing what the players make of their parts and how their notions of them correspond or not with our own preconceived notions. In this respect one has no disappointment to record. Miss Rorke's Candida, like Mr. McKinnell's parson and Mr. Granville Barker's poet, was the very thing; while Miss Sydney Fairbrother revealed much more in Proserpine than one ever guessed to be there, and both the father-in-law of Mr. A. G. Poulton and the curate of Mr. Athol Stewart were as good as could be. The fact is, intelligent actors must revel in Mr. Shaw's plays; they are never called upon to open their mouths without saying something worth saying, and whatever they are called upon to do there can be no doubt in their minds as to what, precisely, it is.

On the other hand, the stage-presentation of *Candida* adds nothing to what is the chief delight of the play—the chief delight of every one of Mr. Shaw's plays—its brilliant dialectic. And in one respect the spectator is actually deprived of a pleasure enjoyed by the reader. The book gives characteristic fragments of exegesis which necessarily disappear on the stage. One example is the account—as good as any "portrait" of La Bruyère—of the father-in-law,[217] Mr. Burgess. Another occurs at the fall of the curtain. The stage direction is "They [husband and wife] embrace. But they do not know the secret in the poet's heart." On the stage the actors can, and do, embrace; but they have no possible means of telling the spectator, by their actions, whether they do or do not know the secret in the poet's heart. On the whole, however, *Candida* on the stage is capital sport. Mr. Shaw maintains that he is quite serious, an out-and-out realist; in short, that in saluting him as a merry sportsman one is like the young lady who, when Sydney Smith said grace, shook him by the hand with a "Thank you so much, Mr. Smith; you are always so amusing." If so, one is evidently in the ignorant position of Candida and her husband when they embrace at the fall of the curtain; one does not know the secret in the playwright's heart.[218]

From "Shaw the Dramatist"

G. K. C H E S T E R T O N

The dramatic volume with which Shaw dazzled the public was called, *Plays, Pleasant and Unpleasant*. I think the most striking and typical thing about it was that he did not know very clearly which plays were unpleasant and which were pleasant. "Pleasant" is a word which is almost unmeaning to Bernard Shaw. Except, as I suppose, in music (where I cannot follow him), relish and receptivity are things that simply do not appear. He has the best of tongues and the worst of palates. With the possible exception of *Mrs. Warren's Profession* (which was at least unpleasant in the sense of being forbidden) I can see no particular reason why any of the seven plays should be held

From *George Bernard Shaw* (New York: The John Lane Company, 1909), pp. 119–25. Reprinted by permission of The Devin-Adair Company, New York.

specially to please or displease. First in fame and contemporary importance came the[119] reprint of *Arms and the Man,* of which I have already spoken. Over all the rest towered unquestionably the two figures of Mrs. Warren and of Candida. They were neither of them pleasant, except as all good art is pleasant. They were neither of them really unpleasant except as all truth is unpleasant. But they did represent the author's normal preference and his principal fear; and those two sculptured giantesses largely upheld his fame.

I fancy that the author rather dislikes *Candida* because it is so generally liked. I give my own feeling for what it is worth (a foolish phrase), but I think that there were only two moments when this powerful writer was truly, in the ancient and popular sense, inspired; that is, breathing from a bigger self and telling more truth than he knew. One is that scene in a later play where after the secrets and revenges of Egypt have rioted and rotted all round him, the colossal sanity of Cæsar is suddenly acclaimed with swords. The other is that great last scene in *Candida* where the wife, stung into final speech, declared her purpose of remaining with the strong man because he is the weak man. The wife is asked to decide between two men, one a strenuous self-confident popular preacher, her husband, the[120] other a wild and weak young poet, logically futile and physically timid, her lover; and she chooses the former because he has more weakness and more need of her. Even among the plain and ringing paradoxes of the Shaw play this is one of the best reversals or turnovers ever effected. A paradoxical writer like Bernard Shaw is perpetually and tiresomely told that he stands on his head. But all romance and all religion consist in making the whole universe stand on its head. That reversal is the whole idea of virtue; that the last shall be first and the first last. Considered as a pure piece of Shaw therefore, the thing is of the best. But it is also something much better than Shaw. The writer touches certain realities commonly outside his scope; especially the reality of the normal wife's attitude to the normal husband, an attitude which is not romantic but which is yet quite quixotic; which is insanely unselfish and yet quite cynically clear-sighted. It involves human sacrifice without in the least involving idolatry.

The truth is that in this place Bernard Shaw comes within an inch of expressing something that is not properly expressed anywhere else; the idea of marriage. Marriage is not a mere chain upon love as the anarchists[121] say; nor is it a mere crown upon love as the sentimentalists say. Marriage is a fact, an actual human relation like that of motherhood, which has certain human habits and loyalties, except in a few monstrous cases where it is turned to torture by special insanity and sin. A marriage is neither an ecstasy nor a slavery; it is a commonwealth; it is a separate working and fighting thing like a nation. Kings and diplomatists talk of "forming alliances" when they make weddings; but indeed every wedding is primarily an alliance. The family is a fact even when it is not an agreeable fact, and a man is part of his wife even when he wishes he wasn't. The twain are one flesh—yes even when they are not one spirit. Man is duplex. Man is a quadruped.

Of this ancient and essential relation there are certain emotional results, which are subtle, like all the growths of nature. And one of them is the attitude of the wife to the husband, whom she regards at once as the strongest and most helpless of human figures. She regards him in some strange fashion at once as a warrior who must make his way and as an infant who is sure to lose his way. The man has emotions which exactly correspond; sometimes looking down at his wife and sometimes[122] up at her; for marriage is like a splendid game of seesaw. Whatever else it is, it is not comradeship. This living, ancestral bond (not of love or fear, but strictly of marriage) has been twice expressed splendidly in literature. The man's incurable sense of the mother in his lawful wife was uttered by Browning in one of his two or three truly shattering lines of genius, when he makes the execrable Guido fall back finally upon the fact of marriage and the wife whom he has trodden like mire:

> Christ! Maria! God,
> Pompilia, will you let them murder me?

And the woman's witness to the same fact has been best expressed by Bernard Shaw in this great scene where she remains with the great stalwart successful public man because he is really too little to run alone.

There are one or two errors in the play; and they are all due to the primary error of despising the mental attitude of romance, which is the only key to real human conduct. For instance, the love-making of the young poet is all wrong. He is supposed to be a romantic and amorous boy; and therefore the dramatist tries to make him talk turgidly, about seeking[123] for "an archangel with purple wings" who shall be worthy of his lady. But a lad in love would never talk in this mock heroic style; there is no period at which the young male is more sensitive and serious and afraid of looking a fool. This is a blunder; but there is another much bigger and blacker. It is completely and disastrously false to the whole nature of falling in love to make the young Eugene complain of the cruelty which makes Candida defile her fair hands with domestic duties. No boy in love with a beautiful woman would ever feel disgusted when she peeled potatoes or trimmed lamps. He would like her to be domestic. He would simply feel that the potatoes had become poetical and the lamps gained an extra light. This may be irrational; but we are not talking of rationality, but of the psychology of first love. It may be very unfair to women that the toil and triviality of potato-peeling should be seen through a glamour of romance; but the glamour is quite as certain a fact as the potatoes. It may be a bad thing in sociology that men should deify domesticity in girls as something dainty and magical; but all men do. Personally I do not think it a bad thing at all; but that is another argument. The[124] argument here is that Bernard Shaw, in aiming at mere realism, makes a big mistake in reality. Misled by his great heresy of looking at emotions from the outside, he makes Eugene a cold-blooded prig at the very moment when he is trying, for his own dramatic purposes, to make him a hot-blooded lover. He makes the young lover an idealistic theoriser about the very things about which he really would have been a sort of mystical materialist. Here the romantic Irishman is much more right than the very rational one; and there is far more truth to life as it is in Lover's couplet—

> And envied the chicken
> That Peggy was pickin'.

than in Eugene's solemn æsthetic protest against the potato-skins and the lamp-oil. For dramatic purposes, G. B. S., even if he despises romance, ought to comprehend it. But then, if once he comprehended romance, he would not despise it.[125]

From The Quintessence
of Bernard Shaw

H. C. D U F F I N

FROM "IMMORALITY AND HERESY"

Shaw's purpose, then, is not necessarily to overturn existing institutions and traditions, but to get men to think for themselves—or at
least to secure freedom to think and speak for themselves for those
who want to. With this aim in view, he seeks first to deprive the word
"morality" of its stupefying power by making it practically synonymous with convention. Immorality then becomes, by definition, not
a form of sin, but a mode of freedom: "Whatever is contrary to established manners or customs is immoral." The definition, once accepted, permits breaches of the established code of thought and
action by the original mind to be examined in the light of reality without prejudice; and this is progress. . . .[37]

. . . . .

But to realize most clearly just what Shaw means by immorality
we may turn to that play which disputes with "Man and Superman" the
claim to be the greatest of his plays—"Candida." The three chief figures
present three progressive stages on the road to immorality. Morell has
not yet left the mark; in spite of his "advanced views" and his admirable qualities, he is completely hidebound. Marchbanks has arrived
at the goal of complete freedom of outlook. Every one of the screens
that commonly stand between man's eyes and naked reality is down
for him: orthodoxy, morality, convention, respectability, good form,
duty; even common sense is sublimated by his fierce instinct for truth.

From *The Quintessence of Bernard Shaw* (London: George Allen and
Unwin, Ltd., 1920), pp. 37, 39–41, 67–69, 98–100, 106–107, and 164. Reprinted by
permission of George Allen and Unwin, Ltd.

Of course, Morell is talking the most dignified common sense when he points out that unless the maidservant is to be a slave every one in the house has to lend a hand in the housework, and Marchbanks undoubtedly ought to have been[39] crushed by his grave reproof, "When there's anything coarse-grained to be done you ring the bell and throw it on to somebody else, eh? That's one of the great facts in your existence, isn't it?" But Marchbanks brushes this transport of Republican enthusiasm and universal philanthropy impatiently aside: "Oh don't torture me. The one great fact now is that your wife's beautiful fingers are dabbling in paraffin oil." Later on he is quite unmoved by Morell's caustic reminder that he is trying to "steal another man's happiness." To label an act or a fact with a popular tag neither alters its nature for him nor throws any new light on it: he has seen it as it is—an unalterable part of reality—from the beginning. He is not afraid to hear his dream of life with Candida described by Morell as "idle, selfish, and useless"; yes, he says, that is, beautiful, free, and happy. He has achieved that acme of immorality—abhorred of the Philistine —irresponsibility.

Candida herself is bound by a sense of many responsibilities. She has a task infinitely more difficult than that of Marchbanks—she has to combine an immoral outlook with life in a workaday world. Her mind is almost as free from conventionality as Marchbanks's own, her slight inferiority in this respect being accounted for by Marchbanks' greater intellectual power. Her breadth of vision, in contrast to Morell's cramped views, is evident in the remarkable scene between[40] the two near the end of the Second Act. She explains, to his bewilderment, that she knows she ought to teach Marchbanks what love really is, and that it is not her "goodness and purity" that prevents her from doing so, but simply her love for her husband. Morell, only halfsatisfied with the one security, and shocked at the repudiation of the other, learns his lesson even too thoroughly, for in his conversation with Marchbanks after the return from the meeting, he acknowledges that Candida would have been held by no sense of "law," and, forgetting her obedience to the higher law of love, suggests that she would probably have yielded to further pressure had the interruption not come. It is noteworthy that Marchbanks, in asking how Morell got past "the flaming sword" that stopped him, seems not only to ignore the conventional difference between his position and Morell's, but to be unaware that it exists.[41]

FROM "SOCIAL RELATIONS INVOLVING SEX"

. . . The leitmotif of all Shaw's work on the theme of woman is her maternal aspect. Whether this is a solitary example in Shaw of simple acceptance[67] of the conventional view (in this case perhaps a convention that imposes even upon Nature herself); whether it is a piece of original and unprejudiced insight; or whether it is a deliberate adoption due to Shaw's obsession by the birth statistics, is not clear. But this dominating note recurs insistently. The two most important of Shaw's women are Candida and Ann Whitefield: the latter is his typical woman—"Every woman is not Ann," he says, "but Ann is Everywoman"; Candida is his ideal woman (if the word "ideal" may be permitted here in its more normal sense). In discussing Ann in the Preface, he says, in effect, "Man's genius is for art in its various forms, woman's for maternity." When Candida is introduced to us, she is described as looking at Marchbanks and Morell "with an amused maternal indulgence which is her characteristic expression"; she is "likely, one guesses, to become matronly later on." With the Virgin of the Assumption, that hangs over the hearth, we are told that not only her husband but she herself would never perceive any spiritual resemblance in Candida. Yet it is Marchbanks who has placed the picture there, and it is suggested that he at least fancies this resemblance. And Marchbanks' dreams have a way of transcending truth. (To his impassioned cry, "Your feet should be beautiful upon the mountains," her reply is apt, but inadequate: "My feet would not be beautiful upon the Hackney[68] Road without boots.") But Marchbanks himself is so impressed by this "maternal" quality of Candida that his idea of a suitable mate for her is some one she can protect. He is not quite consistent, for he has previously suggested an archangel as a worthy lover for her. But Candida gives some support to the other conception. When Marchbanks warns Morell, "She means that she belongs to herself," she turns on him with, "I mean that and a good deal more, Master Eugene"—intending probably to suggest that they belong to her. And indeed these two men, who may be called a man of character and a man of intellect, are children before this woman. But it is to be observed that once the spell of hope is gone, Marchbanks rises easily from tutelage to equality, perhaps to mastery. At the beginning of the scene he has told Morell: "It is she who wants somebody to protect. . . .

Some grown-up man who has become as a little child again. . . . I am
the man, Morell." Now, when she smilingly asks, "Am I *your* mother
and sisters to you, Eugene?" he exclaims, with a fierce gesture of
disgust, "Ah, never." And one feels a sense of satisfaction: a man such
as this should not be any woman's babe, any more than it was fitting
for Nora Helmer to be a man's doll.[69]

　　• • • • •

The discrepancy between Morell and Candida is of a more subtle
nature. To Marchbanks, who appraises their souls, they are profoundly, maddeningly unsuited to each other. Morell, however, is
content—as well he may be—and Candida not only loves her husband,
but is unaware of the distance which separates him from her—at all
events, she gives no sign of feeling it, and certainly does not measure
it with Marchbanks' eyes. Yet she does realize the futility of Morell's
preaching—speaks of it with what appears to him to be soul-destroying
cynicism, and, offended by his Sunday-school morality, she calls him
"a clergyman, a thorough[98] clergyman." It is hard to conceive any
close sympathy between them after that, and, indeed, little sympathy,
except of an unsubstantial emotional sort, exists. A far more natural
and powerful reciprocal attraction draws Candida and Marchbanks
together: they understand, they respond; their reaction to life is alike
joyous, vital, real. It is not quite clear what Marchbanks and Shaw
want to come of this attraction (nothing is actually allowed to come
of it, of course). It is not by any means certain that relations between
Candida and Marchbanks would have been much more permanent
than Nature intended those between her and Morell to be. She loves
his dreams, but they might not have satisfied her practical energetic
character. It is more probable that Shaw and Marchbanks (and
Candida too—everybody, in fact, but Morell) intended nothing more
than that Marchbanks should "learn love" from Candida.

But whatever the intention, it is frustrate, first by Morell's wooden
obstructiveness, and secondly by Candida's acquiescence in his attitude. The situation is of the "Doll's House" type, but Candida is a
Shavian intellectual woman, full-fledged, not an Ibsenite womanly
woman on the point of being reborn. She realizes between herself and
Morell a kindred incompatibility with that of Nora and Torvald Helmer; but she takes, not Nora's line, but Mrs. Alving's: she stays—
probably with success. The lesson of the play seems to be[99] something
of a denial of that of "A Doll's House." A woman (so says this woman,

the greatest of Shaw's women) should *not* leave her husband to seek freedom—not in this case, anyway. She throws Shaw's principles overboard, and sinks self in pity. She is content to seek freedom and self-development within the shell of convention—by flirting with Marchbanks.

Lest it should be supposed that the last sentence contains an intentional or inadvertent bathos, it must be pointed out that Shaw does not use the terms "flirt" and "philander" in the popular derogatory sense. To him flirting and philandering are recognized forms of human activity, and may be carried on by married or unmarried people without more damaging results than those of other modes of artistic experience.[100]

. . . . .

... Having transcended Candida's petty barrier of their difference in years by his conclusive comment, "In a hundred years we shall be the same age," he adds, "But I have a better secret than that in my heart." Fearful, for everybody's sake, of prolonging the intense scene, Candida asks for no explanation of his words—probably knows without asking. We are left to conjecture whether his "better secret" is that but for pity she would[106] have chosen him, or, more probably, that his loss of Candida is an escape to "larger loves and diviner dreams."[1] [107]

FROM "RELIGIOUS MATTERS"

. . . . .

... And of course there is Morell, of whom sufficient has already been said. In the shallow water of the pulpit and the study he is an imposing figure, but, being carried far out of his depth by the surging problems of reality, he flounders helplessly—his buoyant faith betrays him—he sinks, but for the uncanonical hand of his wife.[164]

1 [Shaw's reply appeared in his *Sixteen Self Sketches* (New York, 1949), pp. 158–59. It is reprinted in this book on p. 170.]

From The Real Bernard Shaw

MAURICE COLBOURNE

"Here, then, was the higher but vaguer and timider vision, the incoherent, mischievous, and even ridiculous unpracticalness, which offered me a dramatic antagonist for the clear, bold, sure, sensible, benevolent, salutarily shortsighted Christian Socialist idealism. I availed myself of it in Candida."   G. B. S.[1][127]

FROM "CANDIDA"

If interested enough in the above quotation to ask Where? we shall find no short answer but this: In the English Pre-Raphaelite Movement. And that, though consonant with Candida's subtitle, A Mystery, would be rather too mystifying an answer. Perhaps metaphor will help to fashion an answer that is intelligible without being as tortuous and misty as Shaw's in the Preface to Plays Pleasant.

Picture Candida the play, then, as an arena wherein two gladiators give combat while Candida the woman, aloof yet interested as any Roman empress, watches their trial of strength from the royal box, calling out encouragements and warnings now to one, now to the other, until finally she awards the fight on points, graciously descends, and presents the prize with a little speech explaining her decision. The gladiators, of course, are two of the beings who make up the total Shaw; for all of us, as Sergius Saranoff discovered, are not bundles of contradictions so much as bundles of different beings. Now when Candida was written the most striking pair in Shaw's bundle were the artist and the social reformer. These two rubbed shoulders constantly; as for instance when visits to Florentine art galleries alter-

---

[1] [Preface (1898) to *Pleasant Plays;* reprinted in this book on pp. 91–94].

From *The Real Bernard Shaw* (London: J. M. Dent and Sons, Ltd., 1949), pp. 127–29. Reprinted by permission of J. M. Dent and Sons, Ltd.

nated with prowls round London slums. And both were susceptible, as was the total Shaw, to the eternal religious impulse, the impulse that inspired equally the works of the old Italian painters and the efforts of muscular Christianity to bring hope into the slums. Art, social reform, religion, these three Shaw realized were one, a trinity. It happened that this realization was precipitated by Shaw's sight of the 'pre-Raphaelite' pictures in Birmingham's churches. These not only embodied that trinity, but to Shaw's eyes embodied it in a vigorous and splendidly modern form. The art was modern art; the religion was alive; and because the pictures were painted by his Socialist friends, Burne-Jones and Morris, the social reform was Socialistic. Such a perception was more than enough to generate a play. Without ado, and moved by the religious impulse, Shaw devised the arena in which the artist and the social reformer in him were to take each other's measure and come to grips. Shaw being a dramatist and the essence[128] of drama being conflict; it was through a conflict that this better acquaintance had to be made. The result was the battle of—and for—Candida.

Without fear of much dispute Candida may be cited as Shaw's most perfect play. This is another way of saying it is the least Shavian. It behaves itself, and is devoid of farcical extravagances, its comedy rising naturally from its characters and situations and not from intrusions by Joey the Clown. It is not too long. It does not sermonize. It observes the unities. Its conflict is simple. More extraordinary, it brims with emotion and makes people cry. All this from the arch-satirist, the prolix unorthodox Shaw! No wonder he called it A Mystery.

The play's virtues are almost unending. It not only presents no difficulties to the scenic designer, carpenter, property master, electrician, wardrobe mistress, or to the manager on salary night, but also makes people talk after they leave the theatre. Those not intent upon guessing the poet's secret fall to upon Candida herself. Angel, fool, or bitch? they ask. There is room for most answers between Beatrice Webb's verdict of 'sentimental prostitute' and Shaw's own assurance to Ellen Terry that 'Candida, between you and me, is the Virgin Mother and nobody else.'[129]

From Bernard Shaw: A Chronicle

R. F. RATTRAY

FROM "CANDIDA"

In 1894 Shaw went to Florence in a small group led by Thomas Okey. Shaw occupied himself with the religious art of the Middle Ages and its destruction by the Renaissance. This led him to speculate on how the values of his own day would be superseded. This chimed with the *Doll's House*, which marked for Shaw the end of an epoch.[1]

Shaw's thought turned to the problem of prophecy. Take the human type that, with due allowance for human imperfection, would be accepted as, humanly speaking, ideal, and ask yourself what will supersede it. Shaw chose a devoted Socialist clergyman, modelled on Stopford Brooke with touches of Canon Shuttleworth and Fleming Williams, and his wife, the ideal wife and mother. Shaw has written, "The play is a counterblast to Ibsen's *Doll's House*, showing that in the real typical doll's house it is the man who is the doll. I borrowed the name of Candida from an Italian lady I never met, Candida Barto-lucci, afterwards a British marchioness. Candida is entirely imagined. When I began writing the part of the young poet, I had in mind De Quincey's account of his adolescence in his *Confessions*."[2] But Shaw drew upon his own nature and youth. (When he arrived in Lon-

[1] See his introduction to [William] Archer's *The Theatrical "World" of 1894*, referred to below. [On pages 109–10 of his book Dr. Rattray quotes from this introduction by Shaw and claims that the germ of *Candida* lay in Shaw's description of Ibsen's *Doll's House* as a play in which the wife of a respectable bank manager with an acute feeling of moral superiority over women exposes "the vanity, folly and amorous beglamourment of this complacent person in his attitude towards his wife."]

[2] The *Evening Standard*, 1944, reproduced in the *Radio Times*, 1946, April 12. [This quotation is from Shaw's letter, "Candida Was Not Ellen Terry," reprinted in this book on pp. 158–59.]

From *Bernard Shaw: A Chronicle* (Luton, England: The Leagrave Press, Ltd., 1951), pp. 102–104. Reprinted by kind permission of publishers and author.

don and took a four-wheeler from Euston to Victoria Grove, "the driver accepted four shillings[3] as a[102] reasonable fare."). The young poet is the hero of the play: although naïve, he has great potential intelligence, insight, and capacity for absorbing experience at lightning speed. The plot is the same as that of *Othello*, the awakening of doubt in a husband's mind as to the fidelity of his wife: but whereas in *Othello* it is on the physical plane, in *Candida* it is entirely platonic. The young poet, Marchbanks, has fallen in love with Candida, attributing to her poetic hungers that are left unsatisfied by the empty husks of her husband's rhetoric: his chivalry is appealed to: he must rescue her from this starvation. Marchbanks' power raises in the husband's mind doubt of himself. Instead of the *Othello* "solution" of death, the denouement is explanation and understanding: Marchbanks comes to see that Morell, the husband, is not a mere selfish humbug, but that he loves his wife unselfishly; he also comes to see that Candida does not have the poetic hungers that he attributed to her. Candida reveals that, while her husband has been all the time protecting her, she has been protecting him. Both Morell and Candida are content with their work and domestic happiness: they do not realize the hunger in the young man of genius for experience of greater things: he has assimilated their experience and now must go forward to greater. This is the explanation of the speeches at the end of the play which led Shaw to give it the sub-title, "a Mystery."[4]

---

3 [See *Candida*, Act I. MARCHBANKS: ". . . (the cabman) beamed all over and touched his hat when Morell gave him two shillings. I was on the point of offering him ten." A shilling is worth fourteen U.S. cents.]

4 I have left this passage as it stood in the first edition of this book. In 1950, on November 17, was published in *The Spectator* a letter Shaw had written in 1920: "The secret is very obvious after all—provided you know what a poet is. What business has a man with the great destiny of a poet with the small beer of domestic comfort and cuddling and petting at the apron-string of some dear, nice woman? Morell cannot do without it: it is the making of him: without it, he would be utterly miserable and perhaps go to the devil. To Eugene, the stronger of the two, the daily routine of it is nursery slavery, swaddling clothes, mere happiness instead of exaltation—an atmosphere in which great poetry dies. To choose it would be like Swinburne choosing Putney. When Candida brings him squarely face to face with it, his heaven rolls up like a scroll and he goes out proudly into the majestic and beautiful kingdom of the starry night. Mind, I have no doubt that Eugene found that, though his head was in the stars, he had to keep his feet on the ground as much as Morell, and that some enterprising woman married him and made him dress himself properly and take regular meals. But he did not steal her from a friend." [This letter is reprinted in its entirety in this book on pp. 168–69.]

It is Shaw himself speaking through Marchbanks:[5]

> We all go about longing for love. It is the first need of our natures, the first prayer of our hearts, but we dare not utter our longing, we are too shy. I go about in search of love, and find it in[103] unmeasured stores in the bosoms of others. I see the affection I am longing for given to dogs and cats and pet birds because they come and ask for it. It must be asked for. It is like a ghost: it cannot speak unless it is first spoken to. All the love in the world is longing to speak, only it dare not, because it is shy, shy, shy. That is the world's tragedy.

From the technical point of view of construction, this play is a remarkable specimen. It exhibits great economy. The unities of time, place and action are observed. Instead of the plot being created by a villain, it is created by the hero. For denouement, there is explanation, and understanding for misunderstanding. And yet there is real and powerful action. It is spiritual action. People suffer and are changed by it. It is really poetic drama. The author has lost himself in interpreting Candida, Morell, and other characters. The tense element is relieved by comedy, including a whole comic part, the father of Candida. Minor characters are revelations of life. And yet there are only half a dozen characters and one scene and no change of costume and a domestic setting from contemporary life. It is a valid opinion that has been held by a number of students of Shaw that as a unified, balanced work of art, this is Shaw's best play and one of the best plays that have been written.[104]

---

[5] It is a curious fact that Mr. Iden Payne, who played the part admirably, told me that he regarded the poetic passages as "fustian," whereas Shaw had told him they were real poetry.

Two Letters on Candida

RICHARD MANSFIELD

FROM A LETTER TO WILLIAM WINTER[1]

April 10th, 1895

. . . I have discarded play after play, and I am in despair. I cannot present—I cannot act, the sickening rot the playwright of today turns out. Shaw's *Candida* was sweet and clean—but he's evidently got a religious turn—an awakening to Christianity; and it's just two and one-half hours of preaching, and I fear the people don't want that. Also, there is no part for me but a sickly youth, a poet who falls in love with *Candida*—who is a young lady of thirty-five and the wife of an honest clergyman, who is a socialist! There is no change of scene in three acts, and no action beyond moving from a chair to a sofa, and *vice versa*. O, ye Gods and little fishes! . . .[232]

LETTER TO GEORGE BERNARD SHAW[2]

April 14th, 1895

My dear Shaw,

If we—by we I mean Beatrice and I—had lost a very near and dear friend we could not have sorrowed more than when we discovered "Candida" to be of the impossible.

It has been read—read—read—and reading it would revive our courage—*rehearsed* and hope, faith and even charity dropped below zero. My personal regard for you (which reckoned by the average consideration one male being will bear for another in these business

---

[1] From William Winter, *Life and Art of Richard Mansfield* (New York: Moffat, Yard and Company, 1910), I, 232.
[2] From F. E. Loewenstein, "What Richard Mansfield Thought of *Candida*," *Drama* (British Drama League), New Series, No. 2, (Autumn, 1946), pp. 9–10. Reprinted by permission.

times is really extraordinary) could carry me a long way into the domain of folly and would undoubtedly have slipped me across the frontier in this instance—if dire necessity, and a crisis, hadn't just in the (to you perhaps) unfortunate nick of time built a double-row prickly-pear hedge which won't let "Candida" thro'. Shaw—my light is perhaps very small and very dim—a mere farthing rush or a tallow dip—but viewed by it, and I have no other to view it by—your play of Candida is lacking in all the essential qualities.

The stage is not for sermons—*Not my stage*—no matter how charming—how bright—how clever—how trenchant those sermons may be—

Candida is charming—it is more than charming—it is delightful, and I can well see how you have put into it much that is the best of yourself—but—pardon me—it is *not* a play—at least *I* do not think it is a play—which thinking does not make it any more or any less of a play— its just only what I think and I happen to be skipper of this ship at this time of thinking. Here are three long acts of talk—talk—talk—no matter how clever that talk is—it is talk—talk—talk.

There isn't a creature who seeing the play would not apply Eugene's observations concerning Morell's lecturing propensities to the play itself. If you think a bustling—striving—hustling—pushing— stirring American audience will sit out calmly two hours of deliberate talk you are mistaken—and I'm not to be sacrificed to their just vengeance.

It isn't right to try and build a play out of a mere incident. Candida is only an incident—it doesn't matter how you wad it or pad it or dress it or bedizen it—its an incident—nothing more. All the world is crying out for deeds—for action! When I step upon the stage I want to act— I'm willing to talk a little to oblige a man like you—but I must act— and hugging my ankles for three mortal hours won't satisfy me in this regard. I can't fool myself and I can't fool my audience. I will gather together any afternoon you please a charming assemblage at our Garrick Theatre and read your play to them or play it—as best we may —but I can't put it on for dinner in the evening—people are not satisfied with only the hors d'oeuvres at dinner—where is the soup and the fish and the roast and the game and the salad and the fruit? Shaw—if you will write for me a strong, hearty—earnest—noble—genuine play—I'll play it. Plays used to be written for *actors*—actors who could stir and thrill—and that is what I want now—because I can do that—the world

is tired of theories and arguments and philosophy and morbid sentiment. To be frank and to go further—I am not in sympathy with a
young, delicate, morbid and altogether exceptional young man who
falls in love with a massive middle-aged lady who peels onions. I
couldn't have made love to your Candida (Miss Janet Achurch) if I
had taken ether—I never fall in love with fuzzy-haired persons who
purr and are business-like and take a drop when they feel disposed
and[9] have weak feminine voices—my ideal is something quite different. I detest an aroma of stale tobacco and gin. I detest intrigue
and slyness and sham ambitions. I don't like women who sit on the
floor—or kneel by your side and have designs on your shirt-bosom—I
don't like women who comb their tawny locks with their fingers, and
claw their necks and scratch the air with their chins.

　　You'll have to write a play that a *man* can play and about a woman
that heroes fought for and a bit of ribbon that a knight tied to his lance.

　　The stage is for romance and love and truth and honor. To make
men better and nobler. To cheer them on the way—Life is real, Life
is earnest, and the grave is not its goal. . . .

　　Be not like dumb, driven cattle.

　　Be a hero in the fight!

　　Go on, Shaw; Beatrice and I are with you—you will be always
welcome as a brother. We want a great work from you.

　　Candida *is* beautiful—don't mistake me—we both understand it and
we both appreciate it—there are fine things here—but—we are paid—
alas—Shaw—we are paid to *act*.

Yours, Shaw, truly,

RICHARD MANSFIELD

　　I am perfectly aware that you will not read this letter—you will
gather that I am not about to produce Candida, and there your interest
will cease—you would like to have Candida presented—if I don't
present it—I'm damned—but also—I'm damned if I do. Ah Shaw: Wir
hatten gebauet ein stattliches Haus. I don't want to ruin it all.[10]

From "The Quintessence of Shaw"

JAMES HUNEKER

Candida is not for mixed audiences. Christian socialism is caviare to the general. In characterization there is much variety; the heroine —if there be such an anomaly as a Shaw heroine—is most engaging. Every time I read *Candida* I feel myself on the trail of somebody; it is all in the air. *The Lady from the Sea* comes back when in that last scene, where the extraordinary young poet Marchbanks, a combination of the spiritual qualities of Shelley, Shaw, Ibsen's Stranger, and Shelley again, dares the fatuous James Morell to put his wife Candida to the[246] test. It is one of the oddest situations in dramatic literature, and it is all "prepared" with infinite skill. The dénouement is another of Mr. Shaw's shower baths; withal a perfectly proper and highly moral ending. You grind your teeth over it, as Mr. Shaw peeps across the top of the page, indulging in one of his irritating dental displays.[247]

. . . . .

II

Candida is the very quintessence of her creator. Many prefer this sprightly sermon disguised as a comedy to Mr. Bernard Shaw's more serious works. Yet serious it is. No latter-day paradoxioneer—to coin a monster word, for the Shaws, Chestertons, *et al.*—evokes laughter so easily as the Irishman. He is a[248] cold intellectual wit, a Swiftian wit, minus the hearty and wholesome obscenity of the great Dublin dean. But it is often misleading. We laugh when we should reflect. We laugh when we might better hang our heads—this is meant for the average married and bachelor man. Shaw strikes fire in almost every sentence he puts into Candida's honest mouth. After reading his

From *Iconoclasts: A Book of Dramatists* (New York: Charles Scribner's Sons, 1905), pp. 246–47, 248–56.

eloquent tribute to Ibsen, the crooked places in *Candida* become plainer; her mission is not alone to undeceive but to love; not only to bruise hearts but to heal them.

In a singularly vivid passage in *The Quintessence of Ibsenism*, Mr. Shaw writes: "When Blake told men that through excess they would learn moderation, he knew that the way for the present lay through the Venusberg, and that the race would assuredly not perish there as some individuals have, and as the puritans fear we all shall unless we find a way round. Also, he no doubt foresaw the time when our children would be born on the other side of it, and so be spared the fiery purgation."

This sentiment occurs in the chapter devoted to a consideration of The Womanly Woman. Let us look at the phrases on the printed page of *Candida* that might be construed as bearing upon the above, or, rather, the result of the quoted passage.

Candida speaks to James, her husband, in Act II:—[249]

Don't you understand? I mean, will he forgive me for not teaching him myself? For abandoning him to the bad woman for the sake of my good-ness—my purity, as you call it? Ah, James, how little you understand me, to talk of your confidence in my goodness and purity! I would give them both to poor Eugene as willingly as I would give my shawl to a beggar dying of cold, if there were nothing else to restrain me. Put your trust in my love for you, James, for if that went I should care very little for your sermons—mere phrases that you cheat yourself and others with every day.

Here is one of the most audacious speeches in any modern play. It has been passed over by most English critics who saw in *Candida* merely an attempt to make a clergyman ridiculous, not realizing that the theme is profound and far-reaching, the question put being no more and no less than: Shall a married man expect his wife's love with-out working for it, without deserving it? Secure in his conviction that he was a model husband and a good Christian, the Rev. James Mavor Morell went his way smiling and lecturing. He had the "gift of gab," yet he was no humbug; indeed, a sincerer parson does not exist. He is quite as sincere as Pastor Manders, much broader in his views, and consequently not half so dull.

But he is, nevertheless, a bit of a bore, with his lack of humour and his grim earnestness. No doubt Shaw took his fling at that queer blend-ing of Christianity and socialism, that Karl[250] Marx in a parson's

collar which startled London twenty years ago in the person of the
Christian socialist clergyman. He saw, too, being a man with a sense
of character values and their use in violent contrast, that to the rhap-
sodic and poetic Eugene Marchbanks, Morell would prove a splendid
foil. And so he does. Between this oddly opposed pair stands on her
solid, sensible underpinnings the figure of Candida. Realist as is Mr.
Shaw, he would scout the notion of his third act being accepted as a
transcript from life. For two acts we are in plain earthly atmosphere;
unusual things happen, though not impossible ones. In the last act
Shaw, droll dramatist and acute observer of his fellow-man's foibles,
disappears, only to return in the guise of Shaw the preacher.

And how he does throw a sermon at our heads! The play is arrested in its mid-ocean, and the shock throws us almost off our feet.
Do not be deceived. That mock bidding for the hand of Candida,
surely the craziest farce ever invented, is but this author's cunning
manner of driving home his lesson. Are you worthy of your wife? Is
the woman who swore to love and honour you ("obey" is not in the
Shaw vocabulary, thanks to J. S. Mill) worthy of you? If your love
is not mutual then better go your ways—you profane it! Is this startling? Is this novel? No and yes. The defence of love for love's sake,
coming from the lips of a Shaw character, has a surprising effect, for
no man is less concerned[251] with sex questions, no man has more
openly depreciated the ascendancy of sex in art and literature. He
would be the first to applaud eagerly Edmund Clarence Stedman's
question apropos of Walt Whitman's *Leaves of Grass*: Is there no
other light in which to view the beloved one than as the future mother
of our children? (I trust to a treacherous memory; the meaning is expressed, though not in Mr. Stedman's words.)

Therefore *Candida* is a large exposition of the doctrine that love
should be free—which is by no means the same thing as free love; that
it should be a burden equally borne by both partners in the yoke; that
happiness, instead of misery, would result if more women resembled
Candida in candour. She cut James to the heart with the confounding
of her shawl and personal purity; it was an astounding idea for a
clergyman's ears. She proved to him later that she was right, that the
hundredth solitary sinner is of more consequence than the ninety-nine
reclaimed. Shaw, who is a Puritan by temperament, has, after his
master, Ibsen, cracked with his slingstone many nice little glass houses
wherein complacent men and women sit and sun their virtues in the

full gaze of the world. One of his sharp and disconcerting theories is that woman, too, can go through the Venusberg and still reach the heights—a fact always denied by the egotistical man, who wishes to be the unique sinner so that he may receive the unique consolation. After a gay life, a sober[252] one; the reformed rake; Tannhäuser's return to an Elizabeth, who awaits him patiently; dear, sweet, virtuous Penelope! Shaw sees through this humbug of the masculine pose and turns the tables by making his Candida ride the horse of the dilemma man-fashion. Maeterlinck, in his Monna Vanna and Joyzelle, enforces the same truth—that love to be love should be free.

And the paradoxical part of it all is that Candida is a womanly woman. She is so domestic, so devoted, that the thin-skinned idealist Eugene moans over her kitchen propensities. Shaw has said that "the ideal wife is one who does everything that the ideal husband likes, and nothing else," which is a neat and sardonic definition of the womanly woman's duty. Candida demands as her right her husband's trust in her love, not heavenly rewards, not the consciousness of her own purity, not bolts and bars will keep her from going from him if the hour strikes the end of her affection. All of which is immensely disconcerting to the orthodox point of view, for it is the naked truth, set forth by a man who despises not orthodoxy, but those who profess it only to practise paganism. This Shaw is a terrible fellow; and the only way to get rid of a terrible fellow is not to take him seriously but to call him paradoxical, entertaining; to throw the sand of flattery in his eyes and incidentally blind criticism at the same time. But Bernard Shaw has always refused to be cajoled, and as to the sand or the mud of abuse[253] —well, he wears the very stout spectacles of common sense.

III

What does Mr. Shaw himself think of Candida? Perhaps if he could be persuaded to tell the truth, the vapourish misconceptions concerning her terrible "shawl" speech—about which I never deceived myself—might be dissipated. It was not long forthcoming—his answer to my question, an answer the publication of which was left to my discretion. It may shock some of his admirers, disconcert others, but at the same time it will clear the air of much cant; for there is the

Candida cant as well as the anti-Shaw cant. He wrote me:[1][254]

. . . . .

So here is Shaw on Shaw, Shaw dissecting Candida, Shaw at last
letting in light on the mystery of the "poet's secret!" There may be
grumbling among the faithful at this very illuminating and sensible
exposition, I feel. So thinks Mr. Shaw, for he adds, "As I should certainly be lynched by the infuriated Candidamaniacs[225] if this view
of the case were made known, I confide it to your discretion"—which
by a liberal interpretation means, publish it and be hanged to you!
But "Candidamaniacs!" Oh, the wicked wit of this man who can thus
mock his flock! His *coda* is a neat summing up: "I tell it to you because it is an interesting sample of the way in which a scene, which
should be conceived and written only by transcending the ordinary
notion of the relations between the persons, nevertheless stirs the
ordinary emotions to a very high degree, all the more because the
language of the poet, to those who have not the clew to it, is mysterious
and bewildering and therefore worshipful. I divined it myself before
I found out the whole truth about it." [256]

From George Bernard Shaw: His Plays

H. L. MENCKEN

FROM "BY WAY OF INTRODUCTION"

And so, if we divest ourselves of the idea that Shaw is trying to
preach some rock-ribbed doctrine in each of his plays, instead of
merely setting forth human events as he sees them, we may find his
dramas much easier of comprehension. True enough, in his prefaces
and stage directions, he delivers himself of many wise saws and elabor-
ate theories. But upon the stage, fortunately, prefaces and stage direc-

---

1 [Here follows Shaw's now famous letter of April, 1904, to Huneker; it is
reprinted in this book on pp. 165–66.]

From *George Bernard Shaw: His Plays* (Boston: John W. Luce Company,
1905), pp. xiv, xviii, xix–xxi; 53–59; 60–62.

tions are no longer read to audiences, as they were in Shakespeare's time, and so, if they are ever to discharge their natural functions, the Shaw dramas must stand as simple plays. Some of them, alackaday! bear this test rather badly. Others, such as "Mrs. Warren's Profession" and "Candida," bear it supremely well.[xiv]

. . . . .

In each of the Shaw plays you will find a sham-smasher like Dick.[1] In "Mrs. Warren's Profession," there are three of them—Mrs. Warren herself, her daughter Vivie and Frank Gardner. In "You Never Can Tell" there are the Clandons; in "Arms and the Man" there is Bluntschli, and in "Man and Superman" there are John Tanner and Mendoza, the brigand chief, who appears in the Hell scene as the Devil. In "Candida" and certain other of the plays it is somewhat difficult to label each character distinctly, because there is less definition in the outlines and the people of the play are first on one side and then on the other, much after the fashion of people in real life. But in all of the Shaw plays the necessary conflict is essentially one between old notions of conduct and new ones.[xviii]

. . . . .

As long as a dramatist is faithful to his task of depicting human life as he sees it, it is of small consequence whether the victory, in the dramatic conflict, goes to the one side or the other. . . .[xix] The dramatist, properly speaking, is not concerned about the outcome of the struggle. All he is required to do is to draw the two sides accurately and understandingly and to show the conflict naturally. In other words, it is not his business to decide the matter for his audience, but to make those who see his play think it out for themselves.

"Here," he says, as it were, "I have set down certain human transactions and depicted certain human beings brought face to face with definite conditions, and I have tried to show them meeting these conditions as persons of their sort would meet them in real life. I have endeavored, in brief, to exhibit a scene from life as real people live it. Doubtless, there are lessons to be learned from this scene—lessons that may benefit real men and women if they are ever confronted with the conditions I have described. It is for you, my friends, to work out these lessons for yourselves, each according to his ideas of right and wrong."

---

[1] [Dick Dudgeon, in *The Devil's Disciple*.]

That Shaw makes such an invitation in each of his plays is very plain. The proof lies in the fact that they have, as a matter of common knowledge, caused the public to do more thinking than the dramas of any other contemporary dramatist, with the sole exception of Ibsen. Pick up any of the literary monthlies and you will find a disquisition upon his technique, glance through the dramatic column of your favorite[xx] newspaper and you will find some reference to his plays. Go to your woman's club, O gentle reader! and you will hear your neighbor, Mrs. McGinnis, deliver her views upon "Candida." Pass among any collection of human beings accustomed to even rudimentary mental activity—and you will hear some mention, direct or indirect, and some opinion, original or cribbed, of or about the wild Irishman. All of this presupposes thinking, somewhere and by somebody. Mrs. McGinnis' analysis of Candida's soul may be plagiarized and in error, but it takes thinking to make errors, and the existence of a plagiarist always proves the existence of a plagiaree. Even the writers of reviews in the literary monthlies, and the press agents who provide discourses upon "You Never Can Tell" for the provincial dailies are thinkers, strange as the idea, at first sight, may seem. And so we may take it for granted that Shaw tries to make us think and that he succeeds.[xxi]

. . . . .

"CANDIDA"

"Candida" is a latter-day essay in feminine psychology after the fashion of "A Doll's House," "Monna Vanna" and "Hedda Gabler." Candida Morell, the heroine, is a clergyman's wife, who, lacking an acquaintance with the philosophies and face to face with the problem of earning her daily bread, might have gone the muddy way of Mrs. Warren. As it is, she exercises her fascinations upon a moony poet, arouses him to the mad-dog stage of passion, drives her husband to the verge of suicide—and then, with bland complacency and unanswerable logic, reads both an excellent lecture, turns the poet out of doors, and falls into her husband's arms, still chemically pure. It is an edifying example of the influence of mind over matter.

Arnold Daly's heroic production of the play, at the little Berkeley Lyceum, in New York City,[2] served as the foundation of the present

[2] [In the spring of 1904. Henderson's review of the early New York performances, in *George Bernard Shaw: Man of the Century*, is reprinted in this book on pp. 65–66.]

vogue of Shaw in the United States, and in consequence "Candida" has been the theme of many metropolitan and provincial philosophers and critics. At the start the vast majority of them muddled the play hopelessly. Candida, they decided, was a sublime type of the virtuous wife and mother—a good woman whose thoughts were as innocent as her acts. It[53] remained for Shaw—and he is usually his own best critic—to set them right. Candida, he explained, was a "very immoral female . . . who, without brains and strength of mind . . . would be a wretched slattern or voluptuary." In other words (as he tried to make clear) she remained virtuous, not because there was aught of the vestal or altruist about her, but because she had discovered that it was possible to enjoy all of the ecstatic excitement of a fall from grace, and still, by holding back at the actual brink of the precipice, to retain, in full measure, her reputation as a pattern of fidelity and virtue. She solved the problem of being immoral and respectable at the same time.

The play is well built and thoroughly balanced and mature. Its every scene shows that it is the work of a dramatist whose genius has been mellowed and whose hand has been made sure by experience. The action moves with that certain, natural air peculiar to many of Ibsen's plays. The characters are not sketches, but definitive, finished portraits. They are not obvious types, perhaps, but even the poet, with all his extravagances, is strangely human.

The Reverend James Morell, Candida's husband, is a Christian-socialist of a sort not uncommon on either side of the Atlantic. He has a parish in an unfashionable part of London, and beside the usual futilities of a conscientious clergyman's daily labor, finds time to make frequent addresses to the masses and classes upon the[54] problems of the hour. In his make-up, there is much of the unconscious make-believe of the actor off the stage, though his own belief in himself is unshaken. Public speaking seems to have this uncanny effect upon many men. Beginning in all sincerity, they gradually lay stress upon the manner of saying a thing at the expense of the matter. Their aim is to make an effect by means of the spoken word and in the end, without realizing it, they become stagey and unnatural. Such a man is Morell. By no means, it will be observed, is he to be mistaken for a hypocrite.

Into his home, by some mad, altruistic impulse, he brings Eugene Marchbanks, a moon-struck young man with the romantic ideals and day dreams of a medieval Edgar Allan Poe and the practical common-sense of an infant. Eugene is eighteen. He inhabits a world a mile or so above the pink clouds of the sunset and writes vague, immaterial verses of the sort that all of us invent and some of us set down in pen-and-ink when we are young. At the start, in all probability, Candida regards him as a nuisance. But by the time the play opens she has already lured him on to the rocks. It is pleasant to sit by the fire and listen to his hazy verses. He is a relief from the honest beefiness of Morell. And so Candida has her entertainment and Eugene, poor boy! falls in love with her.

Now, loving another man's wife, since the beginning of written history, has always presupposed or developed[55] a rather ungenial attitude toward that other man, and Eugene, studying Morell, comes to the conclusion that he is a mere vaporish windbag—a silly bundle of stale platitudes, trite ponderosities and pulpit puerilities. Having the valor of youth, he makes open confession.

"I love your wife," he says to Morell, ". . . a woman with a great soul craving reality, truth, freedom, and being fed on metaphors, sermons, stale perorations, mere rhetoric. Do you think a woman's soul can live on your talent for preaching? . . ."

Morell is staggered, not by Eugene's frank avowal of his love for Candida, but by the other things he has said. What if it is true that she is stifled by the atmosphere of the Morell home? What if it is true that she has tired of being shadow and drudge to an obscure, over-earnest clergyman in a semi-slum and has turned her fancy toward the poet?

"It is easy, terribly easy," he says pathetically, "to break a man's faith in himself. To take advantage of that to break a man's spirit is devil's work. Take care of what you are doing. Take care . . . ."

It is a time of torment for the preacher and he sees his house of cards trembling as if for a fall. Eugene, all the while, is defiant and belligerent. He adds the virtue of rescuing Candida to the pleasure of possessing her, and the two together work his swift undoing.

"Send for her!" he roars. "Send for her and let her choose between us!"[56]

Aha, my masters! what a scene is this!—what a scene of mad passion for the gallery to linger over breathlessly, for the orchestra to greet with stares and for the critics to belabor and dissect in the morning!

Candida comes in and the two bid for her heart and helping hand.

"I have nothing to offer you," says Morell, with proud humility, "but my strength for your defense, my honesty of purpose for your surety, my ability and industry for your livelihood, and my authority and position for your dignity. That is all it becomes a man to offer a woman."

"And you, Eugene?" asks Candida quietly. "What do you offer?"

"My weakness!" exclaims the poet passionately. "My desolation! My heart's need!"

"That's a good bid," says Candida judicially. "Now I know how to make my choice."

Then she pauses and looks curiously from one to the other, as if weighing them. Morell, whose lofty confidence has once more changed into heart-breaking dread, loses all power over himself and in a suffocating voice—the appeal bursting from the depths of his anguish—cries "Candida!"

"Coward!" shrieks Eugene, divining the victory in the surrender. And Candida—O most virtuous of wives!—says blandly, "I give myself to the weaker of the two" and falls into her husband's arms. It is a situation that[57] struck the first night audience at the Berkeley Lyceum as one eminently agreeable and refined.

As Shaw explains, the poet, despite the fact that "his face whitens like steel in a furnace that cannot melt it," is a gainer by Candida's choice. He enters the Morell home a sentimental boy yearning for an emotional outlet. He leaves it a man who has shouldered his cross and felt the unutterable stimulus of sacrifice. Candida makes a man of him, says Shaw, by showing him his strength. David finds that he must do without Uriah's wife.

The dramatist makes Candida essay a most remarkable analysis of her own motives. It is after Morell has reproached her, sick at heart and consumed by a nameless fear, to learn if Eugene's fiery onslaught has been born of any unrest that may be stirring within her. She explains freely and frankly, with more genuine honesty and self-revelation, perhaps, than she knows. Eugene, she says, is like a shivering beggar asking for her shawl. He needs love but scarcely knows it, and she conceives it her duty to teach him the value of love, that no worse woman may teach him its pains later on.

"Will he forgive me," she says, "for not teaching him myself? For abandoning him to the bad women for the sake of my goodness— my purity, as you call it? Ah, James, how little you understand me, to talk of your confidence in my goodness and purity. *I would give them both to Eugene as willingly as I would give my*[58] *shawl to a beggar dying of cold*, if there was nothing else to restrain me. . . ."

"Here," says Huneker, "is one of the most audacious speeches in any modern play. It has been passed over by most critics who saw in 'Candida' merely an attempt to make a clergyman ridiculous, not realizing that the theme is profound and far-reaching, the question put being no more or no less than: Shall a married man expect his wife's love without working for it, without deserving it?" To this may be added another and more familiar question: May not the woman who lives in the odor of sanctity be more thoroughly immoral, at heart, than the worst of her erring sisters?

The play has a number of extremely exciting "grand" scenes and in general is admirably suitable for public performance. The minor characters are but three in number—Candida's wine-buying vulgarian of a father, Morell's curate and Proserpine, his typewriter. Proserpine is admirable, and her hopeless love for Morell—a complaint not uncommon among the women he knows—gives the play a note of homely sentiment that keeps it to earth.

As a piece of workmanship "Candida" is Shaw at his best; as a study in the workings of the feminine mind it deserves to rank with some of the best plays the modern stage has to offer.[59]

. . . . .

"HOW HE LIED TO HER HUSBAND"

"How He Lied to Her Husband" is a one-act bit of foolery that Shaw wrote for Arnold Daly after "Candida" had made a success in New York. It was presented for the first time on the evening of Sept. 26, 1904, and during the ensuing week was more vociferously discussed than any other one-act play that ever graced the boards of an American theater.

As he made fun of the vaporing Ibsenites of the early '90's in "The Philanderer," just so Shaw got his joke at the expense of his own ecstatic followers in this little appendix to "Candida." The latter had been presented with huge profit, and thousands of honest playgoers, alert for mysterious "symbolism" and subtle "purposes" had seen in its heroine a great many of the qualities they formerly sought and discovered in the much-mauled Ibsen women. Candida, in brief, became the high priestess of the advanced cult, in all its warring denominational variety. It became a sign of intellectual vigor to go to the Berkeley Lyceum and compare her with Nora Helmer, Hedda Gabler and their company. And so Shaw indited "How He Lied to Her Husband."

The characters in the little farce are a fashionable[60] young poet named Henry Apjohn, an untamed American husband named Bompas, and his wife, Aurora Bompas, a young woman with yearnings. Aurora and Henry have seen a performance of "Candida" and have come away with a feeling that an intrigue after the fashion of Candida and Eugene, is one of those things that no really advanced poet or modern wife should be without. So Henry writes a sheaf of sonnets to Aurora and being determined to play the game according to the rules, proposes that they run off together. They are about to depart, conscientiously leaving the Bompas diamonds behind, when Aurora, at the brink of the precipice, draws back.

Meanwhile Bompas happens upon Henry's sonnets and confronts the poet with the charge of having written them. Henry, determined to save Aurora, "lies like a gentleman"—and incidentally overdoes it. Bompas, mistaking his well-meant prevarication for impolite indifference to Aurora's beauty, or denial of it, flies into a passion, and is on the point of soundly thrashing the amorous bard when Aurora stays his hand. Then Henry confesses, and Bompas is so much pleased by the manner in which the sonnets celebrate his wife's charms that he offers to print them for private circulation among connoisseurs with broad margins and *de luxe* binding.

The play is built upon the lines of broad farce, and in New York it made an uproarious success. The encounter between Bompas and Henry is extraordinarily[61] ludicrous. Aurora throughout is the typical enthusiast of the women's clubs—filled with vague longings and ambitions, but intensely practical and commonplace at bottom. Henry, during one of their tumultuous exchanges, is about to break her fan. She shrieks the warning that it cost a dollar. He ventures upon a dark, melodramatic oath. "How dare you swear in my presence?" she demands. "One would think you were my husband!"

A pretty bit of fooling, *à la* "The Wild Duck," "The Philanderer" and "Alice-Sit-by-the Fire." Shaw calls it "a warning to theatergoers." It is.[62]

A Review of Candida

STARK YOUNG

In a sense, all drama moves toward a condition of farce. This is because the theatre's very essence consists in the heightening of its material. Heightening that is free, fluent, almost abstract, unless it has the restrictions of character and rational measure, floats off into farce; which is thus closer to poetic drama and serious tragedy than to plain everyday prose realism. The usual condition for farce is the lack of strict connection, or the racing ahead of the plot with regard to the characters. *Candida* is fundamentally a farce, a kind of cerebral farce, as it were. It is not so because the immense heightening given to all the characters is too much detached from their actions; the farce appears in the detachability of the reasons—often put into their own mouths—given for their actions. We often sense thoughts, theories, motives assigned by the author to the characters and not wholly necessary to them in the light of what each is and does. These theories and principles make a pattern among themselves, culminating in Candida's explanation of her decision to stay with her husband and its implications, in the last scene.

This last scene is a good example of the point. If we take the play as a farce of ideas pitched delightfully against each other, Candida's explanation of her choice of husband versus poet is capital entertainment, capable of real emotion but remaining a fairly reckless, or at least free, solution of a built-up pattern of theories, ironies, controversial wagers and attacks. This special brand of explanation for the final solution of the problem of her choice between the two men has been, obviously, predicted all along through the play; it arrives

From *Immortal Shadows* (New York: Charles Scribner's Sons, 1948), pp. 193–95. Reprinted with the permission of Charles Scribner's Sons. Copyright 1937 *New Republic*. This is a review of the performance on March 10, 1937, of the McClintic production of *Candida*, starring Katherine Cornell (Empire Theater, New York).

effectively enough. If you choose, however, to overlook the pre-
diction, and to take her explanation as an independent passage in the
play, then you must face one of two interpretations. Here we have a
woman who, as is usual with Mr. Shaw's characters, is from the[193]
ordinary standpoint safely moral, whatever wild words or theories
she may let fly. Candida does the conventional thing: she remains with
her husband instead of going off with the poet. And, like every other
woman in the parish, she loves her husband. She treats him and the
poet, nevertheless, to a full dissection of her decision, which she says
is a matter of choosing the weaker, who needs her most, et cetera, et
cetera. If we do refuse to take the play as cerebral farce, then either she
is a slightly tedious creature (self-illusioned, all-understanding, given
perhaps to a wee sermon now and then) who is now making a perfectly natural choice, but must stir up a lot of semitosh about it, true
or not true; or else, while staying on with her loved husband (not to
speak of her children), she will, from out of a wise and gentle heart,
dilate on the occasion for the two men's good, especially her husband's, who needs the lecture more than Marchbanks does, who can
take it laid on thicker, and who can rather more satisfactorily be
punished a bit.

The whole play indeed is made up of clicks, curtains, balances in
motifs—such as, for the most obvious example, that of Candida's father
finding one by one that the whole house of them is crazy. The single
shortcoming in Miss Cornell's production derives from a refusal of
the full swing to the play's cerebral raciness and frank theatre. Not
seldom during the performance you note the attempt to glide past
some bit of stage trick in structure or dialogue, or to blur effects that,
though not high sad art, are yet good, joyous artifice, healthy and
strictly theatre. On the same basis the least satisfactory performance
is that of Candida's father by Mr. Kaye, which cuts down the full,
gusty content of the role and its business in the whole play.

The abstractions, attitudes and heightening given to each of the
characters clarify their outlines and make them tend toward types.
Thus it is that *Candida* ends by being a play whose roles are capable
of many interpretations and are hospitable to many actors.

As types of what they represent, such roles are always debatable
of course; and in this case it is the poet that heads the debate. Marchbanks is both conventional and unconventional. There are two qualities about him that are true of the poet in general: he responds in-

tensely to things that for most men mean nothing, a sign not of weakness but of strength and significance; he is in the end practical, because he follows what he knows is for him life and[194] reality. The rest of Shaw's poet—not forgetting the persuasive sop of making him the son of a nobleman, which gives another slant to his oddities of course—is a mixture of the Yellow Nineties, with that mauve babble about beauty, plus the stage poet, whose clumsy absurdities make us all feel comfortably indulgent. Thus Mr. Shaw, playing perfectly safe, manages to use Marchbanks to hit the minister—rhetoric, ego, good looks and all—over the head; and while providing a safe happy ending, makes a point for the creative artist by tapping the audience softly on the head with poesy's defense. Mr. Robert Harris' Marchbanks, tormented and comprehending, is well enough, taking the part as it is written.

In fact the casting, directing and playing in Mr. McClintic's production of *Candida* are far above the average. Of all the actresses who have taken the role, Miss Mildred Natwick's Prossie must be very likely the surest and best, and the most delicately and profoundly kept within its due scale of comic and pathetic. Miss Cornell's Candida, as in all characters with a type outline, is one of the many versions possible to the role. By the same token it is more than usually dependent on the player's own quality. Some of her audience seemed to think Miss Cornell's first moments affected. I did not think so; she seemed, rather, a trifle uneasy, whipped up, as if under some kind of sensitive strain in a casual scene. She could take it more simply. In the last scene she takes up all the word battle, sermon, self-confident analysis, et cetera and turns it into a grace and loving wisdom that is rarely seen on our stage, and that sheer acting, no matter how good, as divorced from personal quality, could never achieve.[195]

A Review of Candida

JOSEPH WOOD KRUTCH

To be outmoded but to have written well is, as Max Beerbohm once marked, to be a classic; and Bernard Shaw is one of the few living men who meet that definition. Unlike most great writers, he has survived long enough to achieve within his own lifetime the three inevitable stages: the stage of the bright young man, the stage of the prophet who can say no wrong, and, finally, the stage of being honorably or classically outmoded. Most of the things that were said about him during the first two stages seem now rather silly. To dismiss him as a pyrotechnic trifler is hardly more absurd than to think, as his disciples once did, that he had set down at last any whole and ultimate truth about man or modern society. But what he had it in him to say he said effectively. He wrote well, and he is a classic.

Neither "Pygmalion," which was revived some weeks ago, nor "Candida," now sharing the week with Miss Cornell's "Antigone" at the Cort Theater, is among his best plays. "Candida" was written early, just after the failure of the first "unpleasant" pieces, and was a deliberate attempt to win a public. It is one of his most factitious comedies; in a sense it is probably not really very sincere. But this fact makes even more impressive the test which it passes. Judge it by comparison with some of his other work or judge it by comparison with the best work of his peers belonging to a remoter past, and one may find it lacking in one respect and another. But judge it on Broadway, compare it with those plays now fashionable rather than outmoded, and one immediately becomes aware, not of the things it isn't, but of the things it is. Even quantitatively there is so much more to it. It is, relatively, so substantial, so rich. The mind of the author is working vigorously, continuously. He is giving you more for your time

From *The Nation*, CLXII (April 20, 1946), 487. Reprinted by permission of The Nation Associates, Inc. This is a review of the Katherine Cornell production (Cort Theater, New York, 1946).

and for your money. By any reasonable OPA price regulation the ceiling on such a play should be at least four or five times as high as that for the ordinary commodity, since it surely cost four times as much brains to produce.

The performance which Miss Cornell and her company is offering is good and satisfactory without being especially brilliant; it is certainly the play, not the performance, which carries the evening. Cedric Hardwicke makes a very amusing if rather broad caricature of the heroine's father; Marlon Brando makes the poet Marchbanks as believable and as tolerable as he can well be made; and the always delightful Mildred Natwick gets all there is to be got out of the nearly fool-proof role of Miss Prossy. As for Miss Cornell herself, she, it must be remembered, plays one of those characters who is talked about by the others a good deal more than she actually appears on the stage; but she plays her one big crucial scene at the end warmly and humanly, despite the rather staggering task of preventing Candida from becoming an insufferable prig.

It is, I hope, not necessary at this late date to point out the fact that the author's own sympathies are principally on the side of the clergyman husband, and that it is not the claims of romantic passion which are being defended. I was, however, glad to note that this production seemed to make clearer than other productions did one crucial fact: namely, that the "problem" is never seriously a problem to Candida herself or to the audience. Only the husband and the poet ever imagine that they are really rivals. Candida never takes the latter seriously enough as either a person or a point of view to feel for a moment that she is in the presence of a dilemma, and the audience ought to be constantly aware of this fact if the whole is to remain, as it should, a comedy, not a preposterous problem play.

A comedy, I am sure, is what Shaw wanted it to be; and it is also the only thing he could successfully have made it, since he is, of course, incapable of making any passion which rests upon a sensuous foundation real even when he wants it to be. Even as a comedy, "Candida" would be strengthened if Marchbanks, the poet, were a little more convincing. Shaw tries to give him his moments of eloquence, but they always ring false; for here as elsewhere when he hopes that he has achieved some believable expression of physical love, his images are like those of the famous blind poet who described nature—they convince one that he has heard what others say but not that he has ever seen or felt the thing for himself. To say this or anything else about his limitations is, however, to produce much the same effect as is produced by his own criticism of Shakespeare. What he says is often true; but it is concerned only with what Shakespeare isn't, not with what he is—and what he is keeps him a classic.[487]

From "Varieties of Comic Experience"

ERIC BENTLEY

Shaw's *Candida* (1895), one of the best liked of his plays, is about a trite situation. A young man enters the home of a married couple and falls in love with the wife. In the commodity drama of Shaw's day —the Parisian drama of Emile Augier, Dumas *fils*, and Victorien Sardou—there are two ways of dealing with such a situation. The young man can be the hero, the husband can be either a tyrant or a bore or both, and the play can be a protest against bourgeois marriage: an idea for Dumas *fils*. Alternatively the husband can be a genuine pillar of society, the lover a fool or a scoundrel, and the play can end with a vindication of hearth and home and with the discomfiture of the intruder: an idea for Augier.

In the opinion of his audiences Shaw wrote the Augier play. That is why it is so popular. On the surface the titillations of modernity, underneath an utter conventionality: that is what the literati have made out Shaw to be; that is what the public accepts him as. And the Augier play is actually contained within Shaw's. Shaw does show an attractive modern couple upholding the dignity of marriage. The husband of the triangle is such a socialist as everyone can imagine hobnobbing with Shaw himself at meetings of the Fabian society. Against the talented and generous character of this man, the effeminacy of the lover is calculated to excite the contemptuous laughter of any audience. *Candida* audiences go home fairly glowing with the feeling that after all Shaw did the decent thing in the end.

From *The Playwright as Thinker* (New York: Reynal and Hitchcock, 1946), pp. 165–68. Copyright 1946 by Eric Bentley. Reprinted by permission of Harcourt, Brace & World, Inc.

But did he? A moment's thought tells us that the Reverend James Mavor Morell is not what we thought he was. He has been the victim of a life-illusion of Ibsenite proportions: he has thoroughly misunderstood the marriage on which all his boasted confidence and happiness were based. The aesthetic lover, however, whom audiences, congratulating each other on their[165] normality, invariably laugh at, turns out to be stronger than the famous strong man Morell. That, as it proves, is not saying much. Eugene Marchbanks is strong by any standard. He is all the time acquiring that last ability of noble mind, the ability to live without illusions, and at the end he has acquired it. A look through the play will convince the skeptic that Shaw invariably puts the truth in Eugene's mouth and seldom in anybody else's. Even the things that arouse most derision are truths which nobody in the play—or perhaps in the playhouse—shares with Eugene. Shaw, then, pretends to weight the scales in favor of the husband, when actually the lover is the bigger man. Do we then have the Dumas play? Is Eugene the hero, Morell a millstone round his wife's neck? Obviously not. Eugene's superiority leads not to adultery but to his voluntary departure. This aspect of the play preaches, with Schiller and Ibsen, that the strongest man is he who can stand alone.

All this is to judge by the relative weight given to the male rivals in the triangle. It is to reckon without the eponymous heroine. And, since she is indeed an expression of the feminine enigma, she is best left to the last. On the surface Candida seems to be everything to this play: title, leading role, master of the situation. Her charm is so great that no audience would wish to look behind it. Her mastery of people seems so sure that we are not inclined to pry into its nature and its motivation. On the stage psychological backgrounds are obscured by the corporeal presence of actresses.

Ponder Candida's words and actions, however, for two minutes, and the drama of sentiment falls down like a pack of cards. She is expert at keeping the women away from her husband, yet, aware as she is of her own charms, she does not hesitate to flaunt them before an obviously susceptible young man. She denies all suspicion that he is in love with her long after the fact has become evident, and even if she is sincere in this, one cannot find her the more admirable for possessing so large a capacity for self-deception. A feline cruelty drives her to taunt her husband[166] by declaring that she would give herself to Eugene if necessary, while taunting Eugene by pointing to him and histrionically demanding: Do you call *that* a man? She caps her cruelty by a fake climax in which she portentously pretends to choose between the two men. Obviously she could not do anything else with Morell but keep him, especially since her own chief pleasure in life is bossing him around; and by this time it is doubtful whether Eugene would take her anyway. He has learned better. Eugene, however, has the good grace to be sad about it all. Candida, by way of a parting thrust, admits she would not fancy being permanently linked to a man fifteen years her junior.

The play is not Augier, for marriage is not vindicated. On the contrary, now that the scales have fallen from Morell's eyes, this marriage can never be the same again. It is not easy to be reillusioned. When the play is seen in this light, Morell is the protagonist, and the climax is a typically Shavian stripping-off of illusion. At last we have a possible theme for a Shavian play: The Reverend James's Unconversion. Yet we have seen that in another aspect Eugene is the protagonist, indeed the hero, and that Shaw might have named after him a play: The She-Devil's Disciple. This title leads us back to Shaw's secret. Candida, who is not the heroine that she seems, whose problems are not the main subject of the play as the title of it might suggest, is indeed master of the situation, not, as she thinks, in controlling and understanding all that goes on, but in unintentionally, perhaps inadvisedly, curing both men of their illusions about her and their relation to her. It is by her means that the popular parson is unconverted. It is by her means that the poet learns to live without happiness—that is, without women. The subject of the play is the destiny of the two men. Candida, who alone is unchanged at the end, is the link between them.

Is she, then, the villain of the play? To push the argument so far, simply to invert the more obvious interpretations of the play is to be no nearer to the truth than they. Although we have always been told that Shaw is so much a propagandist that[167] all his characters are merely trumpets of Shavian good or anti-Shavian evil, in actual fact Shaw attains to an astonishing, many-sided objectivity. As skillfully as any other dramatic dialectician who has ever written, he can do full justice to thesis and antithesis alike. That is why people find him contradictory and seldom look for a Shavian synthesis. In *Candida* Shaw shows all the truth there is in the Augier philosophy and all the truth there is in the Dumas philosophy. He himself surpasses both—but not with a third dogma, nor even with a new formula—The Heroine as Villain. He surpasses both by the all-roundness of his vision. If Shaw has on occasion praised partisanship, he has also said: "My plays have only one subject: life; and only one attitude: interest in life." Certainly *Candida* is evidence for this claim.

Candida is not simply a bad woman. The sweetness which she pours over the whole play is not the suspect and poisonous sweetness of a she-devil. It is genuine. But it is combined with other, less amiable qualities. Indeed if the whole play has a sweetness and charm such as James Barrie courted all his life without ever fully achieving, it is because sweetness can be relished only in conjunction with a contrary tartness. Barrie, being wholly saccharine, is emetic. *Candida* is the sweeter for not being all sugar. The *Candida* atmosphere—bland yet delicate, graceful yet gay, tender yet ironical—is an emanation of the *Candida* dialectic.[168]

From "Adventures in Success"

WILLIAM IRVINE

To fail with "Mrs. Warren" was one thing, but to fail with "Arms and the Man"—what more could he do? He was driven back again on bare faith in his own excellence. Genius had to perform anew the old miracle of creating in the welter of public mediocrity and indifference an audience educated and intelligent enough to applaud it. He set to work at once and in the same year (1894) produced "Candida," another "pleasant" masterpiece. Wisely eschewing war, property, and revolution, and touching only in the deftest manner on socialism and municipal[173] corruption, Shaw considers the institution of marriage—and actually upholds it, at least with one hand. As "Arms and the Man" is his "pleasantest," "Candida" is his safest, play.

From *The Universe of G. B. S.* (New York: McGraw-Hill Book Company, 1949), pp. 173–78. Copyright 1949 by William Irvine. Reprinted by permission of McGraw-Hill Book Company, Inc.

Essentially, it is Ibsen's "Doll's House" turned upside down. Ibsen had shown that unhappiness results when a husband treats his wife as a doll. Shaw points out that happiness may result when a wife treats her husband as a doll. His Nora sees her husband as he really is—and retains him. In fact, there is a great scene in which Nora, like the Lady from the Sea, chooses between her husband and another man. But even more than it resembles "A Doll's House" and "The Lady from the Sea," "Candida" resembles Shaw's own *Love Among the Artists*. Yet more desperately unmarried and more desperately unsuccessful at thirty-eight, Shaw returns to the same double problem of marriage and genius and essentially the same triangle situation—and turns a crude juvenility into a masterpiece.

Fortunately, "Candida" has so many excellences that it does not need to be understood to be enjoyed. Acted by Janet Achurch at the Independent Theatre, it soon became a success, but it is still, next perhaps to "Major Barbara," the most widely misunderstood of all Shaw's dramas. As late as 1944, Mr. E. R. Bentley regards Candida as a kind of black-widow spider. The best that can be said is that the play is being progressively more ingeniously and acutely misunderstood. The commonest mistake is to regard Candida's choice as genuine and real. As a matter of fact, Shaw has taken pains not to present her with a choice. Eugene could have been twenty-eight; he is eighteen. He could have been Jovian and red-bearded, like Jack Tanner; he is "slight, effeminate, with a delicate childish voice."[1] His grotesque shyness and absurd cowardice are cruelly if comically insisted on to make the audience see that he could not possibly win a hardheaded woman like Candida. So far as the Morell marriage is concerned, Eugene merely precipitates the conflict between husband and wife; he is no more than a catalytic agent in the domestic rearrangement of atoms. For the real action of "Candida" is based on a very old dramatic device: a misunderstanding. In the course of the play, husband and wife come for the first time genuinely to understand each other and their actual relationship.

In the opening scenes we learn a good deal about the Reverend Morell. Toward Prossy and Lexy, he is wise and indulgent; toward Burgess, vigorous and frank. "He is a first rate clergyman, able to say what he likes to whom he likes, to lecture people without setting

---

[1] Shaw, "Candida," *Plays: Pleasant and Unpleasant* (New York: Brentano's, 1910), II: *Pleasant Plays*, 102. [*Candida*, Act I.]

himself up against them, to impose his authority on them without humiliating them."[2] We learn also that he considers his wife the rock and foundation of his happiness. Meanwhile, she has been down in the country with her children for three weeks. Eugene Marchbanks, a young poet and a friend of the[174] family, has been visiting them there. He comes back thoroughly in love with her, and she, with her mind and ideas thoroughly aired out by him. Conceiving love as a romantic ecstasy which has nothing to do with the domesticities of peeling onions and trimming lamps and little to do with the sublunary detail of physical possession, he cannot understand how a woman like Candida can have any feeling for a windbag like James Morell. He tells James so without delay, having first declared his own love. Morell meets this youthful outburst with magnificent condescension and indulgence. And yet he has apparently himself noticed in Candida's attitude toward him something disturbing, which he has always been reluctant to understand. He concludes an oratorical appeal with: "There are so many things to make us doubt, if once we let our understanding be troubled. Even at home, we sit as if in camp, encompassed by a hostile army of doubts. Will you play the traitor and let them in on me?"[3] Eugene certainly does not come to the rescue: "Is it like this for her always? . . . Do you think a woman's soul can live on your talent for preaching?" Slashing about with truths that are quite irrelevant to Candida's marriage, he cuts deep into the clergyman's self-confidence and therefore into the latter's faith in his wife's love. For James's idea of love is as romantically conventional as Eugene's is romantically poetic. It is an honest, money-down, value-received conception. He possesses Candida's love partly because as a pure woman and a good wife she owes it; and much more, because as a husband, father, and provider, he has earned it.

And what kind of woman is Candida? She is, as Shaw says, "unerring wisdom [one might almost say, Benthamite rationalism and detachment] on the domestic plane,"[4] a realist placed between two romantics, whom she regards with maternal indulgence. Hard facts are her specialty, and the great facts in her life are sex and the home. Therefore she trades a little on her good looks and her good figure, and she regards the great world beyond her fireside as somewhat

[2] *Ibid.*, p. 86. [Act. I.]   [3] *Ibid.*, p. 110. [Act I.]
[4] James Huneker, "The Truth about Candida," *Metropolitan Magazine*, XX (1904), 635 [Shaw's letter to Huneker is reprinted in this book on pp. 165–66.]

shadowy and unreal. Moreover, she is herself a woman of strong instincts. Shaw writes that "without brains and strength of mind she would be a wretched slattern or voluptuary."[5] It is significant that she has married a physically powerful and handsome man. The maternal instinct is particularly strong. And here both Shaw and his critics have gone too far. The stage directions and the symbolism of the play indicate that she is to be regarded primarily as the mother-woman. Her maternal indulgence toward the adult male infant is stressed to the point of objectionable omniscience. Granted that she is predominantly maternal in outward manner and psychological attitude; that the maternal manner, in a beautiful and intelligent woman, is charming to most men—and indeed it is often simply a reassuringly innocent disguise for sex—nevertheless, Candida is[175] much more than a schematization of the mother instinct. If, for example, she were attracted to men simply for their weakness, she would be most fascinated by Lexy, who has nothing but weaknesses. Obviously, she loves Morell because he has been, in some respects at least, stronger and wiser than she. It is clearly indicated that he has formed her mind and therefore encouraged her in that freedom from convention which, he recognizes, will cause her to leave him at once if she is not held by love. Here Chesterton's comment is more accurate than the author's own. He finds in the play

the reality of the normal wife's attitude to the normal husband, an attitude which is . . . insanely unselfish and yet quite cynically clear-sighted. . . . She regards him in some strange fashion at once as a warrior who must make his way and as an infant who is sure to lose his way. The man has emotions which exactly correspond; sometimes looking down at his wife and sometimes up at her; for marriage is like a splendid game of seesaw.[6]

But if Candida sincerely admires her husband, why, when she observes his melancholy after the skirmish with Eugene, does she attack him with such sharp and unfeeling gaiety? She assures him that his work does no good, that his parishioners do not mind him the least bit, that he positively abets them in evil by his sermons, which make them feel good without being good. And all the women are in love

[5] *Loc. cit.*
[6] Chesterton, G. K., *George Bernard Shaw*, John Lane, The Bodley Head, Ltd., London, 1909, pp. 121–123. Reprinted by permission of Dodd, Mead and Company, Inc., New York. Copyright, 1909, by Dodd, Mead and Company. [The Chesterton passage is reprinted in this book in an excerpt on pp. 180–83.]

with him. "And you," she adds, "are in love with preaching because you do it so beautifully. And you think it's all enthusiasm for the kingdom of Heaven on earth; and so do they. You dear silly!"[7]

This is all new to James, because it is all new to Candida. She has just got it from Eugene. But why isn't she disturbed by it, both for herself and for her husband? Partly, perhaps, because she feels that a little truth will be good for James's complacency. But much more, because her rational detachment limits her sympathetic insight; she cannot understand why everybody should not relish truth as keenly as she. And finally, because the masculine world outside is not very real: whether James is winning actual or imaginary victories is not extremely important.

She is equally detached in discussing with Morell Eugene's love for her. Will Eugene forgive her for allowing him to learn what love is from a bad woman? "Forgive you for what?" exclaims her husband. For not having taught him herself, of course. Her decision has been the result of a very Benthamite calculation in moral mathematics. She explains to her husband that she is restrained not by her purity or his preaching but by the preponderant claim of her love for him.

In her too confident superiority and her present subservience to Eugene's thought, she has missed all the storm signals. She does not[176] dream that James cannot grasp her combination of steadfast affection with clear-sighted detachment, that he has understood every word in a personal, emotional context. Morell, on the other hand, is convinced that she cannot love him, since she does not love him for his reasons. The misunderstanding is complete. When she approaches him, he waves her off, telling her with anguish in his voice that she must not touch him. From this point on, Shaw manipulates events to forestall any clarification between husband and wife, until Morell, tortured and degraded by uncertainty and suspicion, demands a "choice" between himself and Marchbanks.

This, the great scene of the play, is, as M. Hamon observes, no more than an appearance for Candida but an agonizing reality for the two men. The spectator is also on the very knife-edge of suspense, for he perceives that Candida, having in her turn been disillusioned about James's conception of their marriage, is beside herself with indignation.

---

[7] Shaw, "Candida," *Plays: Pleasant and Unpleasant,* II: *Pleasant Plays,* 129. [*Candida,* Act II.]

"And pray, my lords and masters," she cries, "what have you to offer for my choice? I am up for auction, it seems. What do you bid, James?"[8] His complacency, though badly shaken, is still monumental, and he is still wedded to his illusions. He replies with "proud humility" and magnificently restrained oratory:

I have nothing to offer you but my strength for your defence, my honesty of purpose for your surety, my ability and industry for your livelihood, and my authority and position for your dignity. That is all it becomes a man to offer to a woman.

At length she decides superbly, "I give myself to the weaker of the two,"[9] which is of course Morell. The spectacle of his bewildered suffering, now showing clearly through the polished speaker and the glossy Christian, has changed her anger to sympathy, but the sense of outrage remains. She must set him right, not with Eugene's truths but with those which are fundamental to her self-respect:

Ask James's mother and his three sisters what it cost to save James the trouble of doing anything but be strong and clever and happy. Ask me what it costs to be James's mother and three sisters and wife and mother to his children all in one. . . . I build a castle of comfort and indulgence and love for him, and stand sentinel always to keep little vulgar cares out. I make him master here, though he does not know it.[10]

Candida has been called a prig and Shaw a preacher for this speech. Yet she must have made it, even though the curtain had fallen and the audience, preceding Eugene, had gone out into the night. It is this grave explanation which makes the play a comedy: now we know how it will[177] be with the Morells in the future; we know also that Candida correctly evaluates her husband, for she can afford to tell him his weakness and her strength. Crushing as the outcome has been to his self-confidence, he is at least temporarily humble and grateful. Clearly, his wife believes that he will rise above his humiliating victory and indeed men like Morell, however noble, have an automatic apparatus for manufacturing self-esteem.

"Candida" is also a study of genius in relation to worldly success and happiness. Burgess is bitter satire. He represents the very worst and shabbiest to whom the world permits the prestige of success. Morell, on the other hand, is the very best that the world admires. He has all

[8] *Ibid.*, p. 155. [Act III.]   [9] *Ibid.*, p. 156.   [10] *Ibid.*, pp. 157–158.

the obvious talents and succeeds because he cannot help it. Finally, Eugene is a genius. He has all the obvious weaknesses and will eventually succeed because the world cannot prevent him. In the extremity of defeat and suffering, he rises suddenly to a realization of his destiny, and rejecting the mere happiness of Candida and her husband, goes out into the night, so that at the very close of the play the theme of the loneliness and self-sufficiency of genius surges up to dominance. Admirably effective as a dramatic instrument, Eugene is psychologically the least satisfactory character in "Candida." As a lover he is, as Chesterton observes, too turgid in his speeches and too finicky about onions. As a genius, he is perhaps too much Shelley made over to fit the definition of a Shavian realist. He "dares to love and trust" and at the same time sees facts without illusion. In so far he tends to inconsistency.

In the late nineteenth century, romantic genius divided into two species: the aesthete who retreated from the world and the superman who conquered it. In "Candida," Shaw has portrayed the first. In "The Man of Destiny," which follows, he portrays the second.[178]

"Candida"

EDMUND FULLER

The next play, *Candida*, was particularly dear to its author's heart. I find it of special interest, in relation both to Shaw and to his audiences. It is probable that *Candida* has long enjoyed and still enjoys a popular rank in the Shaw repertory second only to[25] *Saint Joan*. I have heard a number of persons carp and criticize on the subject of Shaw; decry his public antics; denounce his political thesis; label him overrated and charge that the plays are not plays but tracts, peopled by nothing resembling flesh and blood but by an assortment of Shavian mouthpieces; and wind up, as if in concession to the mystery of his reputation, by adding, "Ah . . . but *Candida!*"

Now *Candida* confronts us with the case of the Reverend James

From *George Bernard Shaw: Critic of Western Morale* (New York: Charles Scribner's Sons, 1950), pp. 25–29. Reprinted with the permission of Charles Scribner's Sons. Copyright 1950 Charles Scribner's Sons.

Mavor Morell, hearty and forthright, a vigorous, uncorrupted, unintimidated Christian Socialist clergyman possessing what would still pass as a broad view of life. He is married to the handsome, self-possessed Candida, the apple of his eye, and regards their relationship as pretty close to the ideal marriage. Into their household comes the dreamy poet, Marchbanks, eighteen years of age as against Candida's thirty-three and Morell's forty. Shaw sees him as "so entirely uncommon as to be almost unearthly; and to prosaic people there is something noxious in this unearthliness, just as to poetic people there is something angelic in it."

Marchbanks declares himself in love with Candida and denounces Morell to his face as a heavy-handed clod, a windbag with the gift of gab, capable of grappling with nothing above the level of sordid realities and speaking only in a jargon of revolting clichés and mediocre sentiments. In addition to which he is manifestly a beast for sullying Candida with such appallingly unfitting tasks as peeling onions and otherwise running a household.

Candida, for reasons I have never been able to ascertain either by reading or witnessing the play, forces the two men into an unhappy contest. With a sublime conceit she demands that each state what he can offer. Morell offers his strength and honesty, his ability and industry, his authority and position. Marchbanks offers: "My weakness! my desolation! my heart's need!"

Whereupon Candida, announcing, "I give myself to the weaker of the two," sends Marchbanks packing with the famous admonition to console himself with the words: "When I am thirty, she will be forty-five. When I am sixty, she will be seventy-five."[26]

Now I propose a great heresy about *Candida*—namely, that it is first-rate theatrical balderdash, as hopelessly romantic as anything against which Shaw ever inveighed for the same sin. He believed in it, indeed. It symbolized for him the inarticulate and consequently ineffective groping of genius toward perceptions transcending the advanced idealism then current. "Here, then, was the higher, but vaguer, timider vision, and the incoherent, mischievous, and even ridiculous, unpracticalness, which offered me a dramatic antagonist for the clear, bold, sure, sensible, benevolent, salutarily shortsighted Christian Socialist idealism."[1]

---

[1] [Preface (1898) to *Pleasant Plays;* reprinted in this book on pp. 91–94.]

But it miscarried. The latter element in the conflict is beautifully realized, for Morell appears in a wonderfully subtle blend of strength with weakness, of vision with blindness. But with Marchbanks, and for that matter with Candida, he lost his grip and sentimentalized to the destruction of his purpose, a charge he probably would not admit even today.

The major weakness is the overdrawn conception of Marchbanks, a role that has caused every ambitious juvenile, and many a super-annuated one, to drool for years. Mansfield put it into rehearsal and then, quite sensibly as an earthly and middle-aged actor, dropped it like a hot potato.

I find myself, presumably in a minority among Shaw enthusiasts, one of the prosaic people to whom Marchbanks is utterly noxious. He is so overdrawn that the "conflict" with Morell loses any convincing semblance of reality. Hence, except on the most sentimentally roman-tic premise, the young poet is insignificant and Candida herself becomes no more than an idle and vain woman with nothing better to do than embarrass a busy husband by cradle-snatching. This extreme view commended itself to prim Beatrice Webb, who asserted that Candida was "simply a woman of bad character."

The conflict between the practical "advanced person" of the moment and the impractical one who has caught a prevision of ad-vanced positions of the future could have been established on a much less exaggerated basis than Marchbanks represents. What, if anything, he perceives is lost in the waves of sentiment that engulf him.[27]

When *Candida* was still a fresh creation Shaw revealed his feelings about it in a series of comments occurring in his letters to Ellen Terry. They are a dead give-away, and it is interesting to see the stress he puts upon the play, contrasted to its avowed didactic thesis.

Sending her the script of his one-acter, *The Man of Destiny*, he observes, "This is not one of my great plays, you must know: it is only a display of my knowledge of stage tricks—a commercial travel-ler's sample. You would like my Candida much better; but I never let people read that: I always read it to them. They can be heard sob-bing three streets off." How the Irishman had run away with the craftsman!

Again, ". . . one does not get tired of adoring the Virgin Mother. Bless me! you will say, the man is a Roman Catholic. Not at all: the man is the author of Candida; and Candida, between you and me, is the Virgin Mother and nobody else."

Again, "It is all very well for you to say that you want a Mother Play; but why didn't you tell me that in time? I *have* written THE Mother Play—Candida—and I cannot repeat a masterpiece."

Very soon after, under the spell of new work, the craftsman has regained control of the Irishman and he reports, "Candida doesn't matter. I begin to think it an overrated play. . . ." And three years later, appalled at Ellen Terry's failure to grasp the worth of the role created for her (Lady Cicely Waynflete, in *Captain Brassbound's Conversion*), he says, "Here you get far beyond Candida, with her boy and her parson, and her suspicion of trading a little on the softness of her contours. . . ."[2]

So perhaps he wrote the play first and invented its meaning afterward. It is a strange product to accompany the declaration of his "conception of romance as the great heresy to be rooted out from art and life—as the root of modern pessimism and the bane of modern self-respect." The "mother play" stress is stranger still, for the whole "wife-mother" theme, much worked over in our time, is a lavishly romanticized concept anyway, even though the phenomenon exists. All romantic phenomena exist, for that matter. Shaw may have contracted the bug from Ibsen[28] (Solveig, in *Peer Gynt*) with whom it is something of an anomaly, too.

Candida has the same romantic weakness as *Cyrano de Bergerac*, also a good piece of theatricality. It tries to build a solid drama on a wholly artificial premise. The esteem in which the play has come to be held is an esteem that Rostand would have welcomed but that is irrelevant for Shaw. That is why those who despise and reject the main body of Shaw's work and its incorporated thesis often will seek eagerly to advance *Candida* as one of Shaw's *real* achievements. With her they are safe.[29]

---

[2] [Excerpts from these and other Shaw-Terry letters are reprinted in this book on pp. 87–91.]

"The Truth about Candida"

A. H. NETHERCOT

The neatest and most concrete specimens of the three types[1] to be found in a single play occur in *Candida*. Indeed, it seems as if this favorite Shavian comedy, written in 1894, must almost have been composed with *The Quintessence* open at the author's elbow, so closely do its chief characters fit into the previously worked out formula.[2]

When Archibald Henderson wrote in both his books on Shaw that a fitting sub-title for *Candida* would be "A Mystery," he was not thinking so much of the famous but ambiguous "secret in the poet's heart" as he was of the motivation and interpretation of the characters as a whole. For of course the tantalizing "secret" is embedded only in the final stage direction and would therefore not challenge the spectator for solution; but the problem of the meaning of the characters and their relationships forms the backbone of the whole play, whether read or seen. Perhaps the fact that for years critic after critic, reader after reader, spectator after spectator have interpreted Candida, Morell, and Marchbanks according to their own[7] temperaments and predilections may help to explain why the play, like the similarly enigmatic *Hamlet* of Shaw's self-selected arch-rival, has proved to be one of the most popular in the repertoire. To judge from most of

[1] [In his preceding paragraphs Professor Nethercot has presented Shaw's own classification of society on the basis of its attitude toward marriage and the family (Chapter II of *The Quintessence of Ibsenism*). Shaw claims that three basic types of human beings—Philistine, idealist, realist—compose society and that in any cross-section of a thousand persons there are 700 Philistines, 299 idealists, and one realist. Shaw's chapter is reprinted in this book on pp. 73–79.]
[2] [The following discussion is a revision and expansion of Professor Nethercot's article, "The Truth about Candida," in the *Publications of the Modern Language Association* (*PMLA*) for September, 1949.]

the printed comments on Shaw's play, and particularly on its heroine, it still remains a mystery. At least, there is little agreement as to its interpretation.

To Duffin Candida is "a Shavian intellectual woman, full-fledged, not an Ibsenite womanly woman on the point of being re-born"; and she has a mind "almost as free from conventionality as Marchbanks' own."[3] As for Marchbanks, "Every one of the screens that commonly stand between man's eyes and naked reality is down . . . : orthodoxy, morality, convention, respectability, good form, duty . . . He has achieved that acme of immorality—abhorred of the Philistine—irresponsibility." And to Duffin the Philistine is Candida's "great baby" of a husband, the Rev. James Mavor Morell, so unlike his wife in almost every respect. So, he says, a "far more natural and powerful reciprocal attraction draws Candida and Marchbanks to-gether," for "their reaction to life is alike vital, joyous, real." For Duffin it is hard to understand how any real sympathy, "except of an unsubstantial emotional sort," can exist between Candida and her husband.

On the other hand, Hamon announces dogmatically: "Candida is commonplace from the intellectual point of view, but has a great soul, is eminently intuitive, reading others' minds, and seeing things naked, just as they are in their pure reality." To Hamon, Morell "symbolizes Christian Socialist idealism, and is clear-sighted, bold, sure of him-self, sensible," but "a man who takes short views." Marchbanks "sym-bolizes poetic idealism," but is "vague and confused in his mind." His love for Candida is "ideal, romantic, and ethereal," and both he and Morell suffer in their loves. But in Candida herself "there is no in-ternal struggle." Although "she is a realist . . . , freed from all conven-tions," she "stays with her husband because she loves him, and not Eugene." For she is also "the mother-woman . . . , the creature of her own natural physiological function, motherhood."

To Henderson, although, as he says, Shaw's "maternal heroine is compact of candor and sympathy," she is scarcely capable of divining what is really going on in Marchbanks' heart. In fact, commonsensical and unscrupulous as she is, she is really lying—or at least deceiving herself—when she tricks the two men into believing that she chooses Morell because he is the weaker of the two. Love alone "dictates her

---

[3] [Duffin's interpretation and most of the others summarized in this selection are reprinted in this book in the three sections: "The Critics (1895–1960)."]

course," although she sees the chance to educate Marchbanks a bit in the process.

Frank Harris goes even beyond Duffin, Hamon, and Henderson in his admiration for the play, which to him is Shaw's greatest and maturest work—"a vital, powerful, humane, and perfectly charming play." Yet Harris (or perhaps his ghost-writer, Frank Scully, who claims to have really written most of the Shaw biography) sums up the meaning of the play by[8] asserting that Morell "hasn't the least inkling that Candida possesses a soul, that she yearns for understanding, for someone to share her idealist dreams and longings. So little conception, indeed, has her husband of his wife's mind and heart, that he closes his offer by saying, self-confident in his manly philistinism: 'That is all it becomes a man to offer a woman.' "

To William Irvine (whose *The Universe of G.B.S.* is the best all-around critical biography of Shaw), Candida is "a realist placed between two romantics, whom she regards with maternal indulgence"; she is, "we might almost say, Benthamite rationalism and detachment" on the "domestic plane." And he quotes with approval G. K. Chesterton's conclusion, as "more accurate than the author's own." For G. K. C. found in the play "the reality of the normal wife's attitude toward the normal husband, an attitude which is . . . insanely unselfish and yet quite cynically clearsighted . . . She regards him in some strange fashion at once as a warrior who must make his way and as an infant who is sure to lose his way."

Preening himself on his unorthodoxy, Edmund Fuller, in his rather elementary and generally imperceptive *George Bernard Shaw: Critic of Western Morale*, proposes "a great heresy about *Candida*— namely, that it is first-rate theatrical balderdash, as hopelessly romantic as anything against which Shaw ever inveighed for the same sin," and summarizes the theme of the play as symbolizing in Marchbanks "the inarticulate and consequently ineffective groping of genius toward perceptions transcending the advanced idealism then current." If the poet really perceives anything, he concludes, it "is lost in the waves of sentiment that engulf him."

As two final specimens of how the critics fall out when considering *Candida*, there are James Huneker and Eric Bentley, among the earliest and the latest of Shaw's enthusiastic missionaries in America. To Huneker in his essay on *Candida* Candida is "a womanly woman," standing "on her solid, sensible underpinnings," and Marchbanks is a "thin-skinned idealist." But Bentley (as anyone knowing Bentley might expect) takes quite a different line in his *Bernard Shaw*. To him Morell represents the person who becomes "utterly disillusioned." Marchbanks represents the one who becomes " 'educated' in the sense of being enabled to see that his true nature is not what he thought it was," and Candida represents the one who "operates as a catalyst . . . , effecting change without being changed . . . ."

Out of all this contradictory welter of intuitive women, intellectual women, womanly women, and mother-women, realists, idealists, and Philistines, disillusioned people, educated people, romanticists, Benthamites, and catalysts, can any truth be distilled or extracted? When one critic labels as a realist a character whom another critic has labeled an idealist, and still another critic labels as an idealist another character whom another critic has labeled a Philistine, who is crazy—the critics, the author, or the audience? What *is* the truth about *Candida* the play and Candida the woman? [9]

I myself have seen and enjoyed such professional actresses as Katherine Cornell and Cornelia Otis Skinner, as well as various amateurs, in the role of Shaw's most admired comedic heroine. I have watched the women in the audience wipe their eyes unashamedly and heard the men sigh secretively over their idol of womanly perfection. And yet I am confident that if the actresses had acted the part as Shaw wrote it and that if the audiences had known Shaw's real opinion of Candida there would have been hisses and boos instead. For there is no doubt that Shaw himself intended his three leading characters to represent, primarily, Marchbanks as the developing realist, Morell as the wavering idealist, and Candida—how disillusioning this will be to the romanticists!—as the static Philistine.

In the chapter on "Ideals and Idealists" in *The Quintessence*, Shaw had analyzed his cross-section of a thousand persons on the basis of their attitude toward marriage and the family, which of course is the prime theme of *Candida*. The Philistines are those who "find the British family arrangement quite good enough for them"; they "comfortably accept marriage as a matter of course," never dreaming of calling it an "institution," either "holy" or otherwise, and thrive happily within it. The idealists realize that marriage, for plenty of those involved in it, is a failure, but do not have the courage to face that fact, and therefore go to all sorts of excessive extremes to defend the "ideal" which for them masks the face of the truth. The isolated realist is the individual "strong enough to face the truth the idealists are shirking"—the man who insists on tearing off the masks and revealing the illusions beneath. And in each case, as already shown, Shaw discusses in detail the characteristic behavior of each type.

Candida, Morell, and Marchbanks all behave in almost perfect conformity with the Shavian formula for their types. Candida is one of the "satisfied ones." As Henderson has acutely observed, there is some doubt of the validity of her advanced principles when judged in the light of her conduct. When she announces to her husband that she would give her "goodness and purity" to poor Marchbanks as willingly as she would give her shawl to a beggar dying of cold, if there were nothing else to restrain her, she knows perfectly well that she is risking nothing, since she will always be restrained by her love of her home and family. As to the way in which the Philistines, according to *The Quintessence*, coerce the idealists "into conformity with the marriage law," recall the way in which Candida's father, Burgess, another Philistine, though of a much coarser brand, a vulgar, materialistic, sharp but naively sincere "old scoundrel," as Morell calls him, brutally reminds the infatuated Prossy, Morell's secretary, that her recent predecessor was "young-er,"—a characteristic which Shaw himself later remarked was sufficient reason for Candida's cannily getting rid of her. Candida has her father's shrewdness, but has refined it in her womanly way. Most of Candida's critics, moreover, promptly admit that she has no[10] ideals, in the Shavian sense. As for her attitude toward art, everyone will recall how she practically hypnotizes herself by gazing at the poker while Marchbanks is absorbed in reading his poetry to her, and how, when awakened to herself, she confesses candidly, "Those sonnets of yours have perfectly addled me." Likewise, when Shaw gives his first affectionate description of his heroine in his stage directions, he emphasizes that when Marchbanks gave the family a large reproduction of Titian's Virgin of the Assumption he "did so because he fancied some spiritual resemblance between" the picture and Candida, and yet, says Shaw, the "wise-hearted observer . . . would not suspect either her husband or herself of any such idea, or indeed of any concern with the art of Titian." Nor is this basic inartisticality in any fundamental contradiction to Burgess's early remark: "I allus had a turn for a bit of poetry. Candy takes arter me that-a-way: huse ter make me tell her fairy stories when she was on'y a little kiddy not that 'igh!" For if Candida's taste in poetry and fairy stories takes after her father's she obviously has no taste at all. It is merely a case of like father, like daughter. No, Candida's concern is with her husband, her two children (who never appear on the stage), her cook, her scrubbrush, her lamp chimneys and paraffin oil, and her red onions. When Morell returns ebulliently from his speech before the Guild of St. Matthew, her main question is, "How much was the collection?"

As for the conflict between the idealist and the realist, so graphically described by Shaw in *The Quintessence*, when the realist insists on shouting from the housetops that marriage is a failure for many people and that its compulsory character ought therefore to be abolished, here, with a slight allowance for the habit of Shavian exaggeration, is a neat picture of the relations among the three main characters in *Candida*—even to Morell the idealist's appealing against Marchbanks the realist to Candida the Philistine, and in his fear actually grasping Marchbanks threateningly by his coat lapel preparatory to making a bodily attack on him. Another of Shaw's tips as to the identifying traits of a Philistine is that when the realist cries out the truth about a great deal of family life the idealist will react against him in the violent fashion previously described, but "The Philistine will simply think him mad." One of the surest laughgetters in *Candida* is the series of passages in which Prossy, shocked by the startling things Marchbanks has said to her about love, informs Burgess that the poet is mad, and Burgess agrees with her. Burgess has already informed Marchbanks sotto voce that Morell is "mad as a 'atter," for Morell has told his father-in-law some realistic home truths about the latter's methods as an employer of labor. When Lexy Mill, the curate, succumbs to the epidemic and announces his fear that Prossy "is a little out of her mind sometimes," Burgess is "overwhelmed," as well he might be. But the remarks draw attention to Burgess, Prossy, and Lexy as minor Philistines in the play.[11]

And how does Morell finally react after the poet has jeered at his illusions that his marriage is a happy one and that such an unearthy angel as Candida (for through much of the play Eugene too has his idealistic illusions so far as she is concerned) could love such a fool and windbag as her husband even if he is wellmeaning? First, Morell exclaims pathetically, "Marchbanks: some devil is putting these words into your mouth. It is easy—terribly easy—to shake a man's faith in himself. To take advantage of that to break a man's spirit is devil's work. Take care of what you are doing. Take care." But when the poet persists in his revelations, the preacher pleads, with a new display of his forensic powers, "In the future—when you are as happy as I am—I will be your true brother in the faith . . . I will help you to believe that every stroke of your work is sowing happiness for the great harvest that all—even the humblest—shall one day reap. And last, but trust me, not least, I will help you to believe that your wife loves you and is happy in her home. We need such help, Marchbanks: we need it greatly and always. There are so many things to make us doubt, if once we let our understanding be troubled. Even at home, we sit as if in a camp, encompassed by a hostile army of doubts. Will you play the traitor and let them in on me?" This sounds suspiciously as if Morell were a member of those "prostitute classes" whom Shaw pillories in the preface to his *Unpleasant Plays* as professional people "who are daily using their highest faculties to belie their real sentiments." Yet Shaw also had a qualified good word to say for the Rev. James some years later in the preface to *Getting Married:* "What an honorable and sensible man does when his household is invaded is what the Rev. James Mavor Morell does in my play . . . He is so far shrewdly unconventional as to recognize that if she chooses the other man, he must give way, legal tie or no legal tie; but he knows that either one or the other must go. And a sensible wife would act in the same way." In a real marriage of sentiment there should be no false shame of seeming conventional in facing the situation.

On the other hand, to revert to the play itself, Candida's innocently cruel and piercing remarks about her husband as her "boy . . . spoiled from his cradle," her ruthless analysis of the reasons the women flock to his services and meetings, her disconcerting appraisal of the actual ineffectiveness of his Sunday sermons—all of which make even Eugene cry out against her insensitiveness to Morell's suffering—have obviously cut deep into the clergyman's self-esteem and confidence in his marriage. But in spite of all sympathy, pleas, and confessions, Marchbanks will have none of Morell's "metaphors, sermons, stale perorations" and pushes forcibly through to a show-down between his ideas and his opponent's. As he says over and over again to Morell, Candida, and Prossy, he wants to get at their "real" selves, he wants "real" answers, but nobody will give him the truth. It is not for nothing that in this chapter in *The Quintessence* Shaw continues to[12] cite Shelley as a specimen of what he calls a realist and the world generally calls an idealist, and that in the early productions of *Candida* in the late nineties Marchbanks was made up to look like Shelley, "femininely hectic and timid and fierce," as Oliver Elton, quoted by Henderson, put it in a review of 1898.

The famous scene in which Candida makes her choice between her two men bears a strong resemblance to a similar scene in Ibsen's *The Lady from the Sea*, which Shaw had interpreted at some length in *The Quintessence*. Here Ellida corresponds to Candida; the sailor who mystically claims her as his wife and wants to draw her away to the sea with him corresponds to Eugene; and the respectable doctor who has married her corresponds to Morell. When the seaman assures her of her own free will and freedom to choose, and her husband "drops his prate about his heavy responsibility for her actions," she decides without any hesitation to stick with her housekeeping. Candida, like Ellida, wishes to "belong to herself," first of all, but she never really appreciates her husband's mental sufferings or his moral courage in going through with the showdown with Eugene. Her "wise-hearted maternal humor" helps her to carry off her domestic crisis with skill and a little pathos, but she has remained essentially impervious to the tremendous tensions which have encircled her. She is the one who at the end announces Shaw's favorite lesson that Eugene has "learnt to live without happiness," but when she and her husband turn to embrace one another after Eugene's flight into the night, Shaw ends his play by reminding his readers what his audiences could only guess: "But they do not know the secret in the poet's heart." The secret, as we shall see, is that Eugene has lost his illusions about Candida—that is, he has lost his ideals. He has become a realist.

So the evidence in *The Quintessence* and in the play itself as to the classification of the main character types matches very accurately. But there is further and even more definite evidence to confirm these conclusions in the later comments of Shaw and his friends on his play. He himself emphasized the "mother incarnate" quality in Candida in his stage directions, and in a letter to Ellen Terry once confided, "Candida, between you and me, is the Virgin Mother and nobody else." In fact, he wrote a whole series of letters to Miss Terry between 1896 and 1899, in which he made it quite clear that he had had her definitely in mind in creating Candida, and suggested that she could therefore scarcely be so ungenerous as to refuse to play the role. He even went so far in pointing the parallel as to assert that she and Janet Achurch were the only two women he had ever met "whose ideal of voluptuous delight was that life should be one long confinement from the cradle to the grave." Candida's instinctive and unscrupulous method of managing people by "engaging their affections" was always his affectionate diagnosis of Terry's character. And when he finally[13] really sent her the manuscript and she read it, she wrote by return mail on October 19, 1896: "I've cried my poor eyes out over your horrid play, your *heavenly* play . . . It has touched me more than I could tell of." When Terry was touched (and it was not a hard thing to do), she really melted. Yet Shaw's equally close but less romantic friend Beatrice Webb, as Shaw promptly informed Terry, had called Candida bluntly "a sentimental prostitute"—probably thinking of the way in which she draws Eugene on to make love to her, knowing all the time that she is arousing his passion only to tantalize him. Terry was left almost speechless. All she could get her pen to trace was an underscored *"Well!"* In spite of her disapproval, however, in another letter to her in 1899, Shaw repeated that even in this mother play, as in most of his plays, he had "prostituted the actress more or less by making the interest in her partly a sexual interest." He left Candida tottering on her pedestal by referring to her wryly as "Candida, with her boy and her parson, and her suspicion of trading a little on the softness of her contours . . ."

More significant, however, is the way in which Shaw describes his comedy's dramatic conflict in the preface which he wrote for his volume of *Pleasant Plays.* "Here, then," he writes, "was the higher, but vaguer, timider vision, and the incoherent, mischievous, and even ridiculous, unpracticalness, which offered me a dramatic antagonist for the clear, bold, sure, sensible, benevolent, salutarily shortsighted Christian Socialist idealism." The "higher vision," with all its weaknesses, must go to the realist, Marchbanks, in spite of his earlier false ideals about Candida; the "benevolent . . . shortsighted Christian Socialist idealism" must obviously go to Morell, who, the commentators inform us, was modeled on the ex-clergyman Socialist litterateur, Stopford Brooke (whom Shaw had known in the Bedford debating society), seasoned, thinks Rattray, with dashes of Fleming Williams and Canon Shuttleworth. It was apparently a characteristic of Christian Socialist clergymen of the Guild of St. Matthew to indulge in emotional humanitarianism and sentimental sermons, if one can judge by

Shaw's review of Wilkie Collins's *The New Magdalen* in 1895.

With Marchbanks as the realist and Morell as the idealist, what is there left for Candida to be but the Philistine? If it be asked why we have to have a Philistine in the play at all, here is how Shaw himself dissected his heroine in a letter he wrote to Huneker in 1904 in explanation of his play, which Arnold Daly's production had at last made the hit of the New York season: [4]

. . . . . [14]

. . . Shaw's implication that when he first wrote his play he was not fully conscious of all its overtones and inner meanings is not a confession of weakness on his part but is in complete harmony with his theory of artistic inspiration. In fact in his own somewhat unorthodox interpretation of Wagner's Ring cycle in *The Perfect Wagnerite*, he quoted Wagner himself on the subject: "How can an artist expect that what he has felt intuitively should be perfectly realized by others, seeing that he himself feels in the presence of his work, if it is true Art, that he is confronted by a riddle about which he, too, might have illusions, just as another might?" And Shaw explained further that by "true Art" Wagner meant "the operation of the artist's instinct, which is just as blind as any other instinct." He had said much the same thing several years before in defending his elucidation of Ibsen. Nevertheless, even though admitting that the artist himself might not always realize the full meaning of his work, Shaw insisted in his articles on stage production for *The Saturday Review* that the first obligation of both the manager and the actor is to fulfill the intentions of the playwright, as shown in his explanations and directions.

In his *Sixteen Self Sketches*, in setting Duffin right on certain[15] interpretative guesses about Eugene's "secret," Shaw corroborates his letter to Huneker when he reiterates that his meaning is that "the domestic life is not a poet's destiny: 'life is nobler than that.' The starry night, and not the cosy room with the paraffin lamp, is the place for him." Duffin's alternative explanation, that Marchbanks is confident that sooner or later Candida will come to him, is, cries Shaw, "wildly silly." Irvine, seeing *Love Among the Artists* as "an early attempt at a 'Candida,'" draws the "secret" from both of them "that artists do not need love."

---

[4] [Shaw's letter to Huneker is reprinted in this book on pp. 165–66.]

This realistic and disillusioning approach to the character of Mrs. Candida Burgess Morell by her creator has remained almost unknown, though Huneker, after printing it in an article in *The Metropolitan Magazine* in 1904, preserved it in his *Iconoclasts* in 1905. Moreover, most of those who remember it wish that Shaw had never written it. Its sardonic analysis has proved much too astringent for them. That clever sentimental sham and perverse liar, Frank Harris, in his biography not only suppresses the most important part of the letter but has the effrontery to claim that the bit he quotes was part of an argument *he* once had with Shaw in which he defended Candida against her author as being "as vital in conception and as powerful and moving in execution as the best of the English classics." Even the generally straight-visioned Henderson turns sentimentalist in the presence of this "maternal heroine" who is so "compact of candor and sympathy," as he puts it in the second version of his biography, where he reduces the letter to one sentence. Yet in the first version he had printed the letter whole, but had cried out pathetically to his readers: "with Shaw's own dissection of his greatest play, I find it quite impossible to sympathize or agree." Searching desperately for some way of salvaging his heroine-worship, he comes up with this lame explanation: "Shaw seems merely to be taking a fling at the 'Candidamaniacs,' as he called the play's admirers; his 'analysis' strikes me as a batch of Shavian half-truths, rather than a fair estimate of the play's true significance." Still sore and sensitive when he wrote his second version, Henderson referred to "the credulous Huneker," apparently forgetting that Shaw himself had chosen Huneker to edit the two volumes of Shavian theatrical criticism, *Dramatic Opinions and Essays*, in 1907, in spite of the fact that in the preface to *The Irrational Knot* he had referred to his American friend as "a man of gorgeous imagination and incorrigible romanticism." Only Eric Bentley in *The Playwright as Thinker* is bold enough to reprint the letter entire and to remark, "This analysis is at many points in accord with mine, at some points not." At the latter points, in fact, he would go even beyond Shaw, and even suggests that the play might have been named *The She-Devil's Disciple*. At this juncture, however, Bentley's temerity and iconoclasm prove too much even for himself, and he also yields to Candida's essential charm. "The sweetness which she pours over the whole play," he concedes, "is not the suspect and[16] poisonous sweetness of a she-devil. It is genuine," even though "it is combined with other, less amiable qualities . . . *Candida* is the sweeter for not being all sugar."

When the Shavian dramatis personae are considered as a whole, it will become apparent that Candida does not stand alone, but that she is actually only one of the most conspicuous and successful representatives of certain of Shaw's chief character classifications. Primarily she is both the mother-woman and the Philistine. Perhaps, too, there is a dash in her of the womanly woman. My guess is also that in her younger days she would have qualified as a specimen of woman as the pursuer. She might almost be described as an Ann Whitefield at a later stage in Ann's career. Many of Shaw's most lovable and "vital" heroines (a favorite epithet of his) fall into these categories. In fact, he implies over and over again that, from this point of view, the perfect wife and mother is practically always a Philistine, plus. Once or twice, as in the case of Jennifer Dubedat from *The Doctor's Dilemma*, she may be an idealist. But never, never can she be a realist.

Finally, let me admit freely that Shaw too has clearly fallen in love with Candida [5]—which only goes to show that it is possible for a man who prides himself on being a realist and even a cynic to fall in love with a Philistine and admire her for the good qualities she has while forgetting those she has not. Shaw was obviously using Prossy as his interpreter when he had her remark, at the very outset of the play, before the audience has yet met its heroine: "It's enough to drive anyone out of their senses to hear a perfectly commonplace woman raved about in that absurd manner merely because she's got good hair, and a tolerable figure . . . She's very nice, very good-hearted: I'm very fond of her and can appreciate her real qualities far better than any man can." The critics have all blindly overlooked the fact that the rest of the characters in the cast, on whose reactions they have based their opinions, are all men.

That is the whole truth about the chief characters in *Candida*. But offering it has anticipated, only for purposes of preliminary illustration, the presentation of the full and varied series of Philistines, idealists, and realists in the Shavian portrait gallery. [17]

---

[5] Irvine even suggests that the ménage à trois in the play may reflect the situation in which Shaw fell temporarily in love with May Morris, the daughter of one fellow Socialist, William Morris, and the wife of another, Henry Halliday Sparling. [Irvine's suggestion is reprinted in this book on pp. 160–61.]

From "Pleasant Plays"

ARCHIBALD HENDERSON

I think that, in writing his next play, Shaw consciously disciplined his wit and tried hard to write a true drama that would genuinely *move* an audience. The successor to *Arms and the Man,* probably Shaw's most perfect piece from the technical standpoint, meets all the classic tests and has achieved international vogue. *Candida* is a penetrating psychological observation upon the emotional reverberations in the souls of three clearly imagined, exquisitely realized characters. The character of Marchbanks (aside from its association with a phase in Shaw's own development) might have been linked with the name of Shelley or with some leading poet (say William Butler Yeats) in the Keltic Renascence. Candida dramatically portrays the conflict between prose convention and poetic anarchy, mirroring that conflict of human wills so essential to authentic drama.

Candida is a little domestic drama, scarcely more than a "scene from private life." Abounding in scenes and situations tense with emotional and dramatic power, it is stamped with the finish and restraint of great art. The characters in this play, so chameleonic in its changing lustres, at every instant turn toward the light new facets of their nature. We catch the iridescent and ever-varying tints of life; and over all is a sparkle of fine and subtle humor, lightening the tension of soul-conflicts with touches of homely veracity. The "auction scene" of the third act, which has a curious parallel in *The Lady from the Sea,* though both were independently conceived, affords the fullest display for Shaw's unexcelled talents as advocate and dialectician. Beneath the glib argumentation lies a texture of deep emotion. Actions,

From *George Bernard Shaw: Man of the Century* (New York: Appleton-Century-Crofts, Inc., 1956), pp. 543–45. Reprinted by permission of Appleton-Century-Crofts Trade Book Division. Copyright 1932 by D. Appleton & Co. Copyright 1956 by Archibald Henderson.

especially in sex relationships, are not governed by the dictates of pure reason. The auction scene is the true obligatory scene; and is a fine example of that thinking aloud the language of the subconscious, since made so notable by Eugene O'Neill's *Desire under the Elms* and *Strange Interlude*.[1]

One day in the late nineties, Shaw called upon Charles Wyndham at his popular theatre, the Criterion, to interest him in *Candida*, which he claimed was written, like most of his plays, on the tops of omnibuses. In declining the play, Wyndham assured Shaw that *Candida* was extraordinarily advanced in thought. Taking a curtain call at the performance of *Candida* by the London Stage Society, July 1, 1900, Shaw triumphantly asserted: "When I read the play to Wyndham, he said that it was twenty years too soon. You have given the contradiction to that statement." He always called it his Virgin Mother play; and half a century ago it was a veritable "tear-jerker." Ellen Terry boohooed over the play, at a first reading; and William Archer, torn between laughter and tears, became hysterical from merely reading it; and even[543] Wyndham shed tears over the last act. Whenever Shaw read it, with all the stops pulled out, to a group of friends, he claimed that they could be "heard sobbing three streets off."

It was obviously influenced by *A Doll's House*, but in reverse. Shaw disclaimed any indebtedness to Ibsen; and it was not until he

---

[1] [In his earlier biography, *Bernard Shaw: Playboy and Prophet* (New York: D. Appleton & Co., 1932), pp. 478, 480, Professor Henderson included the following analysis of Candida and the poet's secret. It is reprinted here by permission of Appleton-Century-Crofts, Inc.]

A fitting sub-title for *Candida* is: a Mystery. This play has mystified would-be interpreters without number. The critics who imagine that Candida "chooses" her husband *because* he is the weaker are wide of the mark. Love dictates her choice. She is bound by none of the conventional grounds for fidelity. She would "choose" Marchbanks without scruple if love bade. Sensing the growing love of the callow young poet and sympathizing with his infatuation, she "seduces" him into worshipful avowals, so that she may bring common sense to bear and show him that love is not the inevitable reward for the higher logic. And Marchbanks, deluded into the belief that Candida has chosen Morell because he is the weaker, reacts in a mood of noble scorn for such cheap, fireside joys. *His* love soars far above the unideal place of Burgess—or is it *bourgeois?*—respectability. In the instant of the Shavian discovery that service, not happiness, is life's higher aim, he passes from youth to manhood. This, indeed, is the "secret in the poet's heart"—else the golden-winged god of dreams shrivels to a pitiful shape of egoism. The names in the play are suggestive: Morell, Burgess, Mill, Prossy, Candida. The maternal heroine is compact of candor and[478] sympathy; but perhaps she scarcely divines the secret in the poet's heart. We never fully understand others. Everyone is hemmed in by the limitations of his own nature.[480]

was eighty that he revealed this particular secret. In a Note to the production in London, with the beautiful American film star, Ann Harding, as Candida, Shaw confesses: "The surprise in *Candida* forty years ago was its turning the tables on *A Doll's House*. For though the cards are not packed against the husband as they were in Ibsen's play, and he is unquestionably a genuine good fellow of high character and unselfish spirit, yet it is shown irresistibly that domestically he is the pet and the doll, and that it is his wife who runs the establishment and makes all his public triumphs possible."

From his unsuccessful novels, Shaw lifted many ideas and situations and used them effectively in his plays. Conolly's farewell to Marian in *The Irrational Knot*, anticipates Marchbanks's farewell to Candida. Mary Sutherland's rejection of the proposal by Owen Jack, the musical genius, evokes a reaction, identical with that of Marchbanks, in thought and violence: "*I* hanker after a *wife! I* grovel after *money!* What dog's appetites have this worldly crew infected me with! No matter: I am free: I am myself again. Back to thy holy garret, oh my soul!"

Candida was drawn from life. And its author approved of it as a first-class type of play, because it "consisted of a situation lasting several hours." Candida was modeled after Kate Salt, a brilliant, fascinating woman. The model for Morell was Edward Carpenter, a Socialist, and for a time an Anglican priest. Shaw was the model for Marchbanks, although he vehemently denied his identity with the poet. Shaw frequently visited the modest home of Henry Salt, the humanitarian; and Shaw vied with Carpenter, who lived nearby, for Kate's favor. They termed themselves her "Sunday husbands." From this trio, Shaw created a sex-triangle play of normal individuals. Carpenter divined Shaw's inspiration at once; and, after a reading of the play by the author, said: "No, Shaw, it won't do." Shaw parried all attempts to discover the models for the principals; but did say once that, when writing the part of the "penny poet," he "had in mind De Quincey's account of his adolescence in his *Confessions*."[2]

[2] When Beverley Baxter, M.P., a prominent editor, repeated the view of some journalists that the three principal characters were drawn from Ellen Terry, Henry Irving, and Shaw, the eighty-eight-year-old dramatist indignantly retorted that this surmise had given him a shock sufficient to "kill any other man of my age," and was "quite the worst shot ever made by a twentieth century critic." See Beverley Baxter, "The Man Who Failed to Understand," *Evening Standard*, November 18, 1944, and Shaw's reply, "Candida Was Not Ellen Terry," same newspaper, November 30, 1944. In his reply, Shaw called upon Heaven to forgive Baxter! [Shaw's reply is reprinted in this book on pp. 158–59.]

Much *réclame* was ingeniously promoted by Shaw, who gave the play the subtitle "A Mystery." This was inevitably associated with the closing words of the last stage direction: *James and Candida embrace; but they do not know the secret in the poet's heart.* In reviewing the play in Germany and Denmark,[544] Georg Brandes dismissed these lines as wholly superfluous. But, singularly enough, there have been many guessing contests over the "secret," which is open— and no secret. To this as a set question at Eton, the interested boys offered six solutions, all of them wrong! Writing a letter to the press, for the benefit of the "sentimental little blighters," Shaw explained that the mood of Candida was nocturnal, night being the true realm of the poet—citing Shakespeare (*The Merchant of Venice*), Byron ("She Walks in Beauty, like the Night"), and Wagner (*Tristan and Isolde*). Did not Marchbanks cry: "Let me go now. The night outside grows impatient." The prime requisite for solving the "mystery" is to know what a poet is:

What business has a man with the great destiny of a poet with the small beer of domestic comfort and cuddling and petting at the apron-strings of some dear nice woman? Morell cannot do without it: it is the making of him: without it he would be utterly miserable and perhaps go to the devil. To Eugene, the stronger of the two, the daily routine of it is nursery slavery, swaddling clothes, mere happiness instead of exaltation—an atmosphere in which poetry dies. To choose it would be like Swinburne choosing Putney. When Candida brings him squarely face to face with it, his heaven rolls up like a scroll; and he goes out proudly into the majestic and beautiful kingdom of the starry night.[3]

Candida presents a domestic problem of universal interest; and has received encomiums in many quarters. Comments by German critics after Agnes Sorma's production at the Neues Theater, Berlin, March 3, 1904, include: a "brilliant success," "a masterpiece," "dazzling fantasy, unique dialogue, bold humor and deep emotion," with Shaw being ranked as "the incarnation of *esprit,* and a many sided literator,

---

[3] George A. Riding, "The Candida Secret," *The Spectator,* CLXXXV (November 17, 1950). Shaw "disclosed" the Candida open-secret to two others; see James Huneker, "The Truth about Candida," *The Metropolitan Magazine,* August 1904; and Henry J. Haskell, "Random Thoughts," *Kansas City Star,* February 20, 1949. [The Riding article which includes two letters from Shaw, and Shaw's letter to Huneker and postcard to Haskell are reproduced in this book on pp. 166–69; 165–66; 169–70.]

a virtuoso of the theater, and in the highest sense a poet." French critics were equally fervent in appreciation. Henri Odier characterizes *Candida* as "one of the most beautiful and finished contributions to the contemporary drama." A reviewer of the production in Brussels, February 7, 1907, describes *Candida* as "une des plus fortes pièces de la scène anglo-saxonne," with the concluding tribute: "Il s'agit d'un nouveau frisson, d'une verbe inédite."[4] [545]

"The Rhetoric of 'Candida'"

WALTER N. KING

Of all the plays in the Shavian canon *Candida* is certainly one of the more provocative, in the sense that it has roused more outraged contempt, more thoughtless praise, than any other Shaw piece. Yet it remains a considerable puzzle, even to critics sympathetic to Shavian ideology and esthetic. That the play has withstood criticism of varying tone and quality attests to its vitality; that it has lured the competent and the incompetent into exegetical adventures underscores its perennial attractiveness. Nevertheless, the fact that the *Candida* controversy is by no means over argues the possibility that somewhere there exists a key for its interpretation, as yet unfound. Whether such a key exists at all is perhaps dubious, but my own impression is that if there be one, it lies within the rhetoric of the play, and that by attending closely to the rhetorical twists and turns of the dialogue and stage directions, we can come as near to the secret of the play as we can ever come to the secret of any piece of verbal art.

Not that I promise any minute analysis of Shaw's diction, syntax or grammar, any cataloguing of tropes and schemes. "The Prose Style of

[4] Candida has been the subject of two critical studies: Gerhard Kutsch, *Der Fall Candida: Eine Kritische Studie über George Bernard Shaw* (Leipzig, 1941) and, in the English language, Chaudhri Aleem Yar, *A Study in Development of George Bernard Shaw, with Special Reference to Candida* (Lucknow, 1954).

From *Modern Drama*, II (2) (September 1959), 71–83. Reprinted by permission of the author and *Modern Drama*. A number of the works to which Professor King refers in footnotes are reprinted in this book.

Bernard Shaw" has yet to be written and will add substantially to our knowledge of Shaw, once it is undertaken successfully. But repeated readings of the play have convinced me that it is a neatly wrought verbal fabric, highly integrated throughout, and that to neglect the verbal patterning is to pass by an essential clue to the play's meaning. Such neglect is in part responsible for the *Candida* controversy, which began in excessive attention to subjective character analysis and threatens to remain there unless another critical approach is attempted.

A resumé of the various interpretations via characterization may not be uncalled for, then, if only to define the problem that rhetorical analysis can perhaps resolve. For in all fairness it must be admitted that sharp attention to rhetoric leads back inevitably to characterization. I should say that previous interpretations fall into three general categories: those broached by Candida haters; those broached by Candida lovers; and those broached by a more cautious set of critics who seek impartial judgment by balancing critical acuity against historical knowledge. But in every case the assumption seems to be that Candida *is* the play, in spite of the statistical fact that she appears less frequently in the first two acts and says less than either Morell or Marchbanks.

Characteristically Beatrice Webb leads the troupe of Candida haters[711] with her school-marmish dictum that Candida is nothing but "a sentimental prostitute;"[1] and no doubt she is to someone like Mrs. Webb who preferred statistics to sentiment and seems frequently to have consoled herself for living in a sentimental world by laying down the law to sentimentalists. Fortunately, Mrs. Webb's name-calling can be dismissed as understandable intemperance. It is less easy to ignore the "heresy," as he calls it himself, of Edmund Fuller, who maintains that "Candida herself becomes no more than an idle and vain woman with nothing better to do than embarrass a busy husband by cradle-snatching."[2] But if it pays to be skeptical with respect to Candida haters, common sense suggests equal skepticism with respect to Candida lovers. G. K. Chesterton long ago set the tone for this group in his brilliantly antithetical comments upon the presence in Candida of the "reality of the normal wife's attitude toward the nor-

---

[1] Quoted by William Irvine in his introduction to *Bernard Shaw, Selected Plays and Other Writings* (New York, 1956), p. xx.
[2] Edmund Fuller, *George Bernard Shaw, Critic of Western Morale* (New York, 1950), p. 27.

mal husband, an attitude which is not romantic but which is yet quite quixotic; which is insanely unselfish and yet quite cynically clear-sighted. It involves human sacrifice without in the least involving idolatry."[3] Undoubtedly there is sound sense in these observations, as there is in much of the criticism of Candida lovers. Yet the chilling light of reflection promotes the suspicion that Chesterton is leading us back willy-nilly to Beatrice Webb's brutal aspersion and that with the addition of another antithesis he would have us almost there.

But we should be equally on our guard against a third kind of critic who tempts us to accept an appealing interpretation of the play grounded in solid historical scholarship combined with shrewd critical acumen.[4] Quite rightly they remind us that to judge *Candida* without taking into account Shaw's definitions, with respect to marriage and the family, of the idealist, the realist and the Philistine, as proclaimed in the second chapter of *The Quintessence of Ibsenism*, is somewhat risky. Morell, they declare persuasively, is obviously the idealist; Marchbanks, the realist; and Candida, for all her charm, the epitome of the Philistine—no other, in fact, than a subtle portrait of Ann Tanner, née Whitefield. Their arguments are by no means easy to assail. They can, and do, cite Shaw's own explanations of the play: his somewhat acidic letter to James Huneker, written in 1904, surely a crucial document; and his scattered remarks in a letter to Ellen Terry, in particular the by-the-way comment in the letter of 6 April, 1896. And to these they could add Shaw's avuncular paragraphs in a letter to a group of Rugby boys, written in 1920, and his succinct statement in the *Sixteen Self Sketches*[72] of what the "secret in the poet's heart" really is. On the critical side, of course, these critics cite relevant stage directions and dialogue from the play itself to suggest that Candida is in part the domestic ghoul of the Candida haters, in part the wife-mother-woman incarnate of the Candida lovers.

Their case seems strong indeed, almost too strong—but this is just the point, and it is on this ground that I feel inclined to take issue with them. With all due respect to their superb contributions to Shavian studies, it seems to me that to interpret *Candida* essentially in terms of key definitions in *The Quintessence* is to court abstractions. Morell is surely something more than a Shavian idealist; Marchbanks, some-

[3] G. K. Chesterton, *George Bernard Shaw* (New York, 1950), p. 118.
[4] See Arthur H. Nethercot, "The Truth about *Candida*," *PMLA*, LXIV (September, 1949), 639–647; and Irvine, *op. cit.*, pp. xvi–xx.

thing more than a Shavian realist; and Candida, something more than a Philistine, an Ann Whitefield matured by housewifery, and husband managing. Much of *The Quintessence*, it should always be remembered, is simply clever sloganeering, aimed at a particular audience living in a particular time, a series of war-cries engineered to push a program of dramatic reform. Like all such war-cries, it is patently shrill here and deliberately shocking there—and somewhat glib throughout. This is not to rush *The Quintessence* into the nearest waste-basket; it remains a critical document that deserves to be well-thumbed. (What would we not give for just such a document from the hand of Marlowe or Shakespeare.) But it should not be accepted without some reservations as a measuring rod for interpretation of a remarkably subtle play. If *Candida* were only an illustration of controversial materials in *The Quintessence*, the Candida controversy would have been settled long ago.

Similarly, Shaw's off-the-cuff comments upon Candida in the Ellen Terry letters should be discounted to a considerable degree, written as they were to further ulterior motives that Shaw himself, in a truly candid moment, would have been the first to confess.[5] When one is a Platonic lover and eager besides to entice a leading actress of the day into the cast of one's off-beat plays, one is likely to write almost anything, so long as it is charmingly written and perhaps may just turn the trick. As for the letter to Huneker,[6] has it in the long run any more relevance to the play than the notorious epilogue to *Pygmalion*[73]

[5] *Ellen Terry and Bernard Shaw, A Correspondence*, ed. by Christopher St. John (Christobel Marshall) (New York, 1931). The key quotation, wedged into a paragraph on a dozen topics in the letter of April 6, 1896, reads: ". . . and Candida, between you and me, is the Virgin mother and nobody else." Surely there is little enough here to fall back upon in support of any thesis.

[6] Printed in his *Iconoclasts* (New York, 1905), pp. 254–6; and in "The Truth about Candida," *Metropolitan Magazine*, XX (1904), 635. A somewhat long quotation from the letter illustrates its exaggerated tone: "Candida is as unscrupulous as Siegfried: Morell himself sees that 'no law will bind her.' She seduces Eugene just exactly as far as it is worth her while to seduce him. She is a woman without 'character' in the conventional sense. Without brains and strength of mind she would be a wretched slattern or voluptuary. She is straight for natural reasons, not for conventional ethical ones. Nothing could be more cold-bloodedly reasonable than her farewell to Eugene: 'All very well, my lad; but I don't quite see myself at fifty with a husband of thirty-five.' It is just this freedom from emotional slop, this unerring wisdom on the domestic plane, that makes her so completely mistress of the situation." In his conclusion, however, Shaw lets the cat out of the bag: "I tell it to you because it is an interesting sample of the way in which a scene [the auction scene], which should be conceived and written only

has to that bewitching work? Written nine years after *Candida* itself, it represents precisely the kind of *ex post facto* judgment Shaw the theoretician could be expected to write, especially in the light of the play's growing popularity, which Shaw was cantankerous enough to resent. And when one considers the propagandistic interpretations of several of Ibsen's plays, blandly presented in *The Quintessence* as incontrovertible truth, and the socialistic blarney Shaw discovered in Wagner's *Ring* cycle, it behooves all of us to be somewhat skittish about his explanations of his own works. The Rugby letter is less extreme; so also is the brief statement in the *Sixteen Self Sketches*.[7] Both possess a mellower tone that induces greater acceptance. Still, it is surely the better part of valor not to depend over much on any or all of these documents as flying buttresses for an interpretation of the play that veers toward allegorical exposition more suitable to *Man and Superman* or even to *The Devil's Disciple*.

Furthermore, play-goers, who after all won for the play its first success and have continued to maintain its reputation ever since, do not react to *Candida* as if it were a geometry problem whose basic axioms can be located in *The Quintessence* and other Shaviana. The same may be said for all the play's general readers. Their reactions stem neither from Shavian theory nor from Shavian commentary written after the fact, but from Shaw's own words as a playwright, three brilliant acts chuck full of them. Here if anywhere can be discovered "the truth about *Candida*"—the truth that Shaw had in him to say while he wrote the play, whether this truth was the conscious product of purer ratiocination or, what is more likely, the unconscious product of

---

by transcending the ordinary motion of the relations between the persons, nevertheless stirs the ordinary emotions to a very high degree, all the more because the language of the poet, to those who have not the clew to it, is mysterious and bewildering and therefore worshipful. *I divined it myself before I found out the whole truth about it.*" (My italics.)

[7] The Rugby letter, published in G. A. Riding, "*Candida's* Secret," *Spectator*, CLXXXV (November 17, 1950), 506, deals only with "the secret in the poet's heart." A short excerpt suggests its moderation. "What business has a man with the great destiny of a poet with the small beer of domestic comfort and cuddling and petting at the apron-string of some dear nice woman? Morell cannot do without it: it is the making of him; without it he would be utterly miserable and perhaps go to the devil. To Eugene, the stronger of the two, the daily routine of it is nursery slavery, swaddling clothes, mere happiness instead of exaltation—an atmosphere in which great poetry dies." In the *Sixteen Self Sketches* (New York, 1949), p. 106, from which I quote later on, Shaw is even more modest in his claims.

genius willing itself into the expression of something deeply felt and believed. Chesterton cannot be lightly dismissed for the suspicion that at the play's climactic moment, the famous auction scene, Shaw was "breathing from a bigger self and telling more truth than he knew."[8]

This truth, elusive as truth always is, springs from the peculiarly translucent rhetoric that garbs the play from first to last. For like all the great Shaw plays *Candida* is a rhetorical *tour de force* and is[74] none the worse for being so. Indeed, the play ought to be rhetorical, since its fundamental conflict is not the conflict between a middle-aged husband and an adolescent boy for the love of the husband's soon-to-be middle-aged wife, but the conflict between two rhetoricians, both of whom misunderstand the nature of the woman, over whom they lock rhetorical horns, for the prime reason that neither understands himself or the rhetoric each holds in esteem.

Morell is a master of rhetorical magniloquence, stuffed to his clerical collar with pulpit metaphors and the periods of conventional socialism, and equipped with the golden voice of the orator who can wow his parishioners on Sunday and radical political societies every other day of the week. Marchbanks is perhaps less magniloquent, but his syntax, diction and imagery, as any astute reader can discover for himself, are as hackneyed as Morell's—a pouring out of tired romantic phrases sodden with the diluted Platonism one would expect in a gifted child growing up in the age when Yeats himself was wallowing in romantic mishmash he outgrew in wiser and more articulate years. Marchbanks can puncture Morell's rhetorical balloon precisely because, when roused, he is a more perceptive rhetorician than Morell. But this is not to say that his perceptions about Candida are any nearer the truth than Morell's. Both are in love with words; and the rhetorical difference between them consists simply in Marchbanks' dogged pursuit, not of the real Candida, whom he thinks he has discovered, but of the real Morell, whom he senses that he understands only superficially—hence, his timid, yet unrelenting investigation into the nature of "Prossy's complaint."

One of the oddest facets in criticism of *Candida* is, in fact, the general recognition that Morell's rhetoric smells of platitudes, while the rhetoric of Marchbanks goes all but unnoticed as the stalest effluvia of post-romantic jargon, forgiveable only because of his almost incredi-

[8] Chesterton, p. 117.

ble youth. His contempt for Morell's rhetorical excesses is not really profound; it is merely a shrewd adolescent nausea over tired truths too polished to invite detection except by someone with a properly rebellious psyche. And this is one of the many ironies in a very ironic play: Shaw's ability to inject vitality into the desiccated rhetoric of Marchbanks, the anti-rhetorician in some respects, and of Morell, the artist in rhetorical legerdemain. For in his own way Morell is a poet too, of low degree certainly, of a degree lower than Marchbanks. But it is just their rhetorical kinship, their Victorian moral earnestness—Morell an exemplar of Arnoldian high seriousness; Marchbanks, of the diluted idealism of William Morris—that sparks Marchbanks into attack and provides him with stamina enough to continue it. Try as he may, he cannot understand why Candida should put up with Morell's[75] rhetorical varnish, when she obviously is not overwhelmed with his own. It is no accident on Shaw's part that she falls into a deep daydream in the third act while Marchbanks is reading his verses to her.

And yet the play is more rhetorical even than this. It is a kind of passacaglia and fugue dependent for ultimate thematic unity and development upon the iteration of a few key words: "fool," "mad," "love," and "happiness," with all of them subsumed in the word "understand." Indeed, the theme of the play might be said to be the conviction that unexamined happiness is not worth enjoying. For *Candida* is a domestic comedy in which the notions about love and happiness held by the two chief male characters have not been understood for what they are. The result is a peculiar folly akin to midsummer madness that precipitates a *Twelfth Night* misunderstanding and psychic confusion, out of which grows the understanding that allows Marchbanks and Morell to see more deeply into themselves, into each other, into Candida, and into the nature of love and happiness.

II

Verbal iteration begins early in Act I when Lexy, the clerical stuffed shirt Morell never really is, remarks to him: "It's so hard to understand you about Mrs. Morell—" To which Morell replies sententiously: "Ah, my boy, get married: get married to a good woman; and then you'll understand. . . . We have no more right to consume happiness without producing it than to consume wealth without pro-

ducing it" (p. 204).[9] And it is Prossy who complains to Lexy a bare
minute later: "Oh, a man ought to be able to be fond of his wife without making a fool of himself about her" (p. 205). By the end of the
act Morell has been branded a fool not only by Prossy, but by Burgess
and Marchbanks. But only Marchbanks' name-calling rankles, and it
is induced by Morell's patronizing blather about "a happy marriage
like ours" (p. 219) and his semi-paternal accusation that Marchbanks
"is making a fool of yourself: a very great fool of yourself" (p. 221)
for proclaiming his love for Candida.

    In his counter-attack to this "wholesome plain speaking" March-
banks lifts the dialogue to rhetorical precision and overtones that far
exceed the usual cut and thrust of comic dialogue.

Do you think that the things people make fools of themselves about are any
less real and true than the things they behave sensibly about? They are
more true: they are the only things that are true. You are very calm and
sensible and moderate with me because you can see that I am a fool about
your wife; just as no doubt that old man who was here just now is very wise
over[76] your Socialism, because he sees that you are a fool about it. Does
that prove you wrong? Does your complacent superiority to me prove that
I am wrong? (p. 221)

Morell's rejoinder trembles with pulpit passion and exposes the unexamined foundations upon which his happiness and self-esteem rest.

In the future, when you are as happy as I am, I will be your true brother in
the faith. I will help you to believe that God has given us a world that
nothing but our own folly keeps from being a paradise. I will help you to
believe that every stroke of your work is sowing happiness for the great
harvest that all—even the humblest— shall one day reap. And last, but trust
me, not least, I will help you to believe that your wife loves you and is
happy in her home. We need such help, Marchbanks: we need it greatly
and always. There are so many things to make us doubt, if once we let our
understanding be troubled. Even at home, we sit as if in camp, encompassed
by a hostile army of doubts. Will you play the traitor and let them in on
me? (pp. 222-3)

    The point, of course, is that Morell's understanding is badly in
need of the shaking up Marchbanks is giving it. On the other hand,

───────────

    [9] Page references in parentheses refer to the text of *Candida* in Bernard
Shaw, *Seven Plays* (New York, 1951).

Marchbanks' retort to Morell's hackneyed plea is a pastiche of hackneyed Shelleyan abstractions also badly in need of an airing.

Is it like this for her always? A woman, with a great soul, craving for reality,
truth, freedom; and being fed on metaphors, sermons, stale perorations,
mere rhetoric? (p. 223)

And Marchbanks, who possesses "the gift of the gab" quite as much as
Morell, rushes headlong into peroration itself.

I'll fight your ideas. I'll rescue her from her slavery to them. I'll pit my
own ideas against them. You are driving me out of the house because you
darent let her choose between your ideas and mine. (p. 224)

It is certainly true that Morell misunderstands the nature of his relationship with Candida, but it is equally true that Marchbanks also
misunderstands it, and more seriously misunderstands his own relationship with her. Otherwise he would not be so sure that Candida "will
understand me, and know that I understand her" (p. 225). Morell's
folly is simply the obverse side of his own.

The *leitmotiv* summed up in the word "fool" goes deeper than
name-calling, however. Implicit to it is the question perennial to all
comedy worthy of the name: what is folly, what is wisdom? If to be
foolish is to misunderstand the nature of others, of oneself, and of
events and things, then Marchbanks and Morell are both fools, balanced
rather neatly at opposite ends of the same seesaw. And if to be wise is
to understand the nature of others, of events and things, and of oneself,[77] then each must fall off the seesaw and awake to some valid
understanding of Candida and of love and happiness—and in the
process awake to the perception that understanding is not just a matter
of intellectualization. Both Marchbanks and Morel rely on a too easy
intellectual approach to human relationships; both couch their arguments in intellectual terms, yet both argue from emotional depths
neither understands. Marchbanks is suffering from something that
cannot be dubbed "calf love," as Morell understands the term. And
Morell enjoys a not-to-be-sneezed-at emotional communion with Candida that baffles Marchbanks, whose mistake is the assumption that his
own relationship with her represents a perfect intellectual partnership.
Of the two, Morell at least is further along toward wisdom, since his
complacent happiness has been sufficiently shattered so that he can
begin to make a sounder estimate of it. Thus, Marchbanks' reckoning

of himself at the end of Act I as "the happiest of mortals" amounts to trenchant dramatic irony, in contrast to Morell's disillusioned curtain line. 'So was I—an hour ago."

And yet Marchbanks, endowed with a subtler intellect than Morell, cannot remain for long in a state of incipient ecstacy. He understands too little, from the mechanism of Prossy's typewriter to "Prossy's complaint." Quite naturally he sets the tone for Act II in his early comment to Prossy that clever, practical people "always had to have love affairs to keep them from going mad" (p. 227). The byplay upon "mad" in this act—Burgess telling Marchbanks that Morell is mad as a March hare; Prossy telling Burgess that Marchbanks is mad as the same creature; Morell concluding that either Marchbanks was "right this morning, or Candida is mad;" and Lexy confiding in Burgess that Prossy is "a little out of her mind sometimes"—is simply a sly extension of the motif of folly reminiscent of Shakespeare's shift from folly to madness, as misunderstanding multiplies, in the middle acts of *Twelfth Night*.

Marchbanks fails to understand, because of his faith in rationality, the nature of love, though he enjoys curious insights into it because of his immersion in himself—the ironic reason why his understanding fails when he exerts it most energetically. Like most teen-agers steeped in Platonic yearnings he conceives of love in terms of his own sensibility.

We all go about longing for love: it is the first need of our natures, the first prayer of our hearts; but we dare not utter our longings: we are too shy. . . . And I see the affection I am longing for given to dogs and cats and pet birds, because they come and ask for it. It must be asked for: it is like a ghost: it cannot speak unless it is first spoken to.[78] All the love in the world is longing to speak; only it dares not, because it is shy! shy! shy! (p. 228)

But all this is only heady generalization, though it forms the substance of Candida's choice in the auction scene; and it is generalization that Marchbanks is edging away from when he pries into "Prossy's complaint." "Tell me," he begs this lovesick maiden lady, "is it really and truly possible for a woman to love him [Morell]? . . . No: answer me. I want to know: I must know. *I* cant understand it. I can see nothing in him but words, pious resolutions, what people call goodness. You cant love that" (pp. 230–1). But this shrewd perception hardly prevents his poetizing his romantic distaste for scrubbing brushes and paraffin oil and actually propels him, in the presence of Candida, into a mawkish, ungrammatical prose lyric in praise of a "tiny shallop to sail away in, far from the world, where the marble floors are washed by the rain and dried by the sun . . ." (p. 236).

Such "poetic horrors" are mild, however, in comparison with those of Morell, when shortly afterwards Candida unwittingly places him on the rhetorical scales and finds him overweight. She too suffers from misunderstanding, in some respects from misunderstanding of a far more egregious sort. Priding herself on her understanding of Marchbanks, she exhibits a faulty perceptiveness that is shocking in direct proportion to the radiant perceptiveness mingled with it. Convinced that Marchbanks is "ready to fall madly in love with me" (p. 241), yet unaware how far matters have already gone, and disappointed in Morell's fatuous faith in her "goodness" and "purity," she speculates rather fatuously herself upon how Marchbanks will "learn what love really is." "Dont you understand?" she asks Morell.

I mean, will he forgive me for not teaching him myself? For abandoning him to the bad women for the sake of my goodness, of my purity, as you call it? Ah, James, how little you understand me, to talk of your confidence in my goodness and purity! I would give them both to poor Eugene as willingly as I would give my shawl to a beggar dying of cold, if there were nothing else to restrain me. Put your trust in my love for you, James; for if that went, I should care very little for your sermons: mere phrases that you cheat yourself and others with every day. (p. 242)

Pleased with herself and delighted that she has pricked Morell's self-composure, she concludes that Marchbanks "is always right. He understands you; he understands me; he understands Prossy; and you, darling, you understand nothing" (p. 243). After such high-flown idiocy, it is significant that when Morell challenges Marchbanks to spend the evening alone with her while he lectures before the Guild of St. Matthew, it is Candida who concludes Act II with "I cant understand—"[79] To which Morell replies: "Ah, I thought it was *I* who couldnt understand, dear."

Significantly, too, it is Candida, the catalytic agent, as Eric Bentley dubs her,[10] who brings Marchbanks and Morell to understanding in Act III, yet fails to penetrate Marchbanks' final perceptions. For it is Candida who remains unchanged and self-satisfied, the saintly fool

[10] Eric Bentley, *Bernard Shaw* (Norfolk, Connecticut, 1947), p. 110.

who survives personal crises almost solely by means of intuition. In spite of her basic hardheadedness Candida is a remarkably limited woman, contrary to the panegyrics squandered on her by Candida lovers. Shaw himself states in the stage direction explanatory to her first act entrance that she has no esthetic appreciation of the copy of Titian's "Virgin of the Assumption," a gift from Marchbanks that hangs over the fireplace. For all she knows or cares the High Renaissance might have been contemporaneous with Pre-Raphaelitism. Nor has she any idea why Marchbanks compares the poker, symbol of domesticity, she holds upright in her hand at the beginning of Act III to a drawn sword—the sword of chastity of medieval romance. Her world is willingly restricted to hearth and family, to the boundaries of the parish of St. Dominic's, with such vicarious forays into the wider world as Morell makes from lecture platform to lecture platform. Her attitude toward Marchbanks is consistently maternal, neither sentimental nor patronizing nor sexually teasing, contrary to the high-minded allegation of Beatrice Webb. It is her very limitedness, not to be mistaken for shallowness, that is all important. Never for a moment could Shaw permit her the slightest shred of intellectuality or esthetic insight; if he had, he could not with any claim to psychological or artistic integrity have presented her as he did in the auction scene. Had she been blessed with any truly rational understanding, she might plausibly have chosen Marchbanks in preference to Morell; which is to say, that in a choice between rival rhetorical bids, Marchbanks' bid would have befuddled her judgment enough to have betrayed her into folly.

Furthermore, there would then have been no point in the consummate irony that underlies the folly, brought on by Morell's moral collapse in Act III, of Marchbanks' exultation prior to the auction scene.

It is she who wants somebody to protect, to help, to work for: somebody to give her children to protect, to help and to work for. Some grown man who has become as a little child again. Oh, you fool, you fool, you triple fool! I am the man, Morell: I am the man. You dont understand what a woman is. Send for her, Morell: send for her and let her choose between— (p. 256)

One hesitates to say that the auction scene is the most misunder-

stood scene in modern English drama; probably it is not, at least emotionally.[80] Audience and reader want Candida to choose Morell, they
are fearful that she may not, and they sense that she chooses Morell for
the simplest and best of reasons—her love for him. Her need for him is
as great as his need for her; her will to protect him from the crassness
of everyday life is as necessary to her as the need to be protected is to
him. But it is not going too far to suspect that the rhetorical niceties of
the scene have not been fully assimilated.

The scene begins in a tangle of misunderstandings: Morell too
overwrought to understand either Candida or Marchbanks, much less
himself; Marchbanks too giddy with personal expectations, still Platonic, to understand either Candida or Morell, and scarcely himself;
and Candida too surprised at Marchbanks' temerity and Morell's
masculine pride and imminent disintegration in the face of what's
happened to understand completely either of them, and only vaguely
aware of her own feckless stimulation of the present crisis.

It is customary to condemn Morell's bid as rhetorical suicide, but
such a judgment seems rather wide of the mark. Shaw himself states
in one of the stage directions that "sincere feeling" lies behind his
debater's points. Morell hardly merits contempt for insisting that he
will not "suffer the intolerable degradation of jealousy" (p. 264); and
if he resorts to oratory, he nevertheless speaks what any devoted
husband can sympathize with.

I have nothing to offer you but my strength for your defence, my honesty
for your surety, my ability and industry for your livelihood, and my
authority and position for your dignity. That is all it becomes a man to
offer a woman. (p. 265)

Except that it is not "all." He has forgotten Candida's warning not to
trust her goodness or purity, but to trust only her love for him, and
he neglects to add his need. He has yet to learn what Marchbanks
already knows, that love must be asked for. It is this that makes March-
bank's bid the stronger of the two: "My weakness. My desolation. My
heart's need" (p. 265). But this is precisely what Morell fails to say, a
truly ironic rhetorical failure, so that Morell is indeed "the weaker
of the two."

Marchbanks, on the other hand, has not spurned rhetoric in his own
bid. He has simply outshone Morell as a rhetorician by welding in-

tellect and emotion into a richly classical appeal. In essence March-banks' bid is the ironic complement of Morell's. Had Marchbanks really understood Candida, he would have known—as the discussion that follows the bidding makes transparently clear—that no woman as innately domestic as she would ever dismiss as totally valueless the kind of bid Morell offers. Candida has sliced too many onions, fended off too many tradesmen and been happy doing so to sacrifice herself[81] to romantic illusions. She is after all Candida, the daughter of a cockney employer, not George Sand.

And she misunderstands Marchbanks to the very end. Platonic to the last, he soars into the rhetoric of self-sacrifice in his final speeches: "I no longer desire happiness: life is nobler than that. Parson James: I give you my happiness with both hands: I love you because you have filled the heart of the woman I loved" (p. 267). His unconscious shift to past tense tells all that needs to be told about the quality of his love. In many ways it was "calf love," but the "calf love" that matures inner vision. For he has finally understood Candida, her cramping maternality, her matronly conventionality. He suddenly understands, too, why Morell "got past the flaming sword that stopped me" (p. 254) earlier in the evening; he understands how lucky he was to have been stopped; and he now understands something about himself—the puzzling "secret in the poet's heart."

Shaw's betrayal of this secret in the *Sixteen Self Sketches*, "that domestic life is not the poet's destiny," is adequate so far as it goes. But the secret embraces as well everything that Marchbanks has learned about himself, about Candida, and about love and happiness. Though Morell had misconceived the quality of his marriage, March-banks had misconceived to a far greater degree the quality of his own devotion to Candida. The Candida Morell loves was always far closer to the real Candida than the Candida Marchbanks loved, who was only an ideal, an illusion manufactured in large part through his adoles-cent need for an illusion to love. Through loving an illusion and being freed from it, he has begun to discover himself, so that in a richer sense than Shaw implies Marchbanks is now on the threshold of a more sensitive perception of why, to use Shaw's own words, "the starry night, and not the cosy room with the paraffin lamp, is the place for him."[11] To remain with Candida implies self-limitation; to leave her implies the self-realization of poetic achievement.

[11] Shaw, *Sixteen Self Sketches*, p. 106.

III

If the interpretation of *Candida* offered here has any validity, what does it suggest in wider terms? For one thing it permits liberation from the subjective interpretations of Candida lovers and haters, and from slavery to Shaw's own *ex post facto* interpretations. For another, it provides a means whereby Shaw's own explanations can be put to use. It would be foolhardy to disagree *in toto* with critics who urge the importance of reading the play in terms of the leads offered in *The Quintessence of Ibsenism*. Morell, Marchbanks and Candida obviously do in some degree belong to the Shavian categories of idealist,[82] realist and Philistine. But if such terms have any application, they apply only when made to overlap—and once they overlap they take on a different relevance. Marchbanks is far more the disillusioned idealist than Morell, who is in many ways far more realistic than Marchbanks. Indeed, if Marchbanks could reconstruct the world according to his own blueprint, which presumably he is now about to tear up, he would wreak as much harm as Ibsen's Brand. The point is that he becomes the Shavian realist by the end of the play.

As for Candida, who in his right mind leaves the theater convinced that she is an out and out Philistine, tinged with Philistinism though she may be? A failure to venerate Titian does not imply abject moral obloquy. Whatever she is—and few people will ever totally agree about her—she is not a walking formula out of *The Quintessence* or any other Shaviana. In essence, she is more the realist, in spite of her limitations and the momentary misconceptions they produce, than either Marchbanks or Morell. For hers is the realism that springs from direct experience with the hard facts of daily life. Temporarily she has been impressed with the anti-rhetoric of Marchbanks, but not enough to be taken in by it. Rhetoric, from whatever source, has no lasting influence upon her judgment. From the start she has understood what love and happiness amount to for herself and for those dear to her: elemental principles of existence that words can never define, illuminate or distort, principles that vary in degree and kind from individual to individual in a way that disregards system of any sort. If Candida represents anything systematically Shavian, she represents the intuitive wisdom of vitality resisting system, of vitality cutting through the fool's rhetoric that gives to system its emotional appeal to system-lovers like Marchbanks and Morell. What saves her in the end, together with Marchbanks and Morell, is her very limited-ness, her freedom from the cant that goes with system.[12] Were she more than she is, she would not be Candida.[83]

"Ibsen, Shaw, and 'Candida'"

JACOB H. ADLER

In an article, "The Truth about Candida,"[1] Arthur H. Nethercot stated that what he was giving was the whole truth. In this paper I propose to see whether more truth cannot be found. Mr. Nethercot bases his interpretation upon the second chapter of *The Quintessence of Ibsenism*, showing that *Candida* illustrates the theories there ex-pressed—Morell being the idealist regarding marriage, Marchbanks the (budding) realist, and Candida the Philistine. This, of course, makes *Candida* a play in which Shaw must have been even more than usually conscious of Ibsen. But Mr. Nethercot does not particularly examine *which* Ibsen. Others have, and the conclusion has generally been *A Doll's House*.[2] But in spite of superficial resemblances, *A Doll's House* is not the play which most closely parallels *Candida* in its

---

[12] See Bentley's comments upon the conflict between vitality vs. system in Shaw's plays, *op. cit., passim.*

[1] *PMLA*, LXIV (September, 1949), 639–47; reprinted under the same title, with additions and in somewhat different form, as the second section of Chapter I ("The Quintessence of Ibseno-Shavianism") in *Men and Supermen: The Shavian Portrait Gallery* (Cambridge, Mass., 1954), pp. 7–17.

[2] E.g., William Irvine, *The Universe of G.B.S.* (New York, 1949), p. 174; Harlan Hatcher, Introduction to *Candida*, in *A Modern Repertory* (New York, 1953), p. 6; John Gassner, Introduction to *Candida*, in *A Treasury of the Theatre*, rev. ed. (New York, 1950), p. 539. Critics have also noted a limited resemblance to *The Lady from the Sea* in the auction scene. See, for example, Nethercot, *Men and Supermen*, p. 13; Irvine, p. 174; Gassner, *Masters of the Drama* (New York, 1940), p. 603.

From the *Journal of English and Germanic Philology* (*JEGP*), LIX (1) (January, 1960), 50–58. Reprinted by permission of the author and *JEGP*. A number of the works to which Professor Adler refers in his footnotes are reprinted (entire or in part) in this book.

realist-idealist-Philistine relationships. That play is *The Wild Duck*. And once one begins to examine *The Wild Duck*, a cluster of other resemblances to *Candida* appear. These resemblances seem worth examining for their own sake, and also for the further light they might shed upon the apparently enigmatical character of Candida,[3] the not perfectly clear characters of Morell and Marchbanks, and perhaps still other problems in the Shaw play.

One quotation relating *Candida* to *A Doll's House* will have to serve for many. William Irvine says of *Candida* that it is "essentially ... Ibsen's 'Doll's House' turned upside down. Ibsen had shown that[50] unhappiness results when a husband treats his wife as a doll. Shaw points out that happiness may result when a wife treats her husband as a doll. His Nora sees her husband as he really is—and retains him."[4] But in *The Wild Duck* too, "happiness results when a wife treats her

---

[3] For a survey of the various interpretations, see "The Truth about Candida," in *PMLA*, LXIV (September, 1949), 639–41; in *Men and Supermen*, pp. 8–9. Nethercot himself apparently concludes that Candida is charming but has unadmirable qualities, including a certain callousness. See especially *Men and Supermen*, pp. 12–13. I hope to show in this paper that, in Nethercot's own terms, Candida can be shown to be more admirable than Nethercot seems to believe.

[4] P. 174. There is Shavian authority—at a rather late date—for this point of view. See Shaw's letter, quoted by Raymond Mander and Joe Mitchenson, *Theatrical Companion to Shaw* (London, 1954) p. 43: "the play is a counterblast to Ibsen's Doll's House, showing that in the real typical doll's house, it is the man who is the doll." But this was written in 1944, almost fifty years after the event; it was written in anger; and in any case, as Milton Crane says ("*Pygmalion*: Bernard Shaw's Dramatic Theory and Practice," *PMLA*, LXVI [1951],879), Shaw "made few statements about his own work of which we may safely believe every word." See also Nethercot's similar view, with particular reference to *Candida* (*Men and Supermen*, p. 15). Shaw's description of *A Doll's House* in *The Quintessence of Ibsenism* (*The Collected Works of Bernard Shaw* [New York, 1931], XIX, 69–71) seems entirely approving. Moreover, *The Wild Duck* is in itself a "counterblast" to *A Doll's House*, in that Nora is an idealist ready to become a realist and Hialmar is not; and Shaw himself points this out in his description of *The Wild Duck* in *The Quintessence* (p. 83). It is difficult to believe that if Shaw really thought himself to be writing a "counterblast" to *A Doll's House* (though "counterblast" is an improbably strong word for Shaw to be using anent Ibsen in the nineties) he would not have realized that this would bring him close to *The Wild Duck*. Finally Shaw says—and surely correctly—that the husband and wife in *A Doll's House* are both idealists and in *The Wild Duck* are respectively idealist and Philistine. It is again difficult to believe that when Shaw wrote *Candida* he did not realize which of these patterns his married couple matched. (In this connection, see Gassner, Introduction to *Candida*, p. 539: Candida "is Ibsen's Nora grown up and self-possessed." But Nora begins as an idealist and ends as a realist. If Nethercot is right in calling Candida a Philistine this would make "growing up" a very strange process!)

husband as a doll," and Gina (who, unlike Nora, is a Philistine) "sees her husband as he really is—and retains him." It seems a bit superfluous to go to an Ibsen play which presents the reverse of Shaw's when there is one which directly parallels it. Moreover, intruders upon marriage exist, and are even the motivating force, in several Ibsen plays; but among these intruders, only two—Mrs. Linde in *A Doll's House* and Gregers in *The Wild Duck*—want to intrude by having the truth (as they see it) brought entirely into the open. And of these two, Gregers is the motivating force of the play and Mrs. Linde is not; and his truth cannot help while hers can. Now Marchbanks in *Candida* is an intruder upon marriage who wants the truth (as he sees it) told; his desire is the motivating force of the play; and his truth is no help to the marriage. Hence Marchbanks most nearly resembles Gregers. The triangles are complete. Surely they are sufficiently congruent to be worth examining side by side.

In terms, then, of the second chapter of *The Quintessence of Ibsenism, The Wild Duck* and *Candida* present similar marriage partners.[51] Shaw himself says that Gina is a Philistine,[5] and she fits his definition perfectly. Her unthinking satisfaction with the married state, her sacrifices which she does not regard as sacrifices, and her lack of culture are all repeatedly stressed. Like no other Ibsen wife, her background is decidedly lower than her husband's. So is Candida's; and Mr. Nethercot's unidealized Candida—the Candida of the onions and the scrubbing brush, the Candida who prefers the poker to Marchbanks' sonnets, who has no interest in Titian, who is good at putting off collectors—belongs, though more polished and charming, clearly in the same Shavian category as Gina.

Similarly the husbands. Hialmar Ekdal and James Mavor Morell are alike idealists regarding marriage; that is, both have illusions about their domestic role, and both have ideals (from Shaw's point of view, false and conventional ideals) about what the basis of marriage and the function of each partner should be. Both magnify the importance of their work. Hialmar has been unjustifiably admired for his voice, his rhetoric, his intelligence, his power of emotion; to a certain extent, the same can be said of Morell. Hialmar was raised by adoring females, which is Ibsen's explanation for his inability to face life; Shaw goes out of his way to have Candida say much the same thing about Morell.

[5] *Quintessence*, p. 81.

Morell is of course a growing power in the world, while Hialmar is a permanent failure; but the resemblances are nevertheless too strong to be overlooked.

If, however, idealism can produce such a weakling as Hialmar, it may seem odd that it can also produce such a dynamo as Morell. But Ibsen himself has many successful idealists, notably Helmer, Manders, and Mayor Stockmann. Shaw's own definition of an idealist (forced upon him, he says, by Ibsen) as one believing strongly in convention is a definition of the frequently successful; for the forcefully conventional can be successful. Moreover, Shaw does not say that an idealist in one direction need be an idealist in all; and Morell has the moral and intellectual advantage of being in some ways a realist (for example, in his relationship to Burgess) and of thinking himself a realist (in the Shavian sense of nonconventionalist) in that he is espousing unpopular ideas.[6] Unlike Ibsen's idealists, therefore, he has a sense of humor and a degree of objectivity, and is hence an unusually pleasant character for an idealist.[7] [52]

In themselves more likable versions of their counterparts in Ibsen, Candida and Morell also strongly resemble Gina and Hialmar in their marital relationship. Like Gina, Candida has preserved in her husband the illusion of being the family power. Each (at least until Candida's plain speaking, to be examined presently) preserves without accepting the idea that her husband's work (Hialmar's "invention," Morell's preaching and socialism) is significant. Each shields her husband from unpleasantness, caters to his whims, yet expects him to share in the manual labor. But the most important resemblance concerns the truth and the wives' attitudes toward it. In *The Wild Duck* the truths are, first, that not Hialmar but Werle has been supporting Hialmar's father; second, that Gina had been Werle's mistress before her marriage; and finally, that Hedwig may or may not be Hialmar's child. Gina has withheld the first of these truths in order to preserve Hialmar in a comfortable illusion; in her Philistine mind, comfort far outweighs truth. She originally withheld the second truth for fear of Hialmar's refusing to marry her: again a Philistine reaction. Since

[6] Cf. Nethercot, *Men and Supermen,* p. 11. Nethercot also pertinently quotes (p. 12) Shaw's preface to *Getting Married,* in which Shaw describes Morell as in some ways unconventional, clearly meaning realistic.

[7] For a similar point of view, see James Huneker, *Iconoclasts: A Book of Dramatists* (New York, 1908), p. 250.

then, however, her silence has been from quite a different cause. The long dormant truth has lost all importance for her; philistinely happy in her marriage, she has "forgotten those old stories." And much the same can be said for her attitude toward the third truth: Hedwig's parentage. Hedwig and Hialmar have a comfortably pleasant relationship; it would not occur to Gina that the identity of Hedwig's blood father is worth considering.[8]

In *Candida*, by coincidence, there are again three truths: first, that Candida thinks Morell's preaching and socialism do no real good; second, the "shawl" speech, in which she tells Morell that only her love for him, not any abstract theories of morality, keep her from giving herself to Eugene; and finally, her revelations at the end of the play about Morell's protected position in the household. Now unlike Gina, Candida reveals each truth with little or no hesitation; and it is precisely this point that has exasperated critics attempting to interpret her character. Some call her cruel,[9] but Philistines in marriage are not deliberately cruel—they simply cannot understand the idealist's position. Others say that she did not realize how seriously Morell would react—in other words that she was *unconsciously* cruel.[10] When this opinion refers to her ignorance of the Morell-Marchbanks quarrel, it is[53] valid but insignificant; character cannot be judged on the basis of facts *necessarily* unknown. When it is meant more generally, the "cruelty" must be judged by the results; and here (it is a point I shall return to) I think criticism has gone far astray in assuming that Morell suffers long or learns much. A reasonable answer will more likely be found by examining each instance of Candida's candor; by comparing her attitude to Gina's; and by examining the actual effects upon Morell.

The first truth—Candida's opinion of the effect of Morell's preaching—is revealed in a quite Philistine context: by persuading Morell of the little good his preaching does, she hopes to induce him to take better care of himself and to spend more time with her! Like Gina, she wants her husband—and herself—to be comfortable.

The second truth (that in the "shawl" speech) Nethercot cor-

---

[8] A realist, like Relling, would agree. But the realist's view, unlike Gina's, would be intellectual and conscious.

[9] E.g., Alick West, *George Bernard Shaw* (New York, 1950), p. 109; Edmund Fuller, *George Bernard Shaw* (New York, 1950), p. 26.

[10] E.g., *Men and Supermen*, pp. 12–13; Irvine, p. 176.

rectly dismisses as essentially meaningless,[11] since Candida knows her love will always keep her faithful. And from the Philistine point of view, what she tells Morell should actually comfort him: it is not, she says, anything so abstract or unflattering as morality—something people constantly violate—which prevents her from being unfaithful; it is her love for him—something she could not possibly violate. The similarity to Gina is again clear: neither of the wives considers "sex" as a matter of abstract morality; both consider a happy marriage far more important than rules about sex.

The third truth (that Candida has given her life to protecting Morell and preserving his position as master) is told, of course, for the sake of helping Eugene to renounce his love and go out and meet his destiny. The objection raised is that in revealing her role as Morell's protectress Candida violates it. But this is not true, for the role that she reveals is quite largely the self-sacrificial role that an idealist-according-to-Shaw would expect of a woman in marriage; and to that extent it should not disturb Morell. From one point of view, indeed, the revelation should actually comfort him. He has doubted that Candida loves him. She is showing him that only a woman who did love her husband and the life she is living, could bear to live it. (There is the further argument that Morell is *not* seriously disturbed—again a point that I shall return to.)

Just as Hialmar and Morell are themselves revealingly similar and different, so are their reactions to the truth. About Gina's past, Hialmar is annoyed, even enraged, but his emotion is temporary and not even particularly genuine; it is rather an expression of what the idealist[54] feels convention requires. He is only too glad to give in gradually, and return to the comfortable fold. And his emotions hardly disturb Gina, except to the extent that *he* might be hurt by them, because she is perfectly aware of their transience. His distrust of Hedwig, as the result of the third revelation, is more serious; but if the wild duck's death would have tricked him into belief again, so would a hundred other things. As Relling points out at the end, Hialmar can idealize his way out of almost any conceivable shock. As we have seen, he is a far more complete idealist than Morell; and the difference in reaction has yet another source: Hialmar (for idealistic reasons) is ashamed of his wife; Morell (for at least partly idealistic reasons) idolizes his.

11 "The Truth about Candida," in *PMLA*, LXIV (September, 1949), 641; in *Men and Supermen*, p. 10. See also Irvine, p. 174.

To the first and second truths—they come swiftly together—Morell's reaction is, as Candida says, "only shock," though the shock is more genuine than Hialmar's. She has apparently seen him similarly shocked before, and apparently knows that he (like Hialmar) will get quickly over it. "How conventional all you unconventional people are!" she exclaims, and that would be the entire key to the reaction, in terms of what Shaw meant by idealism, if Morell had not more to worry about than Candida knows; and her statement points up perfectly both the similarity to Hialmar and the difference. But it is Morell's reaction to the third truth that has particularly concerned critics; and the assumption often made that he is hurt permanently or really and truly changed, seems to me quite mistaken. Bentley, for example, says that Morell is "utterly disillusioned" and ends the play "crushed and speechless."[12] But he is not speechless; immediately after Candida's long exposé, he manages a speech to her that is filled with his ringing cadences. Nor is he crushed; he has enough presence of mind to ask Candida to keep Eugene from doing anything rash, and he and Candida end the play in an embrace which Shaw would seem from his stage direction to intend as an indication of the happiness which Marchbanks eschews. Clearly then, his disillusion, if it exists, is only momentary. His idealism—a Shavian idealist cannot take a woman's truthtelling very seriously—his love for Candida, and her sure-to-be-continued ministrations combine to promise that her revelations will be quickly forgotten. And she knows it; and thus for Eugene's sake she can speak plainly without doing any significant harm.

And so Morell, who is stronger in his idealism than Hialmar, though equally dependent, reacts genuinely but recovers quickly.[55] Hialmar, playing a part and having no shred of strength, takes longer. But the result is the same: both men can be expected to forget the truth and go on as if nothing had happened.

A comparison of Gregers and Marchbanks is also illuminating. Like Gregers, Marchbanks wants the truth told because he feels that the marriage he sees is not a sound one. Each derives his attitude from an unhappy childhood. Each temporarily robs the husband of his sense of security. Each is driven out into the unknown at the play's end. But Gregers, with an Oedipus complex, loves the husband and despises the wife, while Marchbanks, rejected by his entire family and needing

---

[12] *Bernard Shaw* (Norfolk, Conn., 1947), pp. 110, 137; Nethercot seems to agree with this position (*Men and Supermen*, p. 12).

a woman to worship, loves the wife and despises the husband. And from this grows the important difference: Gregors cannot benefit from the truth which the events in the play teach him, but Marchbanks can. Men handicapped as children by female indulgence or general over-admiration—Hialmar, Gregers, Morell, Tesman in *Hedda Gabler*—become idealists. (Others do too, of course.) Rejected by his family, Marchbanks is strong enough to grow into a realist.

Thus *Candida* and *The Wild Duck* both present husbands who are idealists, wives who are Philistines, and intruders who are idealists and who insist that the truth be told. But the Shavian counterparts of Ibsen's characters are more likable or more admirable or both: Candida more articulate, cultured, charming, and clear-sighted than Gina; Morell partly realistic, stronger than Hialmar, far pleasanter; Marchbanks capable, as Gregers is not, of becoming a realist, and younger and therefore more forgivable. Shaw is of course peopling a Shaw world, not an Ibsen world, but more specific reasons for the changes can be found. Regarding Candida, it can be said that Shaw's characters are almost by definition articulate; that he grew distinctly fond of her while he wrote the play;[13] that she had a partly realistic husband from whom she could, as she herself says, learn something;[14] and that, as Nethercot points out, Shaw's womanly women are usually Philistines and usually attractive.[15] But if Candida is to be more admirable than her counterpart, Morell must be also, or the situation will be too poignant (or too farcical) for comedy; and while *Candida*, like *The Wild Duck*, is a perceptive study of illusion versus reality, it is not[56] a harrowing indictment, as *The Wild Duck* is. Marchbanks' personality (which it is quite possible to dislike) represents a more serious problem of interpretation, but it helps to remember that Shaw's example of a realist in *The Quintessence of Ibsenism* is the young Shelley.[16] Moreover, other Shavian realists, such as Vivie Warren, are not entirely likable. And finally, Marchbanks must be in some respects

---

13 Nethercot, "The Truth about Candida," in *PMLA*, LXIV (September, 1949), 646; in *Men and Supermen*, p. 17. See also the remarks quoted by (for example) Fuller, p. 28.

14 "This comes of James teaching me to think for myself. . . ." Irvine notes this, p. 176.

15 "The Truth about Candida," in *PMLA*, LXIV (September, 1949), 646; in *Men and Supermen*, p. 17.

16 Nethercot points this out. See "The Truth about Candida," in *PMLA*, LXIV (September, 1949), 643; in *Men and Supermen*, pp. 12–13.

an idealist in order to behave as he does, and on the other hand must become a realist in order that Shaw may demonstrate dramatically the proposition set forth in *The Quintessence of Ibsenism.*

One last point which can be illuminated by examining *The Wild Duck* in relation to *Candida* is the presence of Burgess. His function in *Candida* is not easily arrived at. "Comic relief" or "a whipping boy for typical Shavian ideas" are both answers with considerable validity, but both seem inadequate in a play with some claim to tightness of construction. Shaw's episodic plays, such as *Caesar and Cleopatra*, do have characters, like Britannus, who contribute little more than their delightful selves and a Shavian attitude; but in other of his tightly constructed plays, such as *Arms and the Man* and *Mrs. Warren's Profession*, there is not one superfluous person.

What Burgess does, and does effectively, is to illuminate character. As noted earlier, his very existence helps establish Candida's Philistinism.[17] And his long conversation with Morell at the beginning of the play predisposes us to regard Morell favorably, since we see Morell at his frankest, his most realistic, his most genuinely effective. Without this scene, Morell's reaction to Eugene's attack would make him seem like a fool; and Eugene's character in turn would suffer diminution.

Burgess also has a function as the complete Philistine. His willingness to take seriously the parade of assertions that members of the household are mad is not only hilariously funny, but also a quite genuine Philistine reaction to people whose concerns seem so utterly beside the point.[18] But Shaw's whole story *is* very close to much ado about nothing; and the presence of a character who feels this way himself is disarming. Paradoxically enough, the audience can take the events more seriously, precisely because Burgess does not.

The counterpart in *The Wild Duck* is of course old Ekdal. First,[57] there is something comic about him. His appearance, his gait, his attitude, pathetic though they are, have also an element of humor. Then, at the very start of the play, his entrance illuminates Hialmar's character, and therefore also, by indirection, Gregers'. In *Candida* we need to know early that both Morell and Marchbanks have strength. In *The Wild Duck* we need to know early that Hialmar is genuinely

---

[17] See also *Men and Supermen*, pp. 10–11.

[18] Nethercot makes a similar point but for a somewhat different purpose (*Men and Supermen*, p. 11).

weak and that Gregers, though by nature morbid, nevertheless badly over-estimates Hialmar. The scene at the party in which Hialmar ignores and disclaims his father performs this function admirably.

Other points of resemblance with Burgess are that Ekdal is an embarrassment socially; that he is wrapped up in a world of his own; and that he stands somewhat outside the action, upon which he offers comment ("the woods avenge themselves"). The parallels are not overwhelming, but they are convincing enough to explain quite considerably the appearance and function of Burgess in Shaw's play.

By comparing *Candida* with *The Wild Duck*, I hope that I have shown, first, that *Candida* is much more closely related to *The Wild Duck* than to *A Doll's House;* second, that such a comparison gives much added support to Nethercot's position, but also modifies it, especially with relation to Candida's character and motivation; and, finally, that, apart from the Philistine-idealist-realist relationships, the comparison provides additional insights into Shaw's characters and their function in his play.

Whether Shaw deliberately used *The Wild Duck* when he wrote *Candida*, I of course cannot say. Saturated as he was with Ibsen, it would have been quite possible for him to transmute some of Ibsen's material without realizing it. On the other hand, *The Wild Duck* provided him (as *A Doll's House* did not) with a fine example of a Philistine-idealist marriage; and it would have appealed to the Shavian sense of humor to make his play ostensibly resemble one Ibsen play so that critics might crow over him in praise or blame, while he carefully covered up the much more cogent resemblances to another. If this was not the intention, it has certainly been the result; and with Shaw such a result is likely to be intentional.

At any rate, if Shaw did not recognize the Ibsenian fowl hovering over his Victoria Park parsonage, he should have. He might have scoffed at both the apparition and the joke. But that would not have kept him from greeting both with relish.[58]

From "'Candida' and 'Pygmalion': Shaw's Subversion of Stereotypes"

PAUL LAUTER

Audiences, as the objects of criticism, reject uncomfortable versions of reality; indeed, too often they refuse to accept even the presence of an irritating point. The recent dispute over the satiric intent of *Lolita* (perhaps abetted by Nabokov's rhetorical masks) illustrates the inability of the mass of readers (and reviewers) to see what strikes them flush on their sensibilities. Anesthetized readers have been the affliction of most twentieth-century writers, and frequently their subjects. But to little avail; indeed, the more writers proclaim the "message" of their work to such audiences, the less they are believed. No contemporary author as diligently applied himself to reshaping his audience's attitudes, none felt impelled so frequently to explain himself in print as Bernard Shaw, yet no writer has been more susceptible to persistent misconstruction.

. . . . .   [14]

A similar dispute obscures Candida. Not so officially, perhaps, but quite as emphatically, Shaw has given us his attitude toward the play. To the inquiries of a Rugby literary society, he explained that the final triumph is Marchbanks': "What business has a man with the great destiny of a poet with the small beer of domestic comfort and cuddling and petting at the apron-string of some dear nice woman?"[1]

[1] Letter of March 8, 1920 quoted in George A. Riding, "The *Candida* Secret," *The Spectator*, CLXXXV (November 17, 1950), 506.

Reprinted from *The Shaw Review*, III (3) (September, 1960), 14–19 by permission of the author and *The Shaw Review*. Copyright 1960 by The Shaw Society of America and the Pennsylvania State University Press. Shaw's letters and Professor Nethercot's essay, referred to in the footnotes, are reprinted in this book.

But Candida could not really be called "nice," he implied to James Huneker:

> Don't ask me conundrums about that very immoral female, Candida. Observe the entry of W. Burgess: 'You're the lady as hused to typewrite for him.' 'No.' 'Naaaow: *she* was younger.' And therefore Candida sacked her. Prossy is a very highly selected young person indeed, devoted to Morell to the extent of helping in the kitchen but to him the merest pet rabbit, unable to get the slightest hold on him. Candida is as unscrupulous as Siegfried: Morell himself sees that 'no law will bind her.' She seduces Eugene just exactly as far as it is worth her while to seduce him. She is a woman without 'character' in the conventional sense. Without brains and strength of mind she would be a wretched slattern or voluptuary. She is straight for natural reasons, not for conventional ethical ones.[2]

But here again Shaw finds himself in a minority. Audiences, particularly in this country, applaud an intellectual, independent, but "nice" Candida, and so she usually appears. Critics, while they do not altogether share the American *hausfrau's* raptures over the Morell dovecote, fall equally in love with this "womanly woman" of great soul, idealist dreams and longings, candor, maternal sympathy, and probing intellect.[3] Candida proves again and again an irresistible romantic heroine.

Perhaps Shaw deserves thus to be misunderstood. Propounder of[15] innumerable rhetorical spoofs and fascinatingly irrelevant prefaces, he has cried up too many wolves for critics to gallop to his defense. Why accept Shaw on Shaw any more seriously than Shaw on any other given subject? But one need not depend upon the playwright's slippery *ex post facto* proclamations of "intention." Solutions of the debates over *Pygmalion* and *Candida* can be located precisely at the sources of confusion: the expectations Shaw generates *and manipulates* in his audience.

Cast in the frame of romantic comedy, *Pygmalion* seems to anticipate, through its title if nothing else, a normally romantic conclusion: boy gets girl, or, to be realistically Shavian, girl gets boy. Galatea, so the pattern requires, triumphs over her cold-blooded creator by capturing him as her man—and they live, and we leave,

---

[2] Letter quoted by Huneker in *Iconoclasts* (New York, 1916), p. 254.
[3] Arthur H. Nethercot neatly sums up critical confusion in his "The Truth about Candida," *PMLA*, LXIV (September, 1949), 639-40.

happily. *Candida,* apparently focussed on an ideally (i.e. responsible) romantic heroine, provides two normal expectations—the moral: a perfectly suited couple are happily reunited, casting out the effete, neurotic, and now disconsolate intruder; the amatory: the husband-burdened nymph flees to the mountaintops with her poet-lover. In either case, the triumph is assuredly Candida's—whatever she chooses must remain golden. Most audiences, conditioned by sentimental fiction and drama, respond in terms of Hollywood and Broadway stereotypes; consequently, they look for such expectations to be fulfilled. Indeed, they refuse to be denied, finding Shaw's statements outside the script to the contrary simply humbug. But critics should remember that audience expectations may profitably be defeated; that, as a matter of fact, a large and important part of English drama works precisely by so irritating its viewers.

Drama, because it is performed before a group more or less homogeneous, must deal with generally held patterns in order to evoke responses. To work with a set of norms and attitudes, however, is not necessarily to accept them; besides, whatever a writer's personal viewpoint, he may adopt or reject patterns of expectation in his work. The audience of *Twelfth Night* or *Macbeth* finds its desires for the defeat of the aspiring servant or the usurper and for the success of the forces of romantic or political normalcy gratified. It is all to Shakespeare's purpose to indulge such expectations, for his plays are essentially conservative and idealistic in outlook. He can, and does, play ironically with his audience's stereotypes—notably in the case of Shylock—but usually his dramas make use of conventional social, moral, and political patterns by accepting them.

Marlowe, on the other hand, perpetually undermines his audience's presumptions. Part One of *Tamburlaine,* for example, takes the form of a medieval tragedy; a mortal rises to the apex of Fortune's wheel from whence he must fall—only Tamburlaine does not fall. Marlowe's playgoer might well have reacted as ours would to a crime-does-pay feature from Hollywood.[4] Not so radically, Jonson twists moral stereotypes in *The Alchemist* by giving the palm, not to mention the gold, to the cleverest rogue. The usual standards of heroes as "moral" and villains as "immoral" disintegrate as the audience

---

[4] Doctor Faustus may similarly be regarded as functioning by disappointing the expectation that Faustus will in the end be saved—as the Morality pattern dictated. For many of these suggestions I am indebted to Professor S. F. Johnson of Columbia University.

finds[61] its normal reactions useless in the new witty framework of Jonson's play. By thus defeating expectations, Marlowe and Jonson challenge stereotyped patterns of cause and effect which underlie conventional, and frequently empty, morality. The audience, deprived of its comfortable precedents, must rediscover within the more real world of the play new bases for ethical behavior.

A similar analysis can, I think, be made of *Pygmalion* and *Candida*. In each case Shaw works to defeat the audience's expectations in order to discompose their stereotypes and to establish the position and function of the creative individual in the modern world.

Romantic comedy—the genre in which Shaw appears to work—normally functions by fulfilling the audience's wish that its surrogate (the hero or heroine with whom we "identify") achieve his reward—usually the lady's hand. Marriage, to a bourgeois audience the foundation of morality *and* society, symbolizes restoration of desired order in the new community focussed on the united hero and heroine.[5] This prototype, which contemporary audiences are conditioned to expect, both assumes *and tends to reenforce* the audience's view that the hero does find happiness ever after in a conventional society grounded on marriage. Making use of this pattern—as Hollywood and Broadway do—in effect lends support to such assumptions. Conversely, to attack such assumptions may well require undermining the pattern: denying the desirability of sterotypic "happiness" for the hero and the possibility of any creative achievement in conventional society, especially in the box of middle-class marriage. But comic expectations are far too deeply ingrained to permit their destruction without seriously impairing the audience's mood. Shaw's problem is to hold his audience in a comic world while pulling the stereotypes on which their responses are built from under them.

Shaw manipulates audience expectations by providing two levels of identification in the play: an apparent hero (heroine in *Candida* and *Pygmalion*) toward whom our sentimental, stereotypic orientation draws us; and the real hero, with whom we are forced to identify if we reflect on the action. In *Candida* and *Pygmalion* one initially identifies with the clever, thriving female, the perfect embodiment of bourgeois virtue and success: Eliza, Cinderella *cum* Pamela, for whom, in the movie version, Shaw wisely provided the magnificent triumph

---

[5] Cf. Northrup Frye, "The Argument of Comedy," English Institute Essays, 1948. ed. D. A. Robertson, Jr. (New York, 1949), p. 58–73.

of the ball scene so that we all could glory in her glitter; Candida, the exemplum of emancipated wifeliness, intrepidly jousting the Muse in defense of her home. Certainly both seem admirably designed in the tradition of comedy heroines and we give them our hearts.

But we cannot give them our heads. For the Morell household *is*, as Shaw growled, a kind of "greasy fool's paradise," whose highest achievement is the barren oratory of Christian socialism, whose apostles are Lexy and Prossy, whose life, however Marchbanks' florid despair befuddles the point, *is* divorced from the heaven of art and intellect:

A wise-hearted observer, looking at her [Candida], would at once guess that whoever had placed the Virgin of the Assumption over her hearth[17] did so because he fancied some spiritual resemblance between them, and yet would not suspect either her husband or herself of any such idea, or indeed of any concern with the art of Titian.[6]

And Candida herself, "addled" by Marchbanks' sonnets, reveals her prissy insensitivity in her smothering pose of confidante:

Come and sit down on the hearth-rug, and talk moonshine as you usually do. I want to be amused.   [ACT III]

I am not afraid, so long as it is your real self that speaks, and not a mere attitude. . . . Now say whatever you want to. . . . And what have you to say to Candida?   [ACT III]

Her motherly envelopment of Morell too must stifle imagination, life itself. Similarly, Eliza's demand for a girl's "right to be loved" too readily dissolves into fetching and slaving, the warmth of the gutter or middle-class "independence," into the life of Freddy Hill and Doolittle. The closer we scrutinize Eliza's dream and Candida's reality, the duller, the more constricting they become—we are driven to seek elsewhere for vitality and vision.

But Shaw makes it difficult for us to do so, because the only characters we can emulate in rejecting the world of Candida and Eliza are notably unsuitable as romantic heroes. Marchbanks is puny and adolescent, Higgins cold and anti-social. To accept either as heroic, to adopt their attitudes, we must surrender our normal conceptions of what constitutes "happiness" and how it may be achieved. And we

---

[6] Shaw's stage direction.

must—if we are to see beyond St. Dominic's Parsonage and railway flower shops, and if we are to respond to the dramas as Shaw wrote them. For Marchbanks' ascendancy from the world of be-good and do-good, from the mother-world to independence, is carefully celebrated in his final triumph over Candida Morell's rhetoric:

> CANDIDA. When I am thirty, she will be forty-five. When I am sixty, she will be seventy-five.
> MARCHBANKS (Turning to her). In a hundred years, we shall be the same age. But I have a better secret than that in my heart. Let me go now. The night outside grows impatient.   [ACT III]
> . . . . .   [18]

The usual perversions of *Candida* and *Pygmalion* are thus understandable: to make the plays suitable for musical comedy audiences, they must be bent into normally sentimental frames and fitted with stereotypic happy endings. The producer must, above all, give his house its dreams. But Shaw was out to make his subversive points; he could not, like his Don Juan, be content with the "romantic vowings and pledgings and until-death-do-us-partings" of sentimental marriage. He recognized, and displayed in both plot and dramaturgy, the need of the artist in a world of bourgeois clichés to adopt the strategies, not of silence, but certainly of "exile and cunning."[19]

APPENDICES

Selected Bibliography

The following list includes the works reprinted in this book and other works which may be used for research papers on the *Candida* theme, on Shaw's ideas and methods, and on various aspects of modern drama. Books available in paperback editions are marked with an asterisk.

BIBLIOGRAPHICAL

The works in this section will guide the student to other works by or on Shaw which supplement those appearing in this selected bibliography.

Broad, C. Lewis and Violet M. Broad. *Dictionary to the Plays and Novels of Bernard Shaw* (New York: The Macmillan Company, 1929). Unfortunately, inaccuracies in this book make it somewhat unreliable.

"A Continuing Check-List of Shaviana" appears in every issue of *The Shaw Review*, published triennially by The Shaw Society of America, Inc. and the Pennsylvania State University Press. This list is invaluable as a guide to the newest critical and biographical material on Shaw, as well as to theater reviews, talks and discussions on Shaw, little-known minor writings, and other kinds of Shaviana.

Indexes like *The Times Index* (London), *The New York Times Index*, *The Reader's Guide to Periodical Literature*, and *The International Index* are mandatory for tracking down elusive Shaw material published in many countries.

Kaye, Julian B. *Bernard Shaw and The Nineteenth-Century Tradition* (Norman, Okla.: University of Oklahoma Press, 1958).

The Saturday Review of Literature, XXVII (July 22, 1944), 28–32, lists all Shaw's separately published works up to this date.

The Shavian, published by the British Shaw Society, and the earlier *Shaw*

Bulletin are available in most college libraries and offer a rich assortment of fascinating side lights on Shaw.

PRIMARY SOURCES (WRITINGS OF BERNARD SHAW)

The editions of *Candida* which follow are among the most generally available. No attempt has been made to list all editions. The variety of editions in which Shaw's plays, novels, and critical or biographical works appear is wide enough to include the two excellent sets of the collected works (the Ayot St. Lawrence Edition published in America and the Standard Edition published in England) and the inexpensive Penguin paperback reprintings of the separate plays. In this country Dodd, Mead and Company have frequently reprinted the works in selected combinations, several to a volume, thus continuing the older, frequently reprinted Brentano edition of Shaw's works.

Candida, in *Plays: Pleasant and Unpleasant*, Vol. II: *Pleasant Plays* (London: Grant Richards, 1898).
Candida, in *Plays: Pleasant and Unpleasant*, Vol. II: *Pleasant Plays* (Chicago: Herbert S. Stone, and Company, 1898). Reprinted, 1904–05.
Candida, in *Plays: Pleasant and Unpleasant*, Vol. II: *Pleasant Plays* (New York: Brentano's, 1905). Reprinted, 1906, 1912, 1918, etc.
Candida, in *Plays: Pleasant and Unpleasant*, Vol. II: *Pleasant Plays* The Ayot St. Lawrence Edition of *The Collected Works of Bernard Shaw*, Vol. VIII (New York: William H. Wise and Company, 1931).
Candida, in *Plays Pleasant and Unpleasant*, Vol. II: *Pleasant Plays*, The Standard Edition of Shaw's Works (London: Constable and Company, Ltd., 1931). Reprinted six times from 1935 to 1952.
Candida, in *Nine Plays by Bernard Shaw* (New York: Dodd, Mead and Company, 1935). Reprinted, 1937, 1940, 1948.
*Candida: A Pleasant Play (Baltimore, Md.: Penguin Books, Inc., 1952), Penguin Book No. 7.
Captain Brassbound's Conversion, in *Selected Plays of Bernard Shaw* (New York: Dodd, Mead and Company, 1948) p. 686.
How He Lied to Her Husband, in *John Bull's Other Island, How He Lied to Her Husband, and Major Barbara*, The Standard Edition of Shaw's Works (London: Constable and Company, Ltd., 1931). Reprinted, 1939, 1947. Also reprinted in **Seven One-Act Plays by Shaw* (Baltimore, Md.: Penguin Books, Inc., 1958). Penguin Book No. 11.
Love Among the Artists, The Standard Edition of Shaw's Works (London: Constable and Company, Ltd., 1931). Reprinted, 1950.

Critical Works

"Epistle Dedicatory" (1903) to *Man and Superman: A Comedy and A Philosophy*, The Standard Edition of Shaw's Works (London: Constable and Company, Ltd., 1931), pp. xviii–xx.

"My Way with a Play," in *The Observer* (London), September 29, 1946; reprinted in *British Thought: 1947*, ed. Ivor Brown (New York: The Gresham Press, 1947), pp. 139–44. Also reprinted in *Shaw on Theatre*, ed. E. J. West, Dramabooks (New York: Hill and Wang, Inc., 1958), pp. 267–73.

Our Theatres in the Nineties, The Standard Edition of Shaw's Works, (3 vols; London: Constable and Company, Ltd., 1954). Reprinted, in part, in *Shaw's Dramatic Criticism: 1895–1898*, ed. John F. Matthews, Dramabooks (New York: Hill and Wang, Inc., 1960).

Preface (1915) to *Androcles and the Lion*, in *Selected Plays of Bernard Shaw* (New York: Dodd, Mead and Company, 1948), p. 769.

Preface (1921) to *Immaturity*, The Ayot St. Lawrence Edition of *The Collected Works of Bernard Shaw*, Vol. I (New York: William H. Wise and Company, 1930), pp. xvi, xx. On Shaw's likeness to Marchbanks and Shelley.

Preface (1898) to *Plays: Pleasant and Unpleasant*, Vol. II: *Pleasant Plays*, The Standard Edition of Shaw's Works (London: Constable and Company, Ltd., 1952), pp. v–viii.

Preface to *Pygmalion* (1912), in *Selected Plays of Bernard Shaw* (New York: Dodd, Mead and Company, 1948), p. 194.

Program for "Don Juan in Hell," Court Theatre, London, 1907. Reprinted in Archibald Henderson, *George Bernard Shaw: His Life and Works* (Cincinnati: Stewart and Kidd Company, 1911), pp. 365–67. Also reprinted in Raymond Mander and Joe Mitchenson, *Theatrical Companion to Shaw* (London: Rockliff Publishing Corporation, 1954), pp. 89–90.

"Religion of the Pianoforte," in *The Fortnightly Reveiw*, LXI (old series) (February, 1894), 264.

The Quintessence of Ibsenism (New York: Brentano's, 1905), pp. 20–47, 82–86, 100–105, 114–17.

The Quintessence of Ibsenism, Now Completed to the Death of Ibsen (1913), Dramabooks (New York: Hill and Wang, Inc., 1957).

"Shaw on Shaw and Molière," in Archibald Henderson, *George Bernard Shaw: Man of the Century* (New York: Appleton-Century-Crofts, Inc., 1956), pp. 740–41.

Sixteen Self Sketches (New York: Dodd, Mead and Company, 1949), pp. 158–59.

Correspondence and Autobiography

"Candida Was Not Ellen Terry," *Evening Standard* (London), November 30, 1944.

Ellen Terry and Bernard Shaw: A Correspondence, ed. Christopher St. John (New York: G. P. Putnam's Sons, 1932), pp. 23, 29–30, 31, 33–34, 80, 81, 181, and 248.

Letter (1900) to Henry J. Haskell, late editor of *The Kansas City Star*, in Richard Burton, *Bernard Shaw: The Man and the Mask* (New York: Henry Holt and Co., Inc., 1916), p. 231; reprinted in the column "Random Thoughts," *The Kansas City Star*, February 20, 1949, p. 16D.

Letter (1904) to James Huneker in Huneker, "The Truth about Candida," *Metropolitan Magazine*, XX (August, 1904), 635; reprinted in Huneker, *Iconoclasts: A Book of Dramatists* (New York: Charles Scribner's Sons, 1905), pp. 254–55.

Letter (1905) to William T. Stead, founder of the English *Review of Reviews*, in the Stead Papers; reprinted in Patrick G. Hogan, Jr., and J. O. Baylen, "G. Bernard Shaw and W. T. Stead: An Unexplored Relationship," *Studies in English Literature: 1500–1900*, I (Autumn, 1961), 137–38. Reply to Stead's review of *Candida*.

Preface to *Salt and His Circle*, by Stephen Winsten (London: Hutchinson and Company, Ltd., 1951), pp. 9–10.

Two letters (1920) to Rugby boys, in George A. Riding, "The *Candida* Secret," *The Spectator* (London) (November 17, 1950), p. 506.

William Morris as I Knew Him, (New York: Dodd, Mead and Company, 1936), pp. 31–37.

SECONDARY SOURCES

Biography

Ervine, St. John. *Bernard Shaw: His Life, Work, and Friends* (London: Constable and Company, Ltd., 1956; New York: William Morrow and Company, 1956), pp. 277–82 and *passim*.

Harris, Frank. *Bernard Shaw: An Unauthorized Biography Based on First-Hand Information* (London: Victor Gollantz, Ltd., 1931), especially Chap. XIII , pp. 181–88 and Chap. XVII, p. 236, on Shaw and Shelley.

Henderson, Archibald. *Bernard Shaw: Playboy and Prophet* (New York: D. Appleton and Company, 1932), pp. 478, 480, 504–505.

——. *George Bernard Shaw: Man of the Century* (New York: Appleton-Century-Crofts, Inc., 1956), pp. 443–44, 476–77, 543–45, 740–41.

Irvine, William. *The Universe of G. B. S.* (New York: Whittlesey House, 1949), pp. 148–49, 173–78.

McKee, Irving. "Bernard Shaw's Beginnings on the London Stage," *Publications of the Modern Language Association (PMLA)*, LXXIV (September, 1959), 474–75.

Pearson, Hesketh. *G. B. S.: A Full Length Portrait* (New York: Harper and Brothers, 1942), p. 79 and *passim*.

Winsten, Stephen. *Jesting Apostle: The Life of Bernard Shaw* (London: Hutchinson and Company, Ltd., 1956); pp. 96–98 contain notes on the writing of *Candida*.

———. *Salt and His Circle* (London: Hutchinson and Company, Ltd., 1951); pp. 103–104 ("Shaw Reads *Candida*") describe some interesting reactions of Shaw's friends to the play.

Criticism: Articles and Reviews

Adler, Jacob H. "Ibsen, Shaw, and *Candida*," *Journal of English and Germanic Philology (JEGP)*, LIX (January, 1960), 50–58.

Bahr, Hermann. A note on *Candida*, in Archibald Henderson, *George Bernard Shaw: His Life and Works* (Cincinnati: Stewart and Kidd Company, 1911), p. 353n.

*Bentley, Eric. "Homage to Scribe," in *What Is Theatre?* (Boston, Mass.: Beacon Press, 1956), pp. 64–67.

*——— (ed.). "The Making of a Dramatist (1892–1903)" (Foreword), *Plays by George Bernard Shaw*, Signet Classics (New York: New American Library of World Literature, Inc., 1960), pp. xxi–xxiv.

Brandes, Georg. "Der Dramatiker Bernard Shaw," *Die Zukunft* (Berlin), XLIII (April 4, 1903), 32–34.

"*Candida*, as Shaw Saw the Play," *The Times* (London), May 25, 1960, p. 6d.

Crane, Milton. "*Pygmalion*: Bernard Shaw's Dramatic Theory and Practice," *PMLA*, LXVI (December, 1951), 879–85.

Elton, Oliver. "Miss Janet Achurch and Mr. Charles Charrington in *Candida*," *The Manchester Guardian*, March 15, 1898.

Engstrom, Elmer. "Shaw and the Well-Made Play" (unpublished Master's thesis, Columbia University, 1948).

Gassner, John. Introduction to *Candida*, *A Treasury of the Theatre* (*Ibsen to Ionesco*), (3d ed.; New York: Simon and Schuster, Inc., 1960), pp. 539–40.

King, Walter N. "The Rhetoric of Candida," *Modern Drama*, II (2) (September, 1959), 71–83.

Krutch, Joseph Wood. "Drama," *The Nation*, CLXII (April 20, 1946), 487.

Lauter, Paul. "*Candida* and *Pygmalion*: Shaw's Subversion of Stereotypes," *The Shaw Review*, III (3) (September 1960), 14–19.

Leblanc-Maeterlinck, Georgette. "Une Conférence," *Le Figaro* (Paris), May 30, 1908.

Loewenstein, F. E. "What Richard Mansfield Thought of *Candida*," *Drama* (new series, No. 2) (Autumn, 1946), pp. 9–10.

MacCarthy, Desmond. *Shaw* (London: MacGibbon and Kee, 1951), pp. 19–27. Contains two theater reviews of *Candida* at the Court Theatre (London), 1904, and Globe Theatre (London), 1937.

Mansfield, Richard. A letter on *Candida*, in William Winter, *Life and Art of Richard Mansfield* Vol. I (New York: Moffat, Yard and Company, 1910), p. 232.

Muret, Maurice. "De Nora à Candida," *Journal des Débats*, June 24, 1904, pp. 1216–18.

Nethercot, Arthur H. "Shaw's Women and the Truth about Candida, *The Shavian* (New series, No. 1) (December, 1953), 12–13.

_____. "The Truth about Candida," *PMLA* LXIV (September, 1949), 639–47.

Riding, George A. "The *Candida* Secret," *The Spectator* (London), CLXXXV (November 17, 1950), 506.

Stanton, Stephen S. "Scribe's *Bertrand et Raton*: A Well-Made Play," *Tulane Drama Review*, II (1) (November, 1957), 58–70.

_____. "Shaw's Debt to Scribe," *PMLA*, LXXVI (December, 1961), 575–85.

Stead, W. T. "*Candida* at the Court Theatre," *Review of Reviews*, XXXI (January, 1905), 38–40.

Valency, Maurice. "Shaw, the Durable Dramatist," *Theatre Arts*, XL (July, 1956), 66–68, 86–87.

Weintraub, Stanley. "Apostate Apostle: H. L. Mencken as Shavophile and Shavophobe," *Educational Theatre Journal*, XII (3) (October, 1960), 184–90.

_____. "The Embryo Playwright in Bernard Shaw's Early Novels," *Texas Studies in Literature and Language*, I (Autumn, 1959), 327–55.

Young, Stark. *Immortal Shadows* (New York: Charles Scribner's Sons, 1948), pp. 193–95. Contains theater review of *Candida* at the Empire Theater (New York), 1937. Reprinted, *Dramabooks (New York: Hill and Wang, Inc., 1958), pp. 177–79.

Criticism: Books

Bentley, Eric. *The Playwright as Thinker* (New York: Reynal and Hitchcock, 1946), pp. 165–68. Reprinted, *Meridian Book M6.

Burton, Richard. *Bernard Shaw: The Man and the Mask* (New York: Henry Holt and Co., Inc., 1916), pp. 66–76 (on *Candida* and *How He Lied to Her Husband*), 231 (letter to late editor of *The Kansas City Star*).

Chesterton, G. K. *George Bernard Shaw* (New York: The John Lane Company, 1909), pp. 119–25. Reprinted, *Dramabooks (New York: Hill and Wang, Inc., 1957).

Colbourne, Maurice. *The Real Bernard Shaw* (London: J. M. Dent and Sons, Ltd., 1950), pp. 127–29.

Duffin, Henry C. *The Quintessence of Bernard Shaw* (London: George Allen and Unwin, Ltd., 1920), pp. 37, 39–41, 67–69, 98–100, 106–107, 164.

Ellehauge, Martin. *The Position of Bernard Shaw in European Drama and Philosophy* (Copenhagen, Denmark: Levin and Munksgaard, 1931), pp. 215–16, 217–38. On Shavian ethics: woman, marriage, flesh vs. spirit, etc.

*Fergusson, Francis. "The Theatricality of Shaw and Pirandello," in *The Idea of a Theatre* (New York: Doubleday Anchorbooks, 1955).

Fuller, Edmund. *George Bernard Shaw: Critic of Western Morale* (New York: Charles Scribner's Sons, 1950), pp. 25–29.

Hamon, Augustin. *The Twentieth Century Molière: Bernard Shaw*, tr. Eden and Cedar Paul (London: George Allen and Unwin, Ltd., 1916), pp. 27–29, 82–205.

Huneker, James. *Iconoclasts: A Book of Dramatists* (New York: Charles Scribner's Sons, 1905), pp. 246–47, 248–56.

Kaye, Julian B. *Bernard Shaw and the Nineteenth-Century Tradition* (Norman, Okla.: University of Oklahoma Press, 1958), pp. 129–31. On Marchbanks, Shelley, and Shaw. Also contains bibliography.

Kronenberger, Louis (ed.). *George Bernard Shaw: A Critical Survey* (New York: World Book Company, 1953), pp. 7–25 (extract from Huneker's *Iconoclasts*, including Shaw's letter to Huneker); *passim* (stimulating essays by G. K. Chesterton, George Jean Nathan, Joseph Wood Krutch, Edmund Wilson, W. H. Auden, Jacques Barzun, and others).

Mander, Raymond and Joe Mitchenson. *Theatrical Companion to Shaw* (London: Rockliff Publishing Corp., 1954), pp. 42–46 (*Candida*: record of early performances, synopsis, and notes); pp. 99–102 (*How He Lied to Her Husband*: early performances, synopsis, and notes); pp. 89–90 (reprint of Shaw's program notes for "Don Juan in Hell," Court Theatre, 1907).

Mencken, Henry L. *George Bernard Shaw: His Plays* (Boston: John W. Luce Company, 1905), pp. xiv, xviii, xix–xxi, 53–59, 60–62.

Nethercot, Arthur H. *Men and Supermen: The Shavian Portrait Gallery* (Cambridge, Harvard University Press, 1954), pp. 7–17. See also Appendix, "What's in a Name?," for brief explications of the names of many of Shaw's characters.

Nicoll, Allardyce. *A History of Late Nineteenth-Century Drama: 1800–*

1850, Vol. I (Cambridge, Eng.: Cambridge University Press, 1930), pp. 90, 194.

Rattray, Robert F. *Bernard Shaw: A Chronicle* (Luton, Eng.: Leagrave Press, 1951), pp. 102–104, 318, 319–20, 327.

*Stanton, Stephen S. (ed.). *Camille and Other Plays*, with "Introduction to the Well-Made Play," Dramabooks (New York: Hill and Wang, Inc., 1957).

———. *English Drama and the French Well-Made Play: 1815–1915* (unpublished Ph.D. dissertation, Columbia University, 1955).

Ussher, Arland. *Three Great Irishmen: Shaw, Yeats, Joyce* (London: Gollantz, 1952). Reprinted, *Mentor Books (New York: New American Library of World Literature, Inc., 1957).

Walkley, Arthur B. *Drama and Life* (London: Methuen and Company, Ltd., 1907), pp. 214–18.

Ward, A. C. *Bernard Shaw* (rev. ed.; London: Longmans, Green and Company, Ltd., 1951).

Sources

Archer, William. *Playmaking: A Manual of Craftsmanship* (New York: Dodd, Mead and Company, 1934). Reprinted, *Dover Publications.

Arvin, Neil C. *Eugène Scribe and the French Theatre: 1815–1860* (Cambridge: Harvard University Press, 1924).

Carlyle, Thomas. *Sartor Resartus: The Opinions of Herr Teufelsdröckh* (1834), Centenary Edition, ed. H. D. Traill, Vol. I (New York: Charles Scribner's Sons; London: Chapman and Hall, Ltd., 1896).

De Quincey, Thomas. *Confessions of an English Opium-Eater* (1821), World's Classics Edition (London, New York: Oxford University Press, 1955).

Franc, M. A. *Ibsen in England* (Boston, The Four Seas Company, 1919).

Horace (Quintus Horatius Flaccus). *Satires, Epistles, and Ars Poetica*, Loeb Classical Library Edition (London: William Heinemann, Ltd., 1955; Cambridge, Mass.: Harvard University Press, 1955), lines 343–46.

Ibsen, Henrik. *The Works of Henrik Ibsen*, ed., with introductions, William Archer and C. H. Herford, Viking Edition (16 vols; New York: Charles Scribner's Sons, 1911), Vol. VIII: *A Doll's House;* Vol. IX: *The Wild Duck;* Vol. X: *The Lady from the Sea*. Reprinted, *Four Plays by Ibsen*, Universal Library (New York: Grosset and Dunlap, Inc.). Reprinted, *Six Plays by Ibsen*, tr. Eva Le Gallienne, Modern Library College Edition T24.

Molière (Jean-Baptiste Poquelin). *Plays by Molière* (New York: The Modern Library, n.d.); *Selected Comedies by Molière*, introd. by Frederick C. Green, Everyman Library Edition (2 vols; London: J.

M. Dent and Sons, Ltd., 1943; New York: E. P. Dutton and Company, 1943). Reprinted, *Modern Library College Edition T29.

*Nietzsche, Friedrich. *The Birth of Tragedy and The Genealogy of Morals* (1887), tr. Francis Golffing (Garden City, N. Y.: Doubleday Anchorbooks, 1956).

_____. *Thus Spake Zarathustra* (1885), tr. Thomas Common (New York: The Modern Library, 1951). Reprinted, *Gateway Editions (Chicago: Henry Regnery).

Ruskin, John. *Sesame and Lilies* (1865) (London: George Allen and Unwin, Ltd., 1933).

Schopenhauer, Arthur. "On Women," in *Essays,* tr. T. Bailey Saunders (London: George Allen and Unwin, Ltd., 1951), pp. 62–75.

Scribe, Augustin-Eugène. *Bataille de Dames,* in *Oeuvres Complètes de Eugène Scribe* (76 vols; Paris: Dentu, 1874), Vol. I: *Comédies-Drames,* 1–115. Tr. Charles Reade as *The Ladies' Battle* (New York: French's Minor Drama, 19—?); tr. T. W. Robertson as *The Ladies' Battle* (London: Lacy's Acting Edition, 19—?). Adapted by Maurice Valency as *The Queen's Gambit: A Romantic Comedy in Three Acts* (New York: Samuel French, 1956).

Shelley, Percy Bysshe. "Even Love Is Sold," A Note to *Queen Mab: A Philosophical Poem* (1813), in *Works of Percy Bysshe Shelley,* Vol. IV, ed. Harry Buxton Forman (London: Reeves and Turner, 1880), pp. 477–82.

*Valency, Maurice. *The Queen's Gambit* (See under Scribe, Augustin-Eugène above).

Suggestions for Study, Discussion, and Writing

TOPICS FOR SHORT RESEARCH PAPERS AND DISCUSSION

Short papers (600–800 words) will help familiarize the student with the basic materials in this book and, by introducing him to simple research projects, will prepare the way for the longer topics listed below. Optional materials from the library may also be used in the preparation of these short topics. All the works referred to in this section are reprinted in this book.

1. How do the Continental critics interpret *Candida?*

2. How do the British critics interpret *Candida?*

3. How do the American critics interpret *Candida?*

4. What general conclusion can be drawn as to the differences in point of view between the Continental, the British, and the American critics?

5. Write a summary of the causes of *Candida*'s early misinterpretation in France.

6. Write a character sketch of Marchbanks.

7. Write a character sketch of Burgess.

8. Explain how you think *Candida* should be acted to emphasize Shaw's meaning without distortion.

9. To what extent does *Candida* fulfill Shaw's own definition of a good acting play? (See "Dramatic Method.")

10. Using Hamon's essay for reference, explain how you think an actor should play the role of Burgess so as to do full justice to Shaw's interpretation of the character and the general meaning of the play.

11. Explain why Shaw gave *Candida* the subtitle "A Mystery."

12. What is Shaw's attitude toward marriage in *Candida?*

13. Evaluate Shaw's attitude toward the clergy in *Candida.*

14. Discuss similarities and differences between Owen Jack's point of view toward marriage in the passage from Shaw's *Love Among the Artists* and that of Marchbanks in the closing scene of *Candida.* Could it be said that Jack, when he relates the story of his near-marriage several years before, is really an older Marchbanks looking back on the experience which is dramatized in *Candida?* Explain.

15. Compare the poet's secret in *Candida* with that described by Lady Cicely in the excerpt from *Captain Brassbound's Conversion.*

16. Demonstrate how one of the following short selections in this book applies to *Candida*:
    a. From the Preface to *Androcles and the Lion*
    b. From the Preface to *Pygmalion*
    c. Miscellaneous Critiques

17. In his chapter "Ideals and Idealists," in *The Quintessence of Ibsenism*, Shaw divides modern society into the categories of Philistine, idealist, and realist. Evaluate the characters in *Candida* on the basis of these social divisions as analyzed by Shaw.

18. In his letter "Candida Was Not Ellen Terry" Shaw said: "When

I began writing the part of the young poet, I had in mind De Quincey's account of his adolescence in his *Confessions.* . . ." What characteristics of Marchbanks are suggested in the selection from *Confessions of an English Opium-Eater?* Where are these characteristics emphasized in *Candida?*

19. What ideas or concepts presented in the selection from Carlyle's "The Everlasting Yea" does Shaw make use of in *Candida?* Does Shaw see these ideas exactly as did Carlyle? In what way does he alter them?

20. Compare or contrast Schopenhauer's and Shaw's conception of woman as revealed in the selection from "On Women" and *Candida.*

21. Demonstrate Shaw's use of Horace's famous formula for being a successful writer.

TOPICS FOR MEDIUM-LENGTH RESEARCH PAPERS
AND DISCUSSION

These topics are for papers of approximately 800–1500 words. While some of these papers can be based on materials in this book, others require the student to avail himself of outside materials, such as plays of Shaw and other dramatists. Use of the library should be encouraged.

1. Compare Candida and Mrs. Bompas in Shaw's companion farce *How He Lied to Her Husband.* (See Selected Bibliography.)

2. Compare Morell and Mr. Bompas in *How He Lied to Her Husband.*

3. Compare Marchbanks and Henry Apjohn in *How He Lied to Her Husband.*

4. In the selection in this book from his chapter "Playlets and Farces," Henderson claims that *How He Lied to Her Husband* was written as a humorous counterpart of *Candida,* not as a travesty on it, and that Shaw warned the New York critics that this farce did not belittle *Candida* in any way. Irvine, on the other hand, states flatly that "In theme [*How He Lied* . . .] is another of Shaw's *Wild Ducks.* It satirizes Ibsen's *Doll's House* and Shaw's own *Candida* and manages to convict both of melodrama." (*The Universe of G. B. S.,* p. 259.) Present an argument supporting either of these points of view.

5. To what extent does Candida dramatize Shaw's conception of woman, as presented in his chapter (reprinted in this book) "The Womanly Woman" from *The Quintessence of Ibsenism?*

6. Study Shaw's playbill notes for a London performance of "Don Juan in Hell," his "Epistle Dedicatory" to *Man and Superman*, and the selections from his correspondence with Ellen Terry (all three works reprinted in this book). To what extent can Burgess, Marchbanks or Morell, and Candida be said to fit the moral or universal states which Shaw uses to explain his own conception of heaven and hell?

7. What ideas or concepts presented in the selection from Ruskin's "The Mystery of Life and Its Arts" does Shaw make use of in *Candida?* In what way does he alter these ideas? How does Ruskin's treatment of these ideas differ from Carlyle's? From Nietzsche's in the selection from "The Sign" [*Thus Spake Zarathustra*)?

8. Compare and contrast Shelley's and Shaw's conception of marriage as revealed in "Even Love Is Sold" and *Candida*. Does Shaw's evaluation of Shelley in the selection "On Shelley and Wagner" throw light on those ideas and values which Shaw admired? (Contextual terms like "pleasurable activity," "high thinking," "high feeling," "skilled voluptuaries," and "plain living" will need to be explained.)

9. Compare or contrast Nietzsche's, Carlyle's, and Shaw's conception of happiness, as revealed in the selections from "Of Higher Man" (*Thus Spake Zarathustra*), "The Everlasting Yea," and *Candida*.

10. Determine by a comparison of the selections from Nietzsche's "What Do Ascetic Ideals Mean?," Shaw's "Epistle Dedicatory" to *Man and Superman*, and his program notes for "Don Juan in Hell" just what Shaw believed with regard to the relations of the artist-man and the mother-woman, and how he differed in this belief from his predecessor, Nietzsche.

11. Read Ibsen's *The Lady from the Sea* and Shaw's analysis of it in the selections from *The Quintessence of Ibsenism*. What are the parallels and differences between *Candida* and *The Lady from the Sea?*

12. Using Shaw's own comparison of himself to Molière (in the section "Dramatic Method"), compare or contrast *Candida* and one of Molière's comedies, such as *Le Misanthrope*.

13. Using Stanton's essay as a guide, compare some of the "well-made"

features of *Arms and the Man, The Devil's Disciple*, or *Captain Brassbound's Conversion* with corresponding features in *Candida*. Then explain how Shaw used these borrowed features to stimulate and teach his audience.

14. Bentley comments on Marchbanks: "As a character, Marchbanks must be reckoned a failure. . . . Though a poorly drawn character, [he] is always an effective stage role, and still seems to correspond to the actors' idea of a poet." (See "The Making of a Dramatist [1892–1903]" in the section "Dramatic Method.") Agreeing or disagreeing with this statement, interpret Marchbanks as a character or as an acting part.

15. In the same essay Bentley claims that only Strindberg could have written a sequel to the ending of *Candida*: "The cruelty of the heroine—merely implicit in [*Candida*]—would have to come to the surface in any continuation of the story. Candida has chosen to let her husband discover his shame: she, as well as he, will have to take the consequences. Let the stage manager hold razors and strait jackets in readiness!" Agreeing or disagreeing with this contention, write a comparative analysis of Candida and one of Strindberg's heroines.

16. Compare all of Shaw's comments in the section "Shaw on the *Candida Secret*" on the meaning of the *Candida* secret. Evaluate them in chronological order so as to reach a conclusion as to his over-all or final interpretation. Do you find any modification or intensification of this attitude over the years?

17. Compare or contrast Shaw's comments in this book on the meaning of the *Candida* secret with the interpretations of it given by one Continental critic (including Hamon in the section "Dramatic Method"), one British critic, and one American critic. (Most of these critics are included in the three sections on "The Critics [1895–1960].")

18. What are the arguments for and against identifying Marchbanks with Shaw? (See Selected Bibliography, *passim*, and Kaye, *Shaw and the Nineteenth-Century Tradition*, pp. 129–31 for further references.)

19. Analyze Shaw's use of satire in *Candida* and *How He Lied to Her Husband*.

20. What faults or incongruities do Mansfield, Walkley, Chesterton, and Krutch find in *Candida?* Which critic is most convincing and

why? What replies might be made to these critics? How effective, for instance, is this answer to Walkley: "We may reply that the characters, especially Candida, merely articulate in rational terms what they must feel for irrational reasons; and that this is the way of real people whose cortex is in good working order. And we may propose a reason different from Walkley's, if perhaps no less facetious, for the humor of the play, apart from the amusing situation: the incongruity of sense in a senseless world is a rich source of comedy." (John Gassner, Introduction to *Candida*, *A Treasury of the Theatre* [3d ed.; New York: Simon and Schuster, Inc., 1960], p. 540.)

21. How do Hamon and Muret differ in their interpretations of the role of Candida? Which critic is more convincing and why?

22. How do Muret, Duffin, Bentley, Irvine, Nethercot, and King differ in their interpretations of Candida's character?

23. In his essay, King distinguishes between three groups of Candida critics: the "Candida lovers" (such as Chesterton), the "Candida haters" (such as Fuller), and the critical-historical scholars (Nethercot, Irvine). Summarize the arguments of two critics in each group whose writings are included in this book.

24. Write an argument defending or rejecting the use of what Lauter in his essay calls "normally sentimental frames" and "stereotypic happy endings" in a popular musical comedy adaptation of *Candida*. (The motion picture version of *Pygmalion*, starring Leslie Howard and Wendy Hiller, was fitted with a Shaw-approved, romantically indulgent ending, similar to that of the Lerner-Loewe musical, *My Fair Lady*.)

25. Adler's essay, "Ibsen, Shaw, and *Candida*," might well have been included in the Ibsen section of this book, under Shaw's sources, since it demonstrates various parallels between *Candida*, and the earlier *Wild Duck* (given its first English performance, incidentally, on May 4, 1894). Can you see why the essay was not included in this section? After reading the writings by Irvine, Nethercot, and King, evaluate Adler's essay. Does it fall into one of the three categories outlined by King? If not, why not?

TOPICS FOR LONG RESEARCH PAPERS AND DISCUSSION

These topics are for papers of more than 1500 words. Materials in this casebook and supplementary materials found in the library should form the basis of these papers.

1. Study the evidence offered in the section "Models from Life" for various women having served as models for Candida. Using biographical and other library sources listed in the Selected Bibliography, write an argument supporting your choice of a particular model (or of no particular model—remembering that Shaw claimed he had no models for Candida).

2. How does Shaw use characterization, plot structure, the ideas of other writers, and satire (irony, paradox) to develop his theme of man's quest for self-realization in Candida?

3. Learn all you can from materials in this book and those mentioned in the Selected Bibliography about Shaw's admiration for, and self-identification with, the poet Shelley. Show how this relationship is reflected in *Candida*.

4. Compare Shaw's view of marriage as revealed in *Candida* with the view of marriage of one other major nineteenth-century playwright as revealed in one or more of his plays.

5. Using Adler's essay as a point of departure, compare or contrast the theme of illusion versus reality in *Candida*, *The Wild Duck*, and *A Doll's House*.

6. What do the selections from Shaw's Preface to *Pleasant Plays*, "Epistle Dedicatory" to *Man and Superman*, and program notes to "Don Juan in Hell" teach us about Shaw's views of religion, life, the relation of the sexes, and the role of art in revealing these universal forces to mankind? (In addition to using materials in the library, read the selection from Colbourne for an explication of the Preface to *Pleasant Plays*.)

7. Find out all you can about either Shelley or Wagner to help you explain Shaw's claim in the selection "On Shelley and Wagner" that these two nineteenth-century artists were, on the one hand, "two arch-voluptuaries" and, on the other, rebels against the social evils of "the average sensual man." (On Shelley, consult, for example, Shaw's essay "Shaming the Devil about Shelley," reprinted in *Pen Portraits and Reviews*, The Standard Edition of Shaw's Works [London: Constable and Company, Ltd., 1949], pp. 236–46.)

8. Study one or more of the following: De Quincey's *Confessions*

of an *English Opium-Eater*, Carlyle's *Sartor Resartus*, Ruskin's *Sesame and Lilies*, Nietzsche's *Thus Spake Zarathustra*, or Schopenhauer's *Essays*. Try to find passages other than those reprinted in this book which would seem to have stimulated Shaw in his writing of *Candida*.